SpringerBriefs in Education

We are delighted to announce SpringerBriefs in Education, an innovative product type that combines elements of both journals and books. Briefs present concise summaries of cutting-edge research and practical applications in education. Featuring compact volumes of 50 to 125 pages, the SpringerBriefs in Education allow authors to present their ideas and readers to absorb them with a minimal time investment. Briefs are published as part of Springer's eBook Collection. In addition, Briefs are available for individual print and electronic purchase.

SpringerBriefs in Education cover a broad range of educational fields such as: Science Education, Higher Education, Educational Psychology, Assessment & Evaluation, Language Education, Mathematics Education, Educational Technology, Medical Education and Educational Policy.

SpringerBriefs typically offer an outlet for:

- An introduction to a (sub)field in education summarizing and giving an overview of theories, issues, core concepts and/or key literature in a particular field
- A timely report of state-of-the art analytical techniques and instruments in the field of educational research
- A presentation of core educational concepts
- An overview of a testing and evaluation method
- A snapshot of a hot or emerging topic or policy change
- An in-depth case study
- A literature review
- A report/review study of a survey
- An elaborated thesis

Both solicited and unsolicited manuscripts are considered for publication in the SpringerBriefs in Education series. Potential authors are warmly invited to complete and submit the Briefs Author Proposal form. All projects will be submitted to editorial review by editorial advisors.

SpringerBriefs are characterized by expedited production schedules with the aim for publication 8 to 12 weeks after acceptance and fast, global electronic dissemination through our online platform SpringerLink. The standard concise author contracts guarantee that:

- an individual ISBN is assigned to each manuscript
- each manuscript is copyrighted in the name of the author
- the author retains the right to post the pre-publication version on his/her website or that of his/her institution

Manuel Förster • Mandy Hommel
Editors

Conceptualisation and Measurement of Financial Competence

A Holistic Approach and Implications for Financial Education

Editors
Manuel Förster
Business and Economic Education, School
of Social Sciences and Technology
Technical University of Munich
Munich, Germany

Mandy Hommel
Vocational Education, Faculty of Electrical
Engineering, Media and Computer Science
OTH Amberg-Weiden
Amberg and Weiden, Germany

ISSN 2211-1921   ISSN 2211-193X (electronic)
SpringerBriefs in Education
ISBN 978-3-031-95689-8   ISBN 978-3-031-95690-4 (eBook)
https://doi.org/10.1007/978-3-031-95690-4

This work was supported by German Research Foundation (DFG), project number: 460770732.

© The Editor(s) (if applicable) and The Author(s) 2026. This book is an open access publication.

Open Access This book is licensed under the terms of the Creative Commons Attribution 4.0 International License (http://creativecommons.org/licenses/by/4.0/), which permits use, sharing, adaptation, distribution and reproduction in any medium or format, as long as you give appropriate credit to the original author(s) and the source, provide a link to the Creative Commons license and indicate if changes were made.
The images or other third party material in this book are included in the book's Creative Commons license, unless indicated otherwise in a credit line to the material. If material is not included in the book's Creative Commons license and your intended use is not permitted by statutory regulation or exceeds the permitted use, you will need to obtain permission directly from the copyright holder.
The use of general descriptive names, registered names, trademarks, service marks, etc. in this publication does not imply, even in the absence of a specific statement, that such names are exempt from the relevant protective laws and regulations and therefore free for general use.
The publisher, the authors and the editors are safe to assume that the advice and information in this book are believed to be true and accurate at the date of publication. Neither the publisher nor the authors or the editors give a warranty, expressed or implied, with respect to the material contained herein or for any errors or omissions that may have been made. The publisher remains neutral with regard to jurisdictional claims in published maps and institutional affiliations.

This Springer imprint is published by the registered company Springer Nature Switzerland AG
The registered company address is: Gewerbestrasse 11, 6330 Cham, Switzerland

If disposing of this product, please recycle the paper.

Acknowledgments

The work reported in this SpringerBrief was funded by the German Research Foundation (DFG, GZ: FO 1039/2-1, project number 460770732). The scientific network "Action-based Financial Literacy—Conceptualization, Assessment and Validation" has been funded from October 2021 to February 2025. On behalf of the network members, we would like to thank the DFG for their support.

Contents

1 **The AFin Network: Advancing Financial Literacy Through Systematisation, Modelling and Assessment—Introduction to the SpringerBrief** 1
Manuel Förster, Mandy Hommel, Carmela Aprea, Bärbel Fürstenau, Roland Happ, and Eveline Wuttke

2 **Untangling the Terminology in the Context of Financial Literacy: Systematising Definitions and Constructs** 11
Mandy Hommel, Eveline Wuttke, Roland Happ, Sebastian Heidel, and Marcel Thum

3 **Financial Literacy Frameworks: A Scoping Review and Critical Appraisal** 47
Carmela Aprea, Clara Vonhof, Nicole Ackermann, Bärbel Fürstenau, Ronja Baginski, and Manuel Vogler

4 **Towards A Generic Financial Competence Process Model** 93
Bärbel Fürstenau, Nicole Ackermann, Mandy Hommel, Christin Siegfried, and Manuel Förster

5 **Complexity in the Measurement of Financial Competence** 111
William B. Walstad, Andreas Kraitzek, Carlo Di Chiacchio, Sabrina Greco, and Manuel Förster

6 **Development and Validation of a Test for Assessing Financial Competence in a Decision-making Process: Using the Example of Purchasing a Mobile Phone** 157
Manuel Förster, Christin Siegfried, and Christoph König

7 **Concluding Remarks on the Work of the Financial Literacy Network AFin**............................... 171
Manuel Förster, Mandy Hommel, Carmela Aprea,
Bärbel Fürstenau, Roland Happ, and Eveline Wuttke

Contributors

Nicole Ackermann, Prof. Dr., Vocational Education with a Focus on Didactics, Department for Research on Educational Sciences, Zurich University of Teacher Education, Zurich, Switzerland

Carmela Aprea, Prof. Dr., Business and Economics Education - Instructional Systems Design and Evaluation & Mannheim Institute for Financial Education (MIFE), University of Mannheim, Mannheim, Germany

Ronja Baginski, Dr., Business and Economics Education - Instructional Systems Design and Evaluation & Mannheim Institute for Financial Education (MIFE), University of Mannheim, Mannheim, Germany

Carlo Di Chiacchio, PhD, International Studies, National Institute for the Evaluation of the Educational System, INVALSI, Rom, Italy

Manuel Förster, Prof. Dr., Business and Economic Education, Technical University of Munich, Munich, Germany

Bärbel Fürstenau, Prof. Dr., Business Education and Management Training, Faculty of Business and Economics, TU Dresden, Dresden, Germany

Sabrina Greco, PhD, International Studies, National Institute for the Evaluation of the Educational System, INVALSI, Rom, Italy

Roland Happ, Prof. Dr., Business Education and Management Training, Faculty of Economics and Management Science, Leipzig University, Leipzig, Germany

Sebastian Heidel, Business Education and Management Training, Faculty of Economics and Management Science, Leipzig University, Leipzig, Germany

Mandy Hommel, Prof. Dr., Vocational Education, Faculty of Electrical Engineering, Media and Computer Science, OTH Amberg-Weiden, Amberg and Weiden, Germany

Christoph König, Dr., Educational Psychology, Department of Psychology, Goethe University Frankfurt, Frankfurt, Germany

Andreas Kraitzek, Dr., Business and Economic Education, School of Social Sciences and Technology, Technical University of Munich, Munich, Germany

Christin Siegfried, Prof. Dr., Business Education for the Vocational Teaching Profession, Faculty of Economics and Social Science, University of Potsdam, Potsdam, Germany

Marcel Thum, Prof. Dr., Economics, Faculty of Business and Economics, TU Dresden, Dresden, Germany

Manuel Vogler, Competence & Career Center, University of Applied Sciences Rhein-Main, Wiesbaden, Germany

Clara Vonhof, Business and Economics Education - Instructional Systems Design and Evaluation & Mannheim Institute for Financial Education (MIFE), University of Mannheim, Mannheim, Germany

William B. Walstad, Prof. Emeritus, PhD, Economics, University of Nebraska–Lincoln, Lincoln, NE, USA

Eveline Wuttke, Prof. Dr., Economics and Business Education, Goethe University Frankfurt, Frankfurt, Germany

Chapter 1
The AFin Network: Advancing Financial Literacy Through Systematisation, Modelling and Assessment—Introduction to the SpringerBrief

Manuel Förster ⓘ, Mandy Hommel ⓘ, Carmela Aprea ⓘ, Bärbel Fürstenau ⓘ, Roland Happ ⓘ, and Eveline Wuttke ⓘ

Abstract Financial literacy is a key competence for individuals and society. Financial literacy empowers citizens to make informed decisions regarding budgeting, saving, and investing, thereby enhancing financial well-being, reducing vulnerability to financial crises, and contributing to economic stability and social equity.

M. Förster (✉)
Business and Economic Education, School of Social Sciences and Technology,
Technical University of Munich, Munich, Germany
e-mail: manuel.foerster@tum.de

M. Hommel
Vocational Education, Faculty of Electrical Engineering, Media and Computer Science,
OTH Amberg-Weiden, Amberg and Weiden, Germany
e-mail: m.hommel@oth-aw.de

C. Aprea
Business and Economic Education – Instructional Systems Design and Evaluation &
Mannheim Institute for Financial Education (MIFE), University of Mannheim, Mannheim,
Germany
e-mail: carmela.aprea@uni-mannheim.de

B. Fürstenau
Business Education and Management Training, Faculty of Business and Economics,
TU Dresden, Dresden, Germany
e-mail: baerbel.fuerstenau@tu-dresden.de

R. Happ
Business Education and Managment Training, Leipzig University, Leipzig, Germany
e-mail: happ@wifa.uni-leipzig.de

E. Wuttke
Economics and Business Education, Goethe University Frankfurt,
Frankfurt, Germany
e-mail: wuttke@em.uni-frankfurt.de

© The Author(s) 2026
M. Förster, M. Hommel (eds.), *Conceptualisation and Measurement of Financial Competence*, SpringerBriefs in Education,
https://doi.org/10.1007/978-3-031-95690-4_1

Despite its importance, there is a lack of clarity in terminology and comprehensive models that reflect the multifaceted nature of financial competence.

To address this gap, the AFin network, funded by the German Research Foundation (DFG), aims to conceptualize financial comptence through three main objectives: (1) developing a holistic competence model that integrates cognitive, emotional, motivational, and behavioral aspects; (2) systematizing existing test instruments and underlying constructs; and (3) designing a holistic assessment approach that includes financial behavior. This interdisciplinary and international network brings together researchers from fields such as economics, educational psychology, and business education. The collaborative structure included working groups, expert inputs from various practitioners, and iterative discussions. Their collective work culminates in a SpringerBrief structured around concepts, frameworks, competence models, assessments, and a technology-based testing prototype. This chapter introduces the AFin research network and lays the groundwork for a more unified and action-oriented approach to financial education that is necessary for both academic advancement and practical implementation in education systems.

Keywords Financial literacy · Financial competence · Financial education · Competence assessment

1.1 The Relevance of Financial Literacy as a Competence, Its Assessment, and Financial Education

Financial literacy is as essential for every citizen in society as it is for society as a whole (Fornero & Lo Prete, 2023). It enables citizens to make informed financial decisions and thus to better plan their income and expenses, to consider financial (emergency) reserves for unpredictable life risks such as illness, and to avoid over-indebtedness (Lusardi & Mitchell, 2014; Lusardi & Streeter, 2023). Informed decisions about budgeting, saving, investing, and retirement planning lead to more financial security, financial wellbeing, and prosperity (Bai, 2023; OECD, 2013). In addition, financially literate people are better at managing financial risks, are less vulnerable to fraud and financial exploitation (Engels et al., 2019; Huston, 2010), and are more resilient in dealing with financial crises (Klapper et al., 2012; OECD, 2020). A society's economy benefits from the financially competent performance of its educated economic citizens (Ackermann, 2021). Overall, a society's financial capability can help to reduce the risk of financial crises and increase social justice (Birkenmaier et al., 2018; Calvo, 2013). This can be promoted by reducing economic inequalities and enabling everyone to participate in economic life as fully as possible (Kaiser et al., 2022; OECD, 2020, 2024).

National financial education strategies are being drawn up and implemented in many countries. These countries include the G20 countries, 35 OECD members, and a large proportion of the countries in the European Union (OECD, 2024). With the current OECD's proposal (2024) for a national financial education strategy, Germany is also on its way to joining the number of countries that recognise the OECD proposal (2024) and thus the relevance of financial literacy with a national education strategy.

In education, integrating financial content into the curriculum enables students to be prepared for financial challenges early (Kaiser et al., 2022; Kaiser & Menkhoff, 2017; Lusardi, 2019). Financial education measures must be based on concrete ideas of which abilities and skills young people need; thus, competence models must first be developed. In order to develop targeted initiatives, valid diagnostics are initially necessary to assess levels of financial literacy, relying on these theory-based competence models. Teachers should be able to assess financial literacy learning levels and adapt teaching accordingly (OECD, 2014). Financial education measures foster awareness of financial issues and promote critical thinking and responsible behaviour. That, in turn, should increase financial well-being and contribute to economic stability and growth with a higher level of financial literacy among the population, enhancing equal opportunities and, thus, economic participation (OECD, 2024, p. 15).

Effective measures should be based on a holistic and application-oriented understanding of financial literacy as a competence (Brimble & Blue, 2015). For better measures to be developed, financial competence should be modelled and measured holistically. This means financial competence should not only include cognitive aspects such as financial knowledge but also motivational, emotional, and volitional facets (Wuttke et al., 2016). These non-cognitive elements are crucial, as they influence how people use their knowledge in real-life financial decision-making situations. Financial literacy, understood as competence, encompasses not only knowledge but also the ability and willingness to solve financial problems and make decisions responsibly (Aprea & Wuttke, 2016). Financial decisions and behaviour are essential components of financial competence as they show how well a person can apply their knowledge in practice. The mere possession of knowledge does not necessarily lead to sound financial decisions (Moreira Costa et al., 2021); instead, people must be able to transfer this knowledge into concrete action (Ali et al., 2014; Bucher-Koenen & Lusardi, 2011; Stolper & Walter, 2017). As a result, research is increasingly calling for financial competence models that not only integrate knowledge and attitudes but also financial behaviour as performance. A competence model should, therefore, not only integrate knowledge and attitudes but also the ability to act as well as concrete steps to evaluate the effectiveness of educational measures and promote financial education in a targeted manner.

1.2 Objectives of the AFin Network and the SpringerBrief

Effective promotion of financial literacy among individuals is necessary. In addition to financial knowledge, non-cognitive dispositions are also essential for responsible financial behaviour (Roa, 2021; Tang et al., 2015). Promoting the individual development of financial literacy requires a holistic basis that includes a comprehensive competence model and valid data collection options for measuring financial literacy. Facing the mentioned challenges, the research network AFin ("Action-based Financial Literacy – Conceptualization, Assessment and Validation") was funded by the German Research Foundation (DFG). Since its foundation in 2021, the research network AFin has pursued the following objectives, which are addressed in this SpringerBrief:

- Objective 1: Development of a holistic personal finance competence model
- Objective 2: Systematisation of existing test instruments and the underlying constructs
- Objective 3: Development of an approach for alternative and holistic assessment concepts that integrate financial behaviour

With the first objective, the network aimed to develop a holistic model for financial competence. The model developed here is intended to combine cognitive and non-cognitive dispositions with a process perspective and further framework conditions. Building on this, the second objective is to review and systematise existing test instruments for the various cognitive and non-cognitive dispositions. Building on the limitations and in parallel to the development of the competence model, the third goal of the network is to develop an alternative and holistic approach for measuring financial competence that integrates behavioural components.

The network was organised explicitly on an interdisciplinary and international basis. Ideas and concepts from the fields of economics, business education, and educational psychology were to be incorporated. The network also aimed to integrate young researchers. It includes the following members in alphabetic order by last name:

- Prof. Dr. Nicole Ackermann (Zurich University of Teacher Education, Upper Secondary Education and Vocational Education, Switzerland),
- Prof. Dr. Carmela Aprea (University of Mannheim, Economic and Business Education; Mannheim Institute for Financial Education (MIFE), Germany),
- Ronja Baginski (University of Mannheim, Economic and Business Education; Mannheim Institute for Financial Education (MIFE), Germany),
- Prof. Dr. Tabea Bucher-Koenen (ZEW—Leibniz Centre for European Economic Research, University of Mannheim, Finance; Mannheim Institute for Financial Education (MIFE), Germany),
- Carlo Di Chiacchio, PhD (National Institute for the Evaluation of the Educational System, INVALSI, International Studies, Italy),
- Prof. Dr. Manuel Förster (Applicant and responsible for the network; Technical University of Munich, Business, Economics and Vocational Education, Germany),
- Prof. Dr. Bärbel Fürstenau (TU Dresden, Business Education and Management Training, Germany),
- Sabrina Greco (National Institute for the Evaluation of the Educational System, INVALSI, International Studies, Italy),

- Prof. Dr. Roland Happ (University of Leipzig; Institute of Business and Economics Education, Germany),
- Sebastian Heidel (University of Leipzig; Institute of Business and Economics Education, Germany),
- Prof. Dr. Mandy Hommel (Co-responsible for the network; OTH Amberg-Weiden, Vocational Education, Germany),
- Prof. Dr. Tim Kaiser (RPTU Kaiserslautern, Economics, especially Economics of Education and Economic Education, Germany),
- Dr. Christoph König (Goethe University Frankfurt, Educational Psychology, Germany),
- Andreas Kraitzek (Technical University of Munich, Business, Economics and Vocational Education, Germany),
- Dr. Andrea Pfändler (formerly Goethe University Frankfurt, Business Education, Germany),
- Prof. Dr. Christin Siegfried (Weingarten University of Education, Business Education, Germany),
- Prof. Dr. Marcel Thum (TU Dresden, Economics, Ifo Institute Dresden, Germany),
- Manuel Vogler (formerly University of Mannheim, Economic and Business Education; Mannheim Institute for Financial Education (MIFE), Germany),
- Clara Vonhof (University of Mannheim, Economic and Business Education; Mannheim Institute for Financial Education (MIFE), Germany),
- Prof. emeritus William B. Walstad, PhD (University of Nebraska–Lincoln, Economics, USA),
- Prof. Dr. Eveline Wuttke (Goethe University Frankfurt, Business and Economic Education, Germany).

The network worked together from 2021 to 2025. The network collaboration was organised in such a way that it met six times during this period for 2 days at one of the network members' locations. Only one meeting had to be held online due to the coronavirus pandemic. The international network members who were unable to attend each meeting in person were connected via a conference system. At the meetings, there was usually an impulse from various external guests from science and practice on financial competence and its facets, which were then discussed. The guests' presentations covered a wide range of topics in the field of financial literacy and financial education. Verena Zepter from Caritas gave insight into financial literacy from the perspective of debt and insolvency counselling, Prof. Dr. Martin Weber from the University of Mannheim shed light into how beliefs and risk-taking develop in boom and bust markets, Prof. Dr. Marco Lehmann-Waffenschmidt and Anna Schütze from TU Dresden threw spotlights on Financial Literacy—from Martin Luther, Immanuel Kant and Max Weber to John Maynard Keynes and the present, Prof. Dr. Andrzej Cwynar from WSEI University Lublin in Poland took a look at financial literacy in Eastern European countries and outlined differences between these and their Western European neighbours, and Sascha Straub from consumer association "Verbraucherzentrale Bayern e.V." reported on his assessment of consumer-oriented financial planning.

Working groups were formed relatively early on to continue working on specific network objectives in the periods between meetings. The results of the working groups were then presented at the meetings and discussed in plenary sessions. These contributions from the network were then the starting point for further developments in the working groups. The working groups that were formed largely corresponded to the author groups in the following chapters. For example, the competence model was discussed, further developed and critically reflected upon in a large number of meetings, so that an iterative process led to the results described below.

The interdisciplinarity and versatility of the network were a great asset. The groups repeatedly received different impulses from the various disciplines. In addition, there was a mixture of experienced and young researchers that added diverse perspectives to the discussions.

The following section outlines the contributions to this SpringerBrief and links to the network's objectives. We want to take this opportunity to thank the DFG for funding the AFin network (GZ: FO 1039/2–1).

1.3 Contents of the Chapters and Structure of the SpringerBrief

The SpringerBrief provides a systematisation of concepts and definitions, frameworks, and measurement instruments for (financial) educators, researchers in the fields of financial literacy, financial competence, and financial education, educational psychologists, economists, professionals in the field of finance, and other interested persons. Our work is based on German and English academic literature.

In order to achieve *Objective 1* and develop a holistic model for personal financial competence, we first take a closer look at the concepts in the context of financial literacy, unravel, and categorise them (Chap. 2). The high degree of heterogeneity of terms and definitions in the German and English literature on financial literacy and financial competence (e.g., Atkinson & Messy, 2012; Lusardi & Mitchell, 2011; Nicolini & Cude, 2022; Oberrauch & Kaiser, 2022; OECD, 2013, 2017, 2022; Seeber & Retzmann, 2017; Walstad & Wagner, 2022) with regard to competence facets and content (e.g., Schuler & Brahm, 2021) is striking. Terms in this context are, for example, financial literacy (in a narrower and broader sense), financial capability, financial education, financial knowledge, and financial competence. The same terms often have different definitions, or definitions with the same meaning use different terminology. Despite all the differences, the definitions appear to have a common core. To achieve the network objectives, it is first necessary to untangle terms, definitions, and underlying constructs. To this end, the concepts used by various authors, the underlying constructs, the financial content addressed, the perspective on financial knowledge or financial literacy (on personal finances or a broader perspective in relation to society or the economy) are compiled and a consideration of financial decisions and behaviour is taken into account.

Chapter 3 provides a structured overview and description of existing financial literacy frameworks, as these frameworks are important tools to achieve a shared understanding of what financial literacy education should entail and to coordinate activities in policy and practice accordingly. The frameworks are analysed in terms of (1) their developers, target group, publication year and outlet, (2) their conceptual and theoretical foundation as well as the methodologies used to develop them, and (3) the components (e.g., content, goals) they delineate. In addition, the strengths and weaknesses of the frameworks are addressed. The findings of this chapter will help practitioners to better understand which frameworks might be adequate to guide their design and assessment decisions, policymakers to better judge which kind of orientation can be expected from existing frameworks and where further development is needed, and researchers to generate new ideas for where additional investigations are indicated.

Chapter 4 introduces a financial competence model. The model is meant as a process model aiming towards capturing the components relevant to individual financial decision-making processes. The model is generic but, at the same time, holistic. It is generic since all its components can be further specified—depending on the purpose of use. It is a holistic model, as it considers (a) both different cognitive and non-cognitive variables, (b) both dispositions and performance (financial behaviour), (c) embeddedness of decision-making in an environment or in different contexts (e.g., personal, social, economic), and (d) consequences of financial behaviour for financial well-being. The development of the model is based on the conceptualisation of financial competence and thus draws on findings presented in Chapters 2 and 3. In addition, the development regards conceptualisations of competence in general as well as already existing competence models. The model and its components are explained and illustrated using different examples from the finance domain.

In line with *Objective 2* of the network, Chap. 5 provides a review of the literature to identify commonly used measurement instruments and operationalisations for constructs related to financial competence. A broad range of instruments used for measuring financial literacy respectively competence and its various facets could be identified. Most focus on a single aspect of financial literacy, mainly knowledge. The number of instruments available depends heavily on which aspect of the financial literacy construct (cognitive vs. non-cognitive) is to be investigated. Cognitive, non-cognitive, and behavioural influences on measuring financial literacy respectively competence and investigated issues related to validity in the systematisation are explored, going beyond previous research by complementing and updating it (e.g., Huston, 2010). The selection of instruments concerning their potential and limitations of financial competence assessments are discussed.

Consequently, in Chap. 6, a technology-based test instrument to assess financial competence employing complex financial decisions for a specific domain is presented. This is a prototype to overcome some of the limitations presented in Chap. 5 and tackles *Objective 3* of our network. The scenario tasks participants with selecting a mobile phone and a contract based on their specified needs. They must decide whether to purchase a phone and sign a mobile phone contract separately or bundled, eliminating impractical combinations. The remaining choices about the specific needs are realistic and yield different favourable options. The scenario concludes with signing the purchase contract. Subsequent queries ask participants to provide reasons for their choices. The process of developing the item based on scientific models (e.g., Wilson, 2005) is presented as the result of the first validation study.

References

Ackermann, N. (2021). Zum Bildungsideal des "mündigen Wirtschaftsbürgers": Kompetenzmodell für ökonomische Bildung und Domänenanalyse des gesamtgesellschaftlichen/gesamtwirtschaftlichen Lebensbereichs [On the educational ideal of the economic citizen: a competence model for economic education and a domain analysis of the societal life sphere]. In C. Fridrich (Ed.), *Wirtschaft, Gesellschaft und Politik* (Sozioökonomische Bildung und Wissenschaft) (pp. 147–178). Springer. https://doi.org/10.1007/978-3-658-32910-5_7

Ali, P., Anderson, M., McRae, C., & Ramsay, I. (2014). The financial literacy of young Australian: an empirical study and implications for consumer protection and ASIC's National Financial Literacy Strategy. *Company and Securities Law Journal, 32*, 334–352.

Aprea, C., & Wuttke, E. (2016). Financial literacy of adolescents and young adults: Setting the course for a competence-oriented assessment instrument. In C. Aprea, E. Wuttke, K. Breuer, N. K. Koh, P. Davies, B. Greimel-Fuhrmann, & J. S. Lopus (Eds.), *International handbook of financial literacy* (pp. 397–415). Springer Science & Business.

Atkinson, A., & Messy, F. (2012). Measuring financial literacy: Results of the OECD/International Network on Financial Education (INFE) Pilot Study. In *OECD working papers on finance, insurance and private pensions, No. 15*. OECD Publishing. https://doi.org/10.1787/5k9csfs90fr4-en

Bai, R. (2023). Impact of financial literacy, mental budgeting and self control on financial wellbeing: mediating impact of investment decision making. *PLoS One, 18*(11), e0294466. https://doi.org/10.1371/journal.pone.0294466

Birkenmaier, J., Sherraden, M., Frey, J. J., Callahan, C., & Santiago, A. M. (2018). *Financial capability and asset building with diverse populations: Improving financial well-being in families and communities*. Routledge.

Brimble, M., & Blue, L. (2015). A holistic approach to financial literacy education. *ACRN Journal of Finance and Risk Perspectives, 4*(3), 34–47. https://eprints.qut.edu.au/115883/

Bucher-Koenen, T., & Lusardi, A. (2011). Financial literacy and retirement planning in Germany. *Journal of Pension Economics and Finance, 10*, 565–584. https://doi.org/10.1017/S1474747211000485

Calvo, G. S. (2013). *Financial crises, social impact, and risk management: Lessons and challenges*. World Development Report. https://openknowledge.worldbank.org/server/api/core/bitstreams/c7fe8641-a96d-5c6b-8b6e-8deb028ba8ec/content

Engels, C., Kumar, K., & Philip, D. (2019). Financial literacy and fraud detection. *The European Journal of Finance, 26*(4–5), 420–442. https://doi.org/10.1080/1351847X.2019.1646666

Fornero, E., & Lo Prete, A. (2023). Financial education: From better personal finance to improved citizenship. *Journal of Financial Literacy and Wellbeing, 1*(1), 12–27. https://doi.org/10.1017/flw.2023.7

Huston, S. J. (2010). Measuring financial literacy. *Journal of Consumer Affairs, 44*, 296–316. https://doi.org/10.1111/j.1745-6606.2010.01170.x

Kaiser, T., Lusardi, A., Menkhoff, L., & Urban, C. (2022). Financial education affects financial knowledge and downstream behaviors. *Journal of Financial Economics, 145*(2), 255–272. https://doi.org/10.1016/j.jfineco.2021.09.022

Kaiser, T., & Menkhoff, L. (2017). Does financial education impact financial behavior, and if so, when? *World Bank Economic Review, 313*, 611–630. https://doi.org/10.2139/ssrn.2753510

Klapper, L., Lusardi, A., & Panos, G. A. (2012). *Financial literacy and the financial crisis*. National Bureau of Economic Research. https://doi.org/10.3386/w17930

Lusardi, A. (2019). Financial literacy and the need for financial education: Evidence and implications. *Swiss Journal of Economics and Statistics, 155*(1), 1–8. https://doi.org/10.1186/s41937-019-0027-5

Lusardi, A., & Mitchell, O. S. (2011). Financial literacy around the world: An overview. *Journal of Pension Economics & Finance, 10*(4), 497–508. https://doi.org/10.3386/w17107

Lusardi, A., & Mitchell, O. S. (2014). The economic importance of financial literacy: Theory and evidence. *Journal of Economic Literature, 52*(1), 5–44. https://doi.org/10.1257/jel.52.1.5

Lusardi, A., & Streeter, J. L. (2023). Financial literacy and financial well-being: Evidence from the US. *Journal of Financial Literacy and Wellbeing, 1*(2), 169–198. https://doi.org/10.1017/flw.2023.13

Moreira Costa, V., De Sá Teixeira, N. A., Cordeiro Santos, A., & Santos, E. (2021). When more is less in financial decision-making: Financial literacy magnifies framing effects. *Psychological Research, 85*(5), 2036–2046. https://doi.org/10.1007/s00426-020-01372-7

Nicolini, G., & Cude, B. J. (Eds.). (2022). *The Routledge handbook of financial literacy*. Routledge.

Oberrauch, L., & Kaiser, T. (2022). Cognitive ability, financial literacy, and narrow bracketing in time-preference elicitation. *Journal of Behavioral and Experimental Economics, 98*, 101844. https://doi.org/10.1016/j.socec.2022.101844

OECD. (2013). *PISA 2012 assessment and analytical framework* (Mathematics, reading, science, problem solving and financial literacy). OECD Publishing.

OECD. (2014). *Financial education for youth: The role of schools*. OECD Publishing.

OECD. (2017). *G20/OECD INFE report on adult financial literacy in G20 countries*. OECD Publishing.

OECD. (2020). *OECD/INFE 2020 international survey of adult financial literacy*. OECD Publishing.

OECD. (2022). *Financial competence framework for adults in the European Union*. OECD Publishing.

OECD. (2024). *Strengthening financial literacy in Germany. Proposal for a national financial literacy strategy*. OECD Publishing.

Roa, M. J. (2021). The role of cognitive and non-cognitive characteristics in financial behaviors and financial literacy. *SSRN Electronic Journal*. https://doi.org/10.2139/ssrn.3964945

Schuler, A., & Brahm, T. (2021). Financial literacy in den Lehrplänen deutscher Schulen - eine bundesländerübergreifende Analyse [Financial literacy in the curricula of German schools - A cross-state analysis]. *Zeitschrift für ökonomische Bildung*, 1–63.

Seeber, G., & Retzmann, T. (2017). Financial literacy – Finanzielle (Grund-)Bildung [Financial literacy - Financial (basic) education]. *Ökonomische Bildung, Vierteljahrshefte zur Wirtschaftsforschung, 86*(3), 69–80.

Stolper, O. A., & Walter, A. (2017). Financial literacy, financial advice, and financial behavior. *Journal of Business Economics, 87*, 581–643. https://doi.org/10.1007/s11573-017-0853-9

Tang, N., Baker, A., & Peter, P. C. (2015). Investigating the disconnect between financial knowledge and behavior: The role of parental influence and psychological characteristics in responsible financial behaviors among young adults. *Journal of Consumer Affairs, 49*(2), 376–406. https://doi.org/10.1111/joca.12069

Walstad, W., & Wagner, J. (2022). Required or voluntary financial education and saving behaviors. *The Journal of Economic Education*. https://doi.org/10.1080/00220485.2022.2144573

Wilson, M. (2005). *Constructing measures: An item response modeling approach*. Routledge.

Wuttke, E., Seifried, J., & Schumann, S. (2016). *Economic competence and financial literacy of young adults: Status and challenges*. Budrich.

Open Access This chapter is licensed under the terms of the Creative Commons Attribution 4.0 International License (http://creativecommons.org/licenses/by/4.0/), which permits use, sharing, adaptation, distribution and reproduction in any medium or format, as long as you give appropriate credit to the original author(s) and the source, provide a link to the Creative Commons license and indicate if changes were made.

The images or other third party material in this chapter are included in the chapter's Creative Commons license, unless indicated otherwise in a credit line to the material. If material is not included in the chapter's Creative Commons license and your intended use is not permitted by statutory regulation or exceeds the permitted use, you will need to obtain permission directly from the copyright holder.

Chapter 2
Untangling the Terminology in the Context of Financial Literacy: Systematising Definitions and Constructs

Mandy Hommel ⓘ, Eveline Wuttke ⓘ, Roland Happ ⓘ, Sebastian Heidel ⓘ, and Marcel Thum ⓘ

Abstract When looking at the German- and English-language literature on financial literacy, one is struck by the heterogeneity in terms and definitions used in different papers, such as financial literacy, financial knowledge, financial capability, financial competence or financial education. Often, different definitions describe the same construct, or definitions with the same content use different terminology. Sometimes, explicit definitions are missing completely. As a result, the constructs behind the terms and the definitions often remain vague. Studies based on these definitions and their findings are hardly comparable, the findings cannot be generalised, and it is difficult to derive educational measures from these findings. Despite all differences, however, the definitions have a common core: financial knowledge is assumed to be a central component of financial literacy in all definitions we encountered. Our chapter takes up definitions, terms and the description of the underlying constructs from studies focussing on financial literacy. Furthermore, we look at the content areas included in each case and analyse whether only personal

---

M. Hommel (✉)
Vocational Education, Faculty of Electrical Engineering, Media and Computer Science, OTH Amberg-Weiden, Amberg and Weiden, Germany
e-mail: m.hommel@oth-aw.de

E. Wuttke
Economics and Business Education, Goethe University Frankfurt, Frankfurt, Germany
e-mail: wuttke@em.uni-frankfurt.de

R. Happ · S. Heidel
Business Education and Management Training, Leipzig University,
Leipzig, Germany
e-mail: happ@wifa.uni-leipzig.de; heidel@wifa.uni-leipzig.de

M. Thum
Economics, Faculty of Business and Economics, TU Dresden, Dresden, Germany
e-mail: marcel.thum@tu-dresden.de

© The Author(s) 2026
M. Förster, M. Hommel (eds.), *Conceptualisation and Measurement of Financial Competence*, SpringerBriefs in Education,
https://doi.org/10.1007/978-3-031-95690-4_2

finances or society-related aspects are taken into account. This is intended to systematically show which constructs are behind which terms and definitions, how broad the content areas are that are considered by the respective authors as an expression of financial literacy and which decisions (personal, societal) are included in each case. We also take a first look at whether the constructs include financial behaviour. Ultimately, the aim is to create a framework in which existing and future studies can also be located and which forms a basis for comparing different studies and deriving evidence-based support measures.

Keywords Financial literacy · Financial competence · Systematic analysis · Terminology in the context of financial literacy · Constructs of financial literacy · Content scope of financial literacy

2.1 Introduction

In the German- and English-language academic literature on financial literacy, the wide scope of terms and definitions is striking. Common terms are financial literacy, financial knowledge, financial capability, or financial competence. Definitions differ by content and in the scope of the construct, e.g. if only cognitive facets are considered, or whether a broad view is taken on financial literacy (that includes motivational, emotional or behavioural factors as well) (Haupt, 2022; Huston, 2010). In particular, the broad spectrum of definitions found under the common umbrella term of financial literacy is striking. The term sometimes refers to just financial knowledge and sometimes takes other characteristics like behaviour, interest in financial topics, values and/or attitudes into account as well. Some definitions have the same content but use different terms for the construct. For example, broader constructs, as mentioned above, are sometimes referred to as financial literacy and sometimes as financial competence. These terminological inconsistencies make it difficult to compare studies and their results, to generalise results, identify deficits and derive educational measures from them.

Geiger et al. (2016, p. 75 f.) provide a first rationale towards differentiating and categorising the terminology. A distinction is made between process-orientation and result-orientation (Fig. 2.1). Financial literacy is seen here as the result of an educational or socialisation process (financial education, financial socialisation). In a narrow sense, financial literacy includes knowledge and affective aspects such as attitudes and motivation. Financial literacy in a broader sense additionally includes behavioural aspects, i.e., the capability to act as well as social competence. The "result" of the educational and/or socialisation process describes the respective learning progress in financial literacy at a specific point in time.

Because we do not consider this differentiation sufficient to systematise existing definitions, terms and constructs and because it does not consider the content areas that are behind the respective definitions, we develop it further. The *aim* of this chapter is to systematise the terms and definitions used, the constructs (behind the terms), and the content areas taken into account in different studies and to provide a

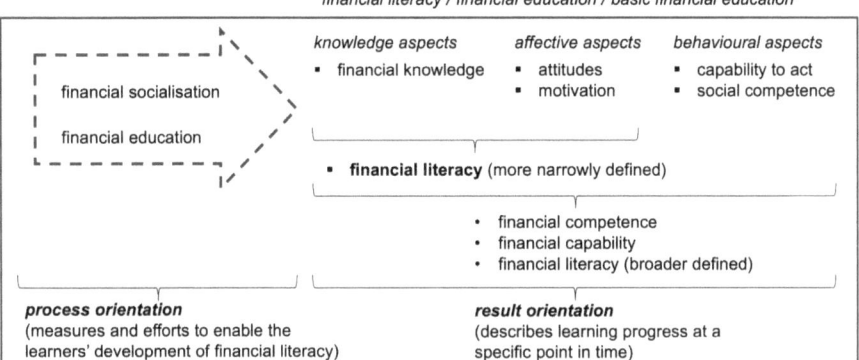

Fig. 2.1 Terms in the context of financial literacy (Geiger et al., 2016, p. 76)

systematisation framework for studies in financial literacy. We conduct a review and an expert survey to validate our systematisation. By applying an inductive approach to the German and English scientific literature corpus around the term financial literacy and familiar terms, we take into account the type of research/study, the terms used by the respective authors, the construct that can be identified behind the terms, the scope of the content considered in the respective studies, the perspective on financial literacy (individual and/or society-related financial requirements) and the proximity to behaviour/performance when confronted with financial decisions.[1] Even though we reviewed a large number of literature sources and a broad range of approaches, we do not claim to have included all relevant sources. Instead, the benefit of the chapter can be seen in the development of criteria for systematisation, which can be used in further studies. In the case of authors or groups of authors of several studies, the contributions are included in our analyses in condensed form and not as a single contribution if the terminology and basic understanding of constructs within a group remain the same. For the sake of clarity and transparency, we provide our table of results in the Appendix Table A1.

2.2 Methodology

2.2.1 Literature Selection

From the beginning of the 1990s, the discussion about financial literacy slowly gained momentum and attracted greater attention (Beck, 1991). We therefore focus on articles that have been published since 1990.

The literature was selected by combining two methodological approaches: a scoping review and an expert survey (for this approach, see Pan et al., 2021). For the

---

[1] The categories are explained in more detail in Sect. 2.2 of this chapter.

review, we searched German and English academic contributions on databases such as Google Scholar, ERIC, EconBiz, and Web of Science, using the keywords (and the German equivalents) financial literacy, financial competence, financial knowledge, financial capability, financial education, and financial behaviour. The snowball method, which allows the identification of further relevant literature by moving backward from a relevant current source, was also applied (Morrison, 2007; Noy, 2008). Identified studies were then reviewed for relevance in an expert survey by members of the AFin research network.[2] Together with these experts, we developed categories in plenary sessions (Pan et al., 2021, pp. 5–6). As a result of this process, 37 contributions were identified as relevant for the subsequent systematisation.

2.2.2 Systematisation Criteria

When analysing the research contributions (see Appendix Table A1), the (groups of) authors (column 1), year(s) of publication (column 2), type of research contribution (column 3), the term(s) used by these authors (column 4), the construct behind the term(s) used (column 5), the content considered (column 6), the content width (column 7), the finance focus (column 8), the consideration of potential behaviour/performance in finance related situations (column 9), the taxonomy level (column 10) and the question of operationalisation in the respective studies (11) were taken into account. Column 12 comprises remarks and the respective references are listed in column 13.

(1) Authors and (2) Year of Publication
Most authors or groups of authors do not publish just one study on the topic of financial literacy. However, each author's (group of authors') background usually evidences a certain understanding of financial literacy that runs through all publications. Instead of always including all potentially relevant publications of this author (group of authors) in our systematisation, which would have quickly become confusing and redundant, we have decided to name the source(s) in which their basic understanding of financial literacy is described.

If studies by the same authors use different terms or have different focuses, we consider these contributions separately. The column year shows the year of publication of one or more central studies of a group or an author.

(3) Type of Research Contribution
We distinguish between empirical studies, reviews, meta-analyses and conceptual studies. In the case of an empirical approach, we further distinguish between (1) qualitative, (2) quantitative, or (3) mixed methods studies. Empirical studies can be distinguished from (4) (systematic) reviews, (5) meta-analyses, and (6) conceptual contributions. If a study falls into more than one category, this is noted in the table. In the case of reviews and meta-analyses, the respective researcher's/research

---

[2] The network "Action-based Financial Literacy - Conceptualisation, Assessment and Validation" (AFin) was funded by the German Research Foundation (DFG, project number 460770732) (Chap. 1)

group's own view must be outlined in the paper. The reference to an already established construct or an existing theoretical background is not listed as an independent study.

(4) Terms/Labels

For this criterion, we adopt the terms used by the author/group of authors in their study, e.g., Financial Literacy (FL), Financial Competence (FC), and/or Financial Education (FE).

(5) Construct and Construct Width

In this category, the width of the respective construct is presented. A distinction can be made between three characteristics:

- Narrow: In a narrow understanding, only knowledge and—if considered in the approach—understanding are included. An example of this is the work of Walstad and Rebeck (2017), who model financial knowledge and understanding for different content areas.
- Intermediate: In this category, only a few facets are included, however, more than just knowledge is taken into consideration. For example, Atkinson and Messy (2012) refer to knowledge, attitudes, and behaviour.
- Broad: In this case, various facets besides financial knowledge are seen as part of the construct, e.g., financial understanding, skills, knowledge application, and/or non-cognitive dispositions such as motivation/interest or attitudes and behaviour/performance. An example of such a construct is the definition of the OECD (2016, p. 47) framework for financial literacy: financial literacy is a "combination of awareness, knowledge, skill, ***attitude*** [sic.] and behaviour necessary to make sound financial decisions and ultimately achieve individual financial well-being". Such a construct would be considered broad.[3]

(6) Content Considered

This category lists the financial content taken into consideration by the respective authors in their contributions (e.g. risk and reward). As an example, the content area of Kraitzek and Förster (2023) is investing.

(7) Content Width

In a *narrow understanding*, from only one up to three content areas are focused. Fürstenau and Hommel (2019), for example, only focus on mortgage loans. Gärling et al. (2009) consider two content areas, namely stock market investments and loans. The *broad approaches* include more than three content areas, e.g. earning/income, spending money, saving money, borrowing money, pension, insurance (Aprea et al., 2015; Wuttke & Aprea, 2018). The classification into narrow and

---

[3] There are also broader approaches based on the definitions of Weinert (2001, more prevalent in German-speaking countries) and Shavelson (2010, more in international studies). Aprea and Wuttke (2016) go even further, seeing financial literacy "as the potential that enables a person to effectively plan, execute, and control financial decisions. As such, it is based on the availability of individual dispositions, that is, knowledge and skills, motivations and interests, attitudes and values and contingent on situational characteristics".

broad does not imply that a broader range of content is "better", this should merely be understood as a description.

(8) Perspective on Finance

Here, we describe which perspective on financial literacy the author(s) focus on. We distinguish between a personal financial perspective and a society-related financial perspective. Approaches focused on personal finance take into account the individual knowledge/competences and or decision-making, which are necessary for financial decisions and financial behaviour. Personal finance thus encompasses areas that are closely connected to the individual life decisions of a person, such as money management, budgeting, and saving (e.g. Atkinson & Messy, 2012; Carmel et al., 2020). Society-related approaches consider skills necessary to understand a social system, for example, to comprehend questions of financing the social/economic system in times of demographic change (Kaminski & Friebel, 2012). Aprea and Wuttke (2016) refer in this respect to responsible economic citizens.

(9) Behaviour/Performance

If behaviour or finance-related performance is considered in the respective instrument used in a study, this is recorded as "performance included". An example would be investment behaviour or borrowing behaviour. "Close to behaviour/performance" refers to decisions that have to be made, for example, in simulations or in situational judgement tests with the perspective "what would you do in a certain situation?". "No behaviour/performance" is recorded if only knowledge elements are included, even if these are embedded in a situation.

(10) Taxonomy Level

With their taxonomy of learning objectives, Anderson and Krathwohl (2001) have laid the foundation for the classification of cognitive process dimensions, the origins of which lie in the work of Bloom (1956). According to Anderson and Krathwohl (2001), a distinction is made between the levels "remember" (knowledge), "comprehend", "apply", "analyse", "evaluate" and "create". The table indicates whether the authors specify a taxonomy level or not ("yes"/"no"). In case no taxonomy levels are mentioned, we categorise this as "not specified".

(11) Operationalisation

Here, we analyse whether and how the respective construct is operationalised, i.e. made measurable. If a construct is measured in a study, we name the type of instrument (qualitative/ quantitative) that was used and the response format (open/closed).

(12) Remarks

This column provides further information regarding the respective contributions. This includes issues of generalisability (e.g., if only households in a specific region have been investigated, as is the case for Carpena et al., 2011), or limitations of instruments (e.g., behaviour measured by means of self-assessment, Grohs-Müller, 2018).

2.2.3 Exemplary Categorisation

These systematisation criteria are applied to the 37 analysed contributions. In the following, we present in detail the results of two examples, namely Walstad and Rebeck (2017; see Table 2.1, Table A1: table sequence number 35) and (below) the approach of the OECD (2013, 2014, 2017, see Table 2.2; Table A1: table sequence number 28):

Walstad and Rebeck investigated financial literacy at 1218 high schools in their 2017 study using the Test of Financial Literacy (TFL) in particular. Table 2.1 shows the categorisation of the contribution based on the aforementioned criteria, supplemented by explanations. The numbers in brackets represent the columns of the table (Appendix, Table A1).

The second example uses the contributions of the OECD (2013, 2014, 2017) and shows their categorisation in Table 2.2. With its conceptual and empirical work, the OECD has laid the foundation for many other contributions

2.3 Results

Type of Research, Terms and Constructs

The contributions (in total 37) are primarily empirical (24). Of these, 16 are exclusively quantitative, 3 conceptual and quantitative, 1 is a meta-analysis and quantitative, 1 is qualitative and conceptual and 3 are mixed methods. Just 7 publications are purely conceptual, 5 are reviews, and one is a meta-analysis and review.

Financial literacy (e.g. Lusardi & Mitchell, 2011; OECD, 2013, 2014, 2017; Walstad & Rebeck, 2017) and financial competence (e.g. Fürstenau & Hommel, 2018, 2019; Hommel et al., 2017; Hommel & Fürstenau, 2020; Kaminski & Friebel, 2012; OECD, 2022) are the most frequently used labels (24 in total). Financial knowledge is also strongly represented (e.g. Carpena & Zia, 2020; Knoll & Houts, 2012; Houts & Knoll, 2020; Bender, 2012; Barry, 2014; Di Domenico et al., 2022) (in total 7). Less common are Financial Decision Making (FDM, mentioned 7 times; e.g. Gärling et al., 2009; Zaleskiewicz & Traczyk, 2020), Financial Behaviour (FB, mentioned 5 times, e.g. Di Domenico et al., 2022; Kaiser & Menkhoff, 2017, 2020; Carpena & Zia, 2020) and Financial Education (FE, mentioned 4 times, e.g. Kaiser & Menkhoff, 2017, 2020; Kaiser, et al., 2022a).[4] Table 2.3 gives a brief overview of the results (the detailed table with all results of the systematisation is available in the Appendix A1; the numbers indicate the lines in the table).

---

[4] The total number of constructs mentioned is higher than the number of articles. This is due to the overlapping and inconsistent use of the constructs within the contributions. To highlight these overlaps and partial inconsistencies, we have mentioned each identified construct.

Table 2.1 Exemplary categorisation of the approach in Walstad and Rebeck (2017)

Criteria	Classification	Explanation
Author (1)	Walstad & Rebeck	
Year (2)	2017	
Type of research (3)	Quantitative	The authors draw on existing constructs (e.g. the learning objectives taxonomy according to Anderson & Krathwohl, 2001). The focus is primarily on the construction and application of measurement instruments. The contribution is based on large quantitative empirical data sets.
Terminology (4)	Financial Literacy (FL)	The authors use the term financial literacy.
Construct (5)	Narrow	The focus is on knowledge and understanding of personal finance, which represents a narrow view of financial literacy.
Content considered (6)	6 content areas	The content areas include using credit; saving; earning income; financial investing; buying goods and services; protecting and insurance.
Content width (7)	Broad	Due to the six different content areas, the content approach is considered broad.
Perspective on finance (8)	Personal finance	The authors describe the target area as personal finance; society-related references are not made.
Behaviour/ Performance (9)	Not included	There is no reference to or assessment of financial performance, the authors only test financial knowledge. Although these knowledge elements are embedded in situations, no performance is required.
Taxonomy level (10)	Knowledge, comprehension, application	The three lower levels (remember, understand, apply) of the taxonomy are addressed according to the test manual (Walstad & Rebeck, 2017, p. 9).
Operationalisation (11)	Various test instruments available	Measurement instruments are available for different target groups: Basic Finance Test (BFT, upper elementary and lower middle school) Test of Financial Knowledge (TFK, upper middle school and high school) Test of Financial Literacy (TFL, Secondary level II and final year high school classes)
Remarks (12)	No behaviour/ performance included, no differentiation between knowledge and literacy; cross-sectional, reliability and validity of self-reported data	Regarding the above-mentioned criteria, the contributions lack the reference to actual behaviour/ performance. Additionally, knowledge and literacy are not differentiated. In a cross-sectional design, statements can only be made at one point in time without taking into account changes due to, e.g., learning effects.

Table 2.2 Exemplary categorisation of the OECD approach (2013, 2014, 2017)

Criteria	Classification	Explanation
Author (1)	OECD	
Year (2)	2013, 2014, 2017	
Type of research (3)	Conceptual (6) and quantitative (2)	The large-scale PISA surveys, which are based on the OECD framework, implement internationally comparative quantitative tests of secondary school students.
Terminology (4)	Financial Literacy (FL)	The OECD uses the label Financial Literacy.
Construct (5)	Broad	The focus of the OECD framework is on knowledge and understanding of finance-related requirements as well as on skills, motivation, confidence to apply and make effective decisions.
Content considered (6)	4 content areas	The OECD focuses on four content areas, namely money and transactions; financial planning; risk and reward, and financial landscape.
Content width (7)	Broad	The range of content can be considered broad with regard to the four content areas.
Perspective on finance (8)	Personal finance	The OECD's focus is on personal finance as a "capacity of students […] to make informed choices" (OECD, 2013, p. 144).
Behaviour/Performance (9)	No (effective) action (performance) included	The OECD covers various task formats, some of which also describe situations. Although the OECD (2013, p. 144) refers to 'effective actions' in its understanding of financial literacy, the items are merely placed in the situational context without requiring any realistic performance/action on the part of the person being tested. Thus, realistic and everyday actions of the person are not covered.
Taxonomy level (10)	Knowledge, comprehension, application	The three lower taxonomy levels (up to "apply") are addressed.
Operationalisation (11)	Various test instruments available	The test includes single and multiple-choice items as well as questions with open-response options.
Remarks (12)	No (effective) action (performance) included; no clear differentiation between knowledge and literacy	The data consists of high school students. Higher taxonomy levels are not represented.

Table 2.3 Results regarding terms (4) and constructs (5)

Term used by author(s)	Construct
Financial Literacy	
	Narrow:
(8) Carpena, Cole, Shapiro & Zia	(8) financial knowledge
(13) Förster, Happ & Maur	(13) knowledge and understanding of personal finance
(21) Oberrauch & Kaiser	(21) financial knowledge
(26) Lusardi & Mitchell	(26) basic financial knowledge
(35) Walstad & Rebeck	(35) knowledge and understanding of personal finance
	Intermediate:
(3) Atkinson & Messy	(3) rather broad (knowledge, behaviour, attitude)
(5) Bender	(5) rather narrow (mainly knowledge)
(7) Carmel, Leiser & Spivak	(7) rather narrow (but modelling the path from knowledge to financial decision-making, considering non-cognitive factors as influencing factors)
(10) Chen & Volpe	(10) rather narrow (personal finance knowledge)
(30) Retzmann & Seeber/Seeber & Retzmann	(30) rather broad (FL as part of economic competence)
	Broad:
(2) Aprea & Wuttke	(2) two perspectives: content and personal resources; four facets: individual cognitive, individual non-cognitive, systemic cognitive, systemic non-cognitive
(11) Cude	(11) knowledge, attitudes, and behaviours
(16) Geiger, Meretz & Liening	(16) knowledge and affect (attitudes and motivation); FC additionally includes action and social competence
(17) Grohs-Müller	(17) following the OECD-definition
(19) Huston	(19) knowledge, ability, confidence to apply or use knowledge
(27) Mania & Tröster	(27) basic financial education covering the basic and practical requirements of everyday monetary matters
(28) OECD	(28) knowledge, understanding, skills, motivation to apply, decisions
(31) Rudeloff	(31) competence model including macroeconomic and microeconomic (individual) facets (cognitive dimension) as well as non-cognitive facets
(32) Schürkmann	(32) financial literacy as competence (knowledge and attitudes)
(34) Silgoner, Greimel-Fuhrmann & Weber	(34) in line with the OECD definition

(*continued*)

Table 2.3 (continued)

Term used by author(s)	Construct
Financial Competence	
	Intermediate:
(1) Ambuehl, Bernheim & Lusardi	(1) evaluation of errors, decision making
	Broad:
(14) Fürstenau & Hommel	(14) knowledge, application, decisions, non-cognitive facets
(16) Geiger, Meretz & Liening	(16) includes FL, additionally action and social competence
(22) Kaminski & Friebel	(22) financial literacy and financial competence (following Weinert)
(24) Kraitzek & Förster	(24) holistic perspective, cognitive and non-cognitive
(29) OECD/EU	(29) "a combination of awareness, knowledge, skill, attitude and behaviour necessary to make sound financial decisions and ultimately achieve individual financial well-being" (p. 3)
(31) Rudeloff	(31) competence model including macroeconomic and microeconomic (individual) facets (cognitive dimension) as well as non-cognitive facets
Financial Knowledge	
	Narrow:
(4) Barry	(4) mainly knowledge
(23) Knoll & Houts	(23) only knowledge
(26) Lusardi & Mitchell	(26) basic financial knowledge
	Intermediate:
(5) Bender	(5) rather narrow (self-regulation in financial decisions)
(20) Kaiser & Menkhoff	(20) rather broad (financial knowledge and behaviour)
	Broad:
(9) Carpena et al.	(9) dimensions numeracy skills, financial awareness and attitudes
(12) Di Domenico et al.	(12) knowledge and non-cognitive facets
Financial Sophistication	
	Narrow:
(6) Calvet, Campbell & Sodini	(6) 3 investment mistakes of households
Financial Decision Making	
	Intermediate:
(25) Luermann, Serra-Garcia & Winter	(25) only intertemporal choice
(37) Zaleskiewicz & Traczyk	(37) emotions included as influence on decision making
	Broad:
(15) Gärling et al.	(15) cognitive abilities and affective influences on decision making
	Not specified
(33) Sekścińska & Markiewicz	(33) Not specified, what FDM is

(*continued*)

Table 2.3 (continued)

Term used by author(s)	Construct
Financial Education	
	Narrow:
(8) Carpena et al.	(8) impacts of 5-week video-based financial education programme
(21) Oberrauch & Kaiser	(21) knowledge scale, FE as intervention
	Intermediate:
(25) Luermann, Serra-Garcia & Winter	(25) rather narrow (modules on money spending, purchase, savings; intertemporal choice)
(36) Walstad & Wagner	(36) rather broad (FE as a means to support FB and decisions)
Financial Behaviour	
	Broad:
(9) Carpena et al.	(9) goal setting, counselling, incentives
(12) Di Domenico et al.	(12) knowledge and non-cognitive factors

Content Considered (6) and Content Width (7)

The content width ranges from contributions that do not address a specific content at all (Cude, 2022; Haupt, 2022; Huston, 2010; Zaleskiewicz & Traczyk, 2020) to contributions with multiple (more than six) content areas. Some of the contributions focus on just one area: Calvet et al. (2009) use investments, in particular asset allocation; Carmel et al. (2020) focus on consumption; Di Domenico et al. (2022) use stocks and funds; Fürstenau and Hommel (2018, 2019) discuss mortgages; Kraitzek and Förster (2023) investing, and Walstad and Wagner (2022) savings (Table 2.4). Most contributions consider more than three content areas, which means that most have a broad content scope.

The terms used for a specific content sometimes vary between the contributions. For example, "money and payments" (Rudeloff, 2019) and "payment transactions" (Schürkmann, 2017) refer to the same content. Similarly, "debt management" (Knoll & Houts, 2012; Houts & Knoll, 2020) and "loans" (Rudeloff, 2019) represent the same core "credit & loans". The content that received the most attention (category "content considered") across all contributions can be traced back to savings & pensions; credit & loans; earning, income & budgeting; investing and insurance.

Perspective on Finance (8)

Most of the contributions focus on personal finance (in total, 28 of the contributions listed). Only a few additionally include a societal perspective, e.g. Aprea and Wuttke (2016), Barry (2014), Bender (2012), Gärling et al. (2009), Grohs-Müller (2018), Kaminski and Friebel (2012), Retzmann and Seeber (2016), and Rudeloff (2019). The latter includes the societal aspect with the category of monetary policy. Kaminski and Friebel (2012, p. 17) take a similar approach, also including social aspects such as questions of financing the social system in times of demographic change and professional biographical aspects.

Table 2.4 Results regarding content width (7)

Content width	Number of areas
Narrow (one or two areas)	one area: Calvet et al. (2009); Carmel et al. (2020); Di Domenico et al. (2022); Fürstenau and Hommel (2018, 2019); Kraitzek and Förster (2023), Walstad and Wagner (2022)
	two areas: Gärling et al. (2009); Lührmann et al. (2018)
Broad (more than two areas)	three areas: Ambuehl et al. (2022); Förster et al. (2017); Grohs-Müller (2018); Lusardi and Mitchell (2011)
	four areas: Atkinson and Messy (2012); Carpena et al. (2011, 2017); Chen and Volpe (1998); Kaiser and Menkhoff (2017); OECD (2016, 2013, 2014, 2017, 2022), Sekścińska and Markiewicz (2020)
	five areas: Bender (2012); Geiger et al. (2016); Rudeloff (2019)
	six areas: Barry (2014); Mania and Tröster (2015), Retzmann and Seeber (2016); Schürkmann (2017); Walstad and Rebeck (2017)
	Multiple areas (more than 6):
	seven areas: Silgoner et al. (2015)
	nine areas: Aprea and Wuttke (2016); Aprea et al. (2015); Kaminski and Friebel (2012)
	ten areas: Knoll and Houts (2012), Houts and Knoll (2020); Oberrauch and Kaiser (2022)

Behaviour/Performance (9)

If behaviour or performance is included, contributions refer above all to financial decision-making (e.g. Ambuehl et al., 2022; Fürstenau & Hommel, 2018; Gärling et al., 2009; Lührmann et al., 2018; Retzmann & Seeber, 2016; Rudeloff, 2019; Sekścińska & Markiewicz, 2020) and self-assessments of financial behaviour (Di Domenico et al., 2022; Grohs-Müller, 2018), only a few to situational questions (e.g. Carpena et al., 2011; Chen & Volpe, 1998), situational judgements (Aprea et al., 2015) and rather complex scenarios (e.g. Fürstenau & Hommel, 2018, 2019; Kraitzek & Förster, 2023).

Taxonomy Level (10)

In the majority of the contributions, no direct reference to the taxonomy level is made (in total 21; e.g. Calvet et al., 2009; Huston, 2010; Geiger et al., 2016; Kaiser et al., 2022a; Kaiser & Menkhoff, 2017, 2020; Carmel et al., 2020; Zaleskiewicz & Traczyk, 2020; Oberrauch & Kaiser, 2022; Kaiser, et al., 2022b; Lührmann et al., 2018; Sekścińska & Markiewicz, 2020; Kaiser, et al., 2022a; Haupt, 2022; Kraitzek & Förster, 2023). In case operators (verbs that describe the quality of the cognitive process like "remember" or "comprehend") are used, we categorise cognitive process dimensions on the basis of these descriptions and item examples. If contributions (explicitly) address taxonomy levels, then predominantly in the case of remembering, comprehension and application (in total 19; Aprea et al., 2015; Atkinson & Messy, 2012; Bender, 2012; Barry, 2014; Carpena & Zia, 2020; Chen & Volpe, 1998; Förster et al., 2018; Fürstenau & Hommel, 2018, 2019; Hommel & Fürstenau, 2020; Knoll & Houts, 2012; Houts & Knoll, 2020; Lusardi & Mitchell,

2011; Walstad & Rebeck, 2017; Schürkmann, 2017; Wuttke & Aprea, 2018; OECD, 2013, 2014, 2017). Higher taxonomy levels such as evaluation of financial decisions (Rudeloff, 2019) are seldomly considered.

Operationalisation (11)

A quantitative approach to operationalisation can be observed in the majority of contributions (in total 19; Ambuehl et al., 2022; Aprea et al., 2015; Atkinson & Messy, 2012; Barry, 2014; Bender, 2012; Calvet et al., 2009; Carpena et al., 2011, 2017; Chen & Volpe, 1998; Di Domenico et al., 2022; Förster et al., 2017; Kaiser & Menkhoff, 2017; Oberrauch & Kaiser, 2022; Knoll & Houts, 2012; Kraitzek & Förster, 2023; Lührmann et al., 2018; OECD, 2013, 2014, 2017; Schürkmann, 2017; Walstad & Rebeck, 2017; Walstad & Wagner, 2022; Wuttke & Aprea, 2018).

In the studies we analysed, literacy or competence is predominantly operationalised and measured using closed items (e.g. Barry, 2014; Bender, 2012; Förster et al., 2018; Lusardi & Mitchell, 2011; OECD, 2013, 2014, 2017). Qualitative surveys or additional qualitative approaches are rather rare (e.g. Grohs-Müller, 2018; Mania & Tröster, 2015). In some cases, a situational approach is used, in which competence is also measured via the response behaviour to closed items.

A stronger situational orientation is implemented by Aprea et al. (2015) using situational judgments in their case for planning and managing of everyday money matters, Fürstenau and Hommel (2018, 2019) applying scenarios for mortgage decisions, Kraitzek and Förster (2023) using complex performance scenarios and Carpena et al. (2011) with short scenarios. A more in-depth analysis regarding the measurement of financial literacy/competence is provided in Chap. 5 of this SpringerBrief.

Remarks (12)

Due to the different research objectives, research designs, samples (regarding age, gender, socio-economic status), as well as geographical and cultural areas of the individual studies, clustering of the limitations is only possible to a restricted extent in terms of content and structure. According to the systematisation criteria, limitations and potential shortcomings were considered for each study.

Clustering can be used to consolidate findings in that the selection of the predominantly quantitative study designs, the selection of the test subjects, (e.g. with regard to age: pupils, students [Förster et al., 2018]; young adults, adults [Calvet et al., 2009]; gender; origin/location: worldwide [OECD, 2013, 2014, 2017]; Europe [e.g. Germany (Förster et al., 2018)]; Sweden [Calvet et al., 2009], Asia [e.g. India (Carpena et al., 2011, 2017)], USA [Walstad & Rebeck, 2017]) require careful consideration. The transferability of the respective study findings must be carefully and critically examined in each case.

2.4 Discussion and Conclusion

Our chapter describes the systematisation of definitions, terms, constructs and content that are all related to financial literacy (used here as a common generic term). These were categorised according to a previously developed criteria grid. Despite the striking heterogeneity, two central results can be identified:

1. a categorisation system for further classification of contributions to the topic, but also a basis for the further development of this categorisation system;
2. a systematisation of contributions that illustrate the diversity and inconsistency of the terms, constructs and research approaches that are addressed.

As presented at the beginning of the chapter, the heterogeneity of terms and constructs behind the terms should be noted. The terminology refers to different constructs, and, conversely, the same constructs comprise different facets or refer to different terminology. These differences continue in the other categories considered, such as the differences in the consideration of financial behaviour/performance, cognitive, emotional, or volitional facets of financial literacy. Subsequently, the differences persist in the content scope and content considered and the way in which the underlying construct is operationalised in measurements. There are various approaches to assessing and investigating financial literacy. Additionally, the different regions from which the selected contributions originate also contribute to the inconsistent use and description of terminology, e.g. due to regional or culturally determined traditions in concepts and linguistic terms. As it stands, the results are not comparable with each other, and it is almost impossible to derive coherent educational measures from the results of the studies.

Despite all the differences, the definitions have a common core: financial knowledge is a central (and sometimes the only) component of financial literacy in all the definitions known to us. In Weinert's (2001) definition of competence, knowledge is only one facet needed for competent action/performance. It can, therefore, be stated that knowledge as the identified common core of the definitions could serve as a starting point for sound financial action. What is often missing is a connection to real performance and "effective actions" (OECD, 2013, p. 144).

The results of our working group establish connections to the working group "Frameworks" (Chap. 3) and the working group "Instruments" (Chap. 5), the results of which are presented in the following chapters. Furthermore, the aim of the network is to develop a performance-oriented approach to financial literacy. Therefore, it is necessary to establish a competence framework and define the measurement instruments. For all this, a foundation based on existing terminology, frameworks, and measurement approaches is essential.

Appendix

Table A1 Systematising terminology

(sequence no.)	1) Author/s	2) Year	3) Type of research contribution	4) Terms/Labels (used by authors)	5) Construct (behind the concepts) and width	6) Content considered	7) Content width	8) Perspective on finance	9) Behaviour/ Performance	10) Taxonomy level	11) Operationalisation	12) Remarks
definition of the category	name of authors	year(s) of publication	based on the focus of the paper	name or concept used by authors	short description of the construct used and classification (categories: narrow, rather narrow, rather broad, broad)	short description of the financial content areas	narrow, broad	perspective on finance: e.g. focussing personal finance or/and society or/and additional perspectives such as well-being; responsible corporate citizen; levels within?	Does the survey instrument contain financial behaviour (close to reality), decision making or references to behaviour?	explicitly mentioned by authors? (yes/no) AND if applicable, then: cognitive process dimension required, namely: remember, comprehend, apply, analyse, evaluate, create	type of the instrument/test: knowledge, competence, situational judgement; response format: open/closed	observations related to concept, content, etc., evaluation of approaches
coding categories and coding instructions		year(s) of publication	(1) qualitative, (2) quantitative, (3) mixed-methods, (4) reviews, (5) meta-analyses, (6) conceptual (e.g. a contribution that is 2/3 conceptual and uses empirical data to illustrate)	Financial Literacy FL, Financial Competence FC, Financial Education FE, Financial Decision Making FDM, Financial Understanding FU, Fin. Attitudes FAtt, (e.g. risk attitude), Financial Knowledge FK, Financial Behaviour FB, Financial Action FA, Financial Confidence FConf (Perception of own FL, confidence in own knowledge)	**narrow:** construct focuses e.g. merely knowledge and understanding **intermediate:** rather narrow/rather broad **broad:** construct includes several facets, e.g. besides knowledge and understanding also behaviour, and e.g. non-cognitive dispositions (financial interest, motivation, self-efficacy, ...)	number (if applicable) and area (e.g. money and transactions; managing finances; risk and reward, financial landscape) (more than 6 areas coded as "multiple")	**narrow:** one up to three content areas **broad:** more than three content areas	personal finance (budgeting, insurance)	e.g. decision tasks in a third perspective or complex situational judgments	e.g. remember, comprehend	e.g. observing choices	e.g. one name of a concept can cover several definitions (e. g. FL); author(s) use a different understanding related to the concept x in the sense of y

#	Author	Year		FC (deliberative financial competence)				personal finance	reference to decisions (in an experimental setting)	not specified	FL questionnaire	distance to real action situations, behaviour/ performance
1	Ambuehl, Bernheim & Lusardi	2022	(2) quantitative	FC (deliberative financial competence)	intermediate (rather broad), (evaluation errors), decision making quality	3 areas: savings, interest, inflation	narrow	personal finance		not specified	FL questionnaire (5 items, savings, compound interest, inflation) [appendix of the working paper 20618, p. 14], education intervention experiments; self-reported behaviour (regarding the experiment)	distance to real action situations, behaviour/ performance
2	Aprea, Wuttke, Leumann & Heumann / Aprea & Wuttke / Wuttke & Aprea	2015/ 2016/ 2018	(6) conceptual and (2) quantitative	FL	broad, two perspectives: content and personal resources; four facets: individual cognitive, individual non-cognitive, systemic cognitive, systemic non-cognitive	9 areas: individual cognitive (8): earning/income & planning and managing everyday money matters, spending money, avoiding indebtedness and over-indebtedness, saving money/ building up assets, borrowing money/ taking out loans, making provisions for old age, taking out insurance, using information and counselling services; plus individual systemic (7): money and financial policies, real economy interrelationships, macroeconomic interrelationships, knowledge of finance-related facts, framework conditions of the political system, social security system, tax system	broad	personal finance and society, so far only instrument for personal finance	SJT close to action	comprehend, apply, act	Situational judgement for the facet "plan and manage everyday money matters"	in test: cognitive facets explicit, affective facets are addressed, holistic action and decision-making situation

(continued)

Table A1 (continued)

(sequence no.)	1) Author/s	2) Year	3) Type of research contribution	4) Terms/Labels (used by authors)	5) Construct (behind the concepts) and width	6) Content considered	7) Content width	8) Perspective on finance	9) Behaviour/ Performance	10) Taxonomy level	11) Operationalisation	12) Remarks
3	Atkinson & Messy	2012	(2) quantitative	FL	intermediate (rather broad) (knowledge, behavior, attitude)	4 areas: budgeting, money management, short and long term financial plans, financial product choice	broad	personal finance	no	not specified	questionnaire with 8 questions; tested in 14 countries across 4 continents	mainly knowledge in test, attitude and behaviours
4	Barry	2014	(2) quantitative	FK, FAtt	narrow (mainly knowledge and attitudes towards money)	6 areas: (subjective meaning of money issues; interest, inflation, stocks and bonds, social care, investment, credit, guarantee, pension plans, gross and net)	broad	personal finance, societal aspect with the category of monetary policy	no	not specified	5 scales	limited to attitudes towards money
5	Bender Bender & Barry	2012 2013	(2) quantitative	FK, FDM (attitudes towards money)	intermediate (rather narrow) self regulation in financial decisions/ in money management	5 areas: money management, managing everyday money matters, income and spending, gross and net; interest, inflation, shares, bonds, insurance, retirement provisions	broad	personal finance the societal aspect with the category of monetary policy	behaviour (no action)	knowledge dimension: metacognition (planning and self-monitoring) for financial behaviour; in addition: motivation and volition/effort and self-efficacy (relevant for self-regulated decisions)	TRSQ (trait self-regulation-questionnaire) for financial behaviour	self-regulation measured separately, quality of knowledge test not evaluated, no validated and reliable knowledge test that assesses cognitive elements such as knowledge in addition to attitudes and other non-cognitive elements

6	Calvet, Campbell & Sodini	2009	(2) quantitative	FS (financial sophistication)	narrow	1 area: asset allocation (three types of investment mistakes: underdiversification, inertia in risk taking, and the disposition effect in direct stockholdings)	narrow	personal finance	yes	not specified	actual investment descisions of Swedish households	1) cannot be replicated in other countries/ environments as few countries have such detailed data as Sweden 2) narrow focus on a household's wealth allocation (neglecting other dimensions such as investments, consumption choices, …)
7	Carmel, Leiser & Spivak	2020	(6) conceptual	FL (knowledge and sophisticated skills) --> FDM	intermediate (rather narrow) but modelling the way from FL to FDM and considering various facets in between; orientation to the OECD framework: broad (knowledge and understanding skills, motivation, confidence to apply, decisions)	1 area: consumption related and managerial behaviour	narrow	personal finance	not clearly	not specified	tasks	FC is measured, not specified; FDM not really specified

(*continued*)

Table A1 (continued)

(sequence no.)	1) Author/s	2) Year	3) Type of research contribution	4) Terms/Labels (used by authors)	5) Construct (behind the concepts) and width	6) Content considered	7) Content width	8) Perspective on finance	9) Behaviour/ Performance	10) Taxonomy level	11) Operationalisation	12) Remarks
8	Carpena, Cole, Shapiro & Zia	2011	(2) quantitative	FL, FE, FDM	narrow (financial knowledge)	4 areas: budget, savings, loan, insurance	broad	personal finance	"suggest an action to a friend" (fin. attitudes)	(knowledge), comprehend, apply	dimensions of financial knowledge: numeracy skills (computing interest), basic financial awareness, attitudes towards financial decisions; questionnaires (single choice questions and short scenarios on which a comment must be made); impacts of five-week video-based financial education programme	study includes only households in India (Ahmadabad)
9	Carpena, Cole, Shapiro & Zia / Carpena & Zia	2017/ 2020	(2) quantitative	FK (FAtt; numeracy, awareness), FB	broad (financial behaviour and attitudes; financial incentives, goal setting, counselling; financial knowledge includes 3 dimensions: numeracy skills, financial awareness and attitudes towards personal finance)	4 areas: FB: Household Budgeting, Savings, Borrowing, Insurance FK: Financial Numeracy, Financial Awareness, Financial Attitudes	broad	personal finance	"suggest an action to a friend" (fin. attitudes), household financial outcomes	(knowledge), comprehend, apply	3 dimensions of financial knowledge: numeracy skills, basic financial awareness, attitudes towards financial decisions; questionnaires (single choice questions and short scenarios on which a comment must be made)	study includes only households in India (Ahmadabad)

10	Chen & Volpe	1998	(2) quantitative	FL	intermediate (rather narrow) FL as personal finance literacy, in particular personal finance knowledge, opinions and decisions	4 areas: [general knowledge], savings and borrowing, insurance, investment	broad	personal finance	situational question and decision making	knowledge, decision making	comprehensive questionnaire with 36 knowledge questions and 8 questions on opinion and decision (924 university students)	mainly cognitive facets in test
11	Cude	2022	(6) conceptual	FL (existing definitions, components [knowledge, attitudes and behaviours, self-efficacy] and related concepts)	broad (knowledge, attitudes and behaviours)	no specific content	not specified	personal finance	no	(knowledge), not specified	conceptual, no instrument but literature review	conceptual, not empirical
12	Di Domenico et al.	2022	(2) quantitative	FK, FB, FDM	broad (motivation; interaction of knowledge and non-cognitive facets, depletion/self-control)	1 area: stocks and funds (basic economic concepts, interest rates)	narrow	personal finance	FB (self-reported)	no	knowledge based on 6 Lusardi items; FB, financial well-being self-reported	
13	Förster, Happ & Molerov/ Förster, Happ & Maur	2017/ 2018	(2) quantitative	FL	narrow knowledge and understanding of personal finance	3 areas: banking, everyday money management, insurance – these areas were formed from the 6 content areas of Walstad et al. (2013)	narrow	personal finance	no	two categories (knowledge and comprehension; application)	Test of Financial Literacy (TFL, secondary level II and final year classes high school)	no clear differentiation between knowledge and literacy

(continued)

Table A1 (continued)

(sequence no.)	1) Author/s	2) Year	3) Type of research contribution	4) Terms/Labels (used by authors)	5) Construct (behind the concepts) and width	6) Content considered	7) Content width	8) Perspective on finance	9) Behaviour/ Performance	10) Taxonomy level	11) Operationalisation	12) Remarks
14	Fürstenau & Hommel; Hommel & Fürstenau/ Hommel, Fürstenau, Leopold, Ponce & Lopez.	2018/ 2019/ 2020/ 2020/ 2017	(3) mixed-methods	FL/FC	broad (competence-oriented view on FL; potential to plan, execute, control decisions; Weinert, 2001: Wuttke & Aprea, 2018); individual-cognitive competence facet; acknowledges knowledge and application); (2017: knowledge and application, economic reasonable decisions; non-cognitive facets), (2010: competence construct adapted from Shavelson)	1 area: mortgage loans	narrow	personal finance	decision about taking a mortgage (calculation of free monthly income, comparison rent vs. buy, affordable purchase price, annuity calculation); informal learning from websites and decision about a mortgage	comprehend, apply	situational judgement	limited to content mortgages, focus group only young adults (students)

			FDM (financial decision making)				focus on financial decisions			
15	Gärling, Kirchler, Lewis & van Raaij	2009	(4) review		broad (psychological antecedents of financial decisions; decision making as influenced by cognitive and other resources [cognitive abilities, affective influences, overconfidence, overoptimism, risk aversion, loss aversion, money illusion as influence of nominal represenation])	2 areas: stock market investments, loans (rather a psychological investigation with focus on debt and credit usage and value of money)	narrow	personal and global (financial crisis)		not specified	no instrument but literature review	no aggregation into a model of FL/FC or financial decision making
16	Geiger, Meretz & Liening	2016	(6) conceptual	FL, FC	broad FL includes aspects of knowledge and affect (attitudes and motivation); FC additionally includes action and social competence	5 areas: money management, handling life risks, wealth accumulation and old-age provision, handling loans	broad	personal finance (private households)	reference to necessary actions	no	no instrument but literature review	

(*continued*)

Table A1 (continued)

(sequence no.)	1) Author/s	2) Year	3) Type of research contribution	4) Terms/Labels (used by authors)	5) Construct (behind the concepts) and width	6) Content considered	7) Content width	8) Perspective on finance	9) Behaviour/ Performance	10) Taxonomy level	11) Operationalisation	12) Remarks
17	Grohs-Müller/ Grohs-Müller & Greimel-Fuhrmann	2018	(3) mixed-methods	FL, FB	broad (orientation towards OECD - FL), (equated with FE); not only knowledge and problem-solving skills but also money attitudes, the willingness and motivation to deal with relevant questions and problems and to make responsible, reflective decisions (happiness and power, financial planning, quality achieved for money, anxiety), and financial behaviour (rational, demonstrative and compensatory)	3 areas: consumption behaviour, savings behaviour, tendency towards debt (money attitudes)	narrow	personal finance; societal aspect with the category of monetary policy	self-assessment of financial behaviour (money matters, consumption and saving) - action not included	self-assessed behaviour (application?)	(1) qualitative access - financial experiences and perceptions of money matters + attitudes towards money (2) quantitative study, consumption and saving, self-reporting	behaviour measured by means of self-assessment
18	Haupt	2022	(4) review	FL (measurement of FL mostly focus on financial knowledge, financial mathematics, and mathematical skills)	overview about the field of measuring financial literacy, therefore various concepts	no focus on content areas (discussing different components of FL)	not specified	personal finance	no	not possible to determine	review article, various measurement approaches are mentioned.	not possible to determine, depends on the measurement approach, broad scope from knowledge to action

19	Huston	2010	(4) review	FL (knowledge dimension and application dimension)	broad (knowledge and "ability and confidence to effectively apply or use knowledge related to personal finance concepts and products" (p. 307), make decisions)	no specific content	not specified	personal finance		no	recommendation: quantitative test with 12 to twenty items	
20	Kaiser & Menkhoff / Kaiser, Lusardi, Menkhoff & Urban	2017/ 2020/ 2022	(5) meta-analyses and (4) review	FE --> FK --> FB / FK --> FB	intermediate (rather broad) financial knowledge and behaviour; focus: treatment effects on FB	4–6 areas: FB: borrowing, budgeting and planning, saving and investing, insurance, remittances, FE: classroom, online, counselling, educative nudge	broad	personal finance	downstream outcome is financial behaviour (i.e., the result of actions)	no	partly (knowledge tests, measures of behaviour)	
21	Oberrauch & Kaiser / Kaiser, Menkhoff & Oberrauch	2022	(2) quantitative / (5) meta-analysis and (2) quantitative	FL (via FE as intervention)	narrow (financial knowledge scale)	10 areas: interest, inflation, time value of money, investing, housing, annuities, retirement saving, debt management, diversification of risk, life insurance	broad	personal finance	I. article investigates the relationship between financial literacy and time-preferences (beta, delta) and narrow bracketing in an incentivized decision-experiment II. article investigates the causal effect of (financial) education intervention on patience (delta) in incentivized decision-experiments	no	I. 14 items in the FK test and 18 choices eliciting intertemporal preferences II. time preferences using Convex Time Budgeting Task (CTB)	focus on CTB (Convex Time Budgeting Task) in laboratory conditions

(continued)

Table A1 (continued)

(sequence no.)	1) Author/s	2) Year	3) Type of research contribution	4) Terms/Labels (used by authors)	5) Construct (behind the concepts) and width	6) Content considered	7) Content width	8) Perspective on finance	9) Behaviour/ Performance	10) Taxonomy level	11) Operationalisation	12) Remarks
22	Kaminski & Friebel	2012	(6) conceptual	FC/FL	broad (FC and FL), education serves the development of competence, competence analogous to Weinert as knowledge, abilities, skills, attitudes, motivation, values	9 areas: dealing with money, dealing with life risks, asset accumulation and old-age provision, dealing with loans/credits, procuring/processing and evaluating financial information, dealing with advisory and sales situations, the role of the state and influences of international financial interdependencies, functions and interests of financial service providers	broad	individual/ personal und society	rather no (in the description of the competence objectives there is a lot of "explain", "grasp", "analyse")	differentiation between competences and sub-competences according to learning objectives related to economic education	conceptual, no instrument	conceptual, not empirical, action dimension missing; construct also contains non-cognitive facets
23	Knoll & Houts	2012/ 2020	(2) quantitative	FK	narrow (knowledge)	10 areas: interest, inflation, time value of money, investing, housing, annuities, retirement saving, debt management, diversification of risk, life insurance	broad	personal finance	no (but items based on simple actions: having a savings account, or buying a stock)	knowledge, apply	20 item scale (selected response), Knoll and Houts Financial Knowledge Scale (FKS), 10 items short version	covers a similar construct as the Big Three (and Big Five) but at the cost of more response burden among respondents; psychometric properties of shorter scales are similar (own empirical observation)

24	Kraitzek & Förster	2023	(6) conceptual and (2) quantitative	FC	broad ("holistic perspective on the construct of financial competence", p. 222), cognitive and non-cognitive	1 area: investing (as one part of the CEE 2021 content areas)	narrow	personal finance	scenarios	knowledge, apply - no concrete reference to taxonomy levels, but to complex problem solving	performance in a financial competence test with: a standardized test for measuring knowledge and understanding (TFL); a complex performance scenario according to the seven facets of competence assessments (Shavelson, 2012)	focus on one content area
25	Luermann, Serra-Garcia & Winter	2018	(2) quantitative	FE --> FDM	intermediate (rather narrow) FDM, only intertemporal choice	2 areas: focus on created modules by the authors: 1. money spending and purchasing decisions, planning (conscious planning of income and expenditures), 2. saving (saving motives and investment)	narrow	personal finance	yes, decision tasks intertemporal choice (e.g. earlier payment with lower interest rates)	not mentioned	task where money is being allocated	narrow content area with view on financial decision making
26	Lusardi & Mitchell	2011	(4) review	FK	narrow (basic financial knowledge)	3 areas: interest, inflation, risk diversification (addressing risk in financial action)	narrow	personal finance	no	no (mainly remember and comprehend, partly apply knowledge)	closed single items (3 test items - thereof two basic items: (1) ability to calculate compound interest (numeracy), (2) understanding of inflation; – one more sophisticated: (3) knowledge risk diversification, buying a single stock or a stock fund (criteria: simplicity, relevance, brevity; to use in telephone and face-to-face interviews)	limited to basic financial knowledge and numeracy (interest), comprehension of the concept of the concept inflation and simple ideas relate to risks at the stock market

(continued)

Table A1 (continued)

(sequence no.)	1) Author/s	2) Year	3) Type of research contribution	4) Terms/Labels (used by authors)	5) Construct (behind the concepts) and width	6) Content considered	7) Content width	8) Perspective on finance	9) Behaviour/ Performance	10) Taxonomy level	11) Operationalisation	12) Remarks
27	Mania & Tröster	2015	(1) qualitative and (6) conceptual	FL	broad ("basic financial education" covers the "existentially basic and directly practical requirements of everyday behaviour and lifestyle in monetary matters", transl. Mania & Tröster, 2014, p. 140)	6 areas: income, money and transaction, expenses and buying, managing money, credit and debt, provision and insurances	broad	personal finance	yes, interviewpartners debt councellors, continuing education advisors, advice seekers	not specified, but operators such as comprehend, evaluate, calculate, etc.	expert interviews (debt councellors, continuing education advisors, advice seekers) to gather the contents of FL as basic financial education	purpose was developing curricula based on a competence model, measuring FC not included
28	OECD	2013/ 2014/ 2017	(6) conceptual and (2) quantitative	FL	broad (knowledge and understanding of financial concepts, risks; skills, motivation, confidence to apply, effective decisions)	4 areas: money and transactions, financial planning, risk and reward, financial landscape	broad	personal finance	no	comprehension and application	test available, 40 items, short answers (constructed responses) calculations, selected responses; focus on cognitive facets, probands are asked about their savings behavior and access to information on money and financial products after the test	mainly cognitive facets in test

29	OECD/EU	2011/ 2022	(6) conceptual	FC	broad (financial competence; framework for adults): "a combination of awareness, knowledge, skill, attitude and behaviour necessary to make sound financial decisions and ultimately achieve individual financial well-being", p. 3)	4 areas: money and transactions; planning and managing finances; risk and reward, financial landscape (e. g. regulation and consumer protection)	broad	personal finance	category of skills and behaviour is defined for every content area	essential competences, advanced competences, expert competences (highlighted in the Excel version)	conceptual (categories awareness, knowledge and understanding; skills and behaviour; confidence, motivation and attitudes)	
30	Retzmann & Seeber / Seeber & Retzmann	2016/ 2017	(6) conceptual	FL (FE as part of economic education, FL as part of economic competence)	intermediate (rather broad) FL as part of Economic Competence (competence areas consists of financial education: acknowledging individual decisions; acknowledging economic interaction with others and knowing legal aspects)	6 areas: markets, economic systems, political regulations; role of consumer, earner, economic citizen	broad	decisions and rationality of individuals (personal finance); relations and interactions with others; and system and order of the whole (economy)	decision and interaction	no explicit reference to taxonomy levels, but learning objectives that address reasoned decisions, acknowledging relationship and interaction with others, and knowing/ understanding the financial and legal system	conceptual, no instrument	conceptual, not empirical

(*continued*)

Table A1 (continued)

(sequence no.)	1) Author/s	2) Year	3) Type of research contribution	4) Terms/Labels (used by authors)	5) Construct (behind the concepts) and width	6) Content considered	7) Content width	8) Perspective on finance	9) Behaviour/ Performance	10) Taxonomy level	11) Operationalisation	12) Remarks
31	Rudeloff	2019	(3) mixed-methods	FL, FC	broad (competence model including macroeconomic and microeconomic [individual] facets [cognitive dimension] as well as non-cognitive facets [see operationalisation])	5 areas: money and payments, saving, loans, insurance, monetary policy	broad	personal and society (monetary policy)	decisions	reproduce, apply, analyse/elaborate/validate, evaluate (Rudeloff, 2019, p. 114)	free response and multiple choice, testitems available, competence model evaluated (2 dimenstions)	non-cognitive facets measures separately (PANAS for emotion, Prenzel for motivation, money by Barry, economic interest, self-efficacy)
32	Schürkmann	2017	(2) quantitative (monograph)	FL	broad (FL as competence and attitudes towards money management)	6 areas: debt, asset formation, insurance, taxes, payment transactions, monetary policy, online service offers	broad	rather personal finance	no	yes, competence model includes cognitive requirements with reference Blooms taxonomy (Schürkmann, 2017, pp. 15, 73)	competence test, dichotomised, Rasch scaled	level suitable only for certain classes and not widely applicable in the school sector
33	Sekścińska & Markiewicz	2020	(4) review	FDM (FB (influence of individual dispositions, and emotion, motivation)	narrow (not precisely specified what FDM is or if general mechanisms are assumed)	4 areas: saving, investing, borrowing, financial cheating	broad	personal finance	yes, decision making	not specified	not specified, should work in all decisions making processes	general
34	Silgoner, Greimel-Fuhrmann & Weber	2015	(2) quantitative	FL	broad (in line with the OECD definition; survey as part of an OECD initiative)	(7 areas: different content areas mentioned but not explicitly listed: money management, savings, financial products as loans, credit cards, stocks and shares, bonds, current account, pension funds, ...)	broad	personal finance	yes, questions regarding FB ("Which of the following statements best describes how you last chose a product?", p. 46)	not specified	11 items covered FK (inflation, interest rates, risk-return lin, exchange rates 6 items regarding FB (holding pension funds, shopping around, taking out a loan, ...)	distance to real behaviour

35	Walstad & Rebeck	2017	(2) quantitative	FL	narrow (knowledge and understanding of personal finance)	6 areas: using credit; saving; earning income; investing; buying financial goods and services; protecting and insurance	broad	personal finance	no	knowledge (remember and comprehension; application)	various test instruments available: Basic Finance Test (BFT), Test of Financial Knowledge (TFK), Test of Financial Literacy (TFL)	behaviour not included; no clear differentiation between knowledge and numeracy
36	Walstad & Wagner	2022	(2) quantitative	FE	intermediate (rather broad) FL and FE as impact for FB and FDM	1 area: focus on saving behaviours	narrow	personal finance	downstream outcome is financial behaviour (i.e., the result of actions)	no	based on NFCS dataset	no behaviour/ performance included, no differentiation between knowledge and literacy; cross-sectional; reliability and validity of self-reported data
37	Zaleskiewicz & Traczyk	2020	(6) conceptual	FDM (influence of emotions)	intermediate (rather broad) emotions are included as influence and target variable of FDM	no specific content	not specified	not specified, more personal	role of emotions in financial decision making; review of results on different stages of the decision process; integral and incidental emotions in financial decision making	not specified	not specified, should work in all decision making processes	general
999	Noctor, Stoney & Stradling	1992	frequently cited, but primary source (despite intensive search) not found	FL (informed judgements and effective decisions in using and managing money)								

References

Ambuehl, S. B., Bernheim, D., & Lusardi, A. (2022). Evaluating deliberative competence: A simple method with an application to financial choice. *American Economic Review, 112*(11), 3584–3626. https://doi.org/10.1257/aer.20210290

Anderson, L. W., & Krathwohl, D. R. (2001). *A taxonomy for learning, teaching, and assessing: A revision of Bloom's taxonomy of educational objectives*. Longman.

Aprea, C., & Wuttke, E. (2016). Financial literacy of adolescents and young adults: Setting the course for a competence-oriented assessment instrument. In C. Aprea, E. Wuttke, K. Breuer, N. Keng Koh, P. Davies, B. Greimel-Fuhrmann, & J. Lopus (Eds.), *International handbook of financial literacy* (pp. 397–414). Springer.

Aprea, C., Wuttke, E., Leumann, S., & Heumann, M. (2015). Kompetenzfacetten von Financial Literacy: Sichtweisen verschiedener Akteur [Competency facets of financial literacy: Perspectives of different actors]. In J. Seifried, S. Seeber, & B. Ziegler (Eds.), *Jahrbuch der berufs- und wirtschaftspädagogischen Forschung 2015* (pp. 11–22). Barbara Budrich.

Atkinson, A., & Messy, F. (2012). Measuring financial literacy: Results of the OECD/International Network on Financial Education (INFE) Pilot Study. In *OECD working papers on finance, insurance and private pensions, No. 15*. OECD Publishing. https://doi.org/10.1787/5k9csfs90fr4-en

Barry, D. (2014). Die Einstellung zu Geld bei jungen Erwachsenen [Young adults' attitudes towards money]. Eine Grundlegung aus wirtschaftspädagogischer Sicht [A foundation from the perspective of business education]. Springer VS.

Beck, K. (1991). Economic literacy in German speaking countries and the United States. First steps to a comparative study. *Economia, 1*, 17–23.

Bender, N. (2012). *Selbstreguliertes Geldmanagement bei jungen Erwachsenen*. Dissertation, JGU Mainz, Peter Lang.

Bender, N., & Barry, D. (2013). Adaption of the TRSQ for financial behavior. In K. Beck & O. Zlatkin-Troitschanskaia (Eds.), *From diagnostics to learning success. Proceedings in vocational education and training* (pp. 213–224). Sense.

Bloom, B. S. (1956). *Taxonomy of educational objectives: The classification of educational goals* (1st ed.). Longman Group.

Calvet, L. E., Campbell, J. Y., & Sodini, P. (2009). Measuring the financial sophistication of households. *American Economic Review, 99*(2), 393–398. https://doi.org/10.1257/aer.99.2.393

Carmel, E., Leiser, D., & Spivak, A. (2020). The arrested deployment model of financial literacy. In T. Zaleskiewicz & J. Traczyk (Eds.), *Psychological perspectives on financial decision making* (pp. 89–105). Springer Nature.

Carpena, F., Cole, S. A., Shapiro, J., & Zia, B. (2011). *Unpacking the causal chain of financial literacy*. World Bank Policy Research Working Paper (5798).

Carpena, F., Cole, S., Shapiro, J., & Zia, B. (2017). The ABCs of financial education: Experimental evidence on attitudes, behavior and cognitive biases. *Management and Science, 65*(1), 346–369. https://doi.org/10.1287/mnsc.2017.2819

Carpena, F., & Zia, B. (2020). The causal mechanism of financial education: Evidence from mediation analysis. *Journal of Economic Behavior & Organization, 177*, 143–184. https://doi.org/10.1016/j.jebo.2020.05.001

Chen, H., & Volpe, R. P. (1998). An analysis of personal financial literacy among college students. *Financial Services Review, 7*(2), 107–128. https://doi.org/10.1016/S1057-0810(99)80006-7

Cude, B. (2022). Defining financial literacy. In G. Nicolini & B. J. Cude (Eds.), *The Routledge handbook of financial literacy* (pp. 5–17). Routledge.

Di Domenico, S. I., Ryan, R. M., Bradshaw, E. L., & Duineveld, J. J. (2022). Motivations for personal financial management: A self-determination theory perspective. *Frontiers in Psychology, 13*, 977818. https://doi.org/10.3389/fpsyg.2022.977818

Förster, M., Happ, R., & Maur, A. (2018). The relationship among gender, interest in financial topics and understanding of personal finance. *Empirische Pädagogik, 32*(3/4), 293–309. https://doi.org/10.1177/2047173419892209

Förster, M., Happ, R., & Molerov, D. (2017). Using the U.S. test of financial literacy in Germany – Adaptation and validation. *The Journal of Economic Education, 48*(2), 123–135. https://doi.org/10.1080/00220485.2017.1285737

Fürstenau, B., & Hommel, M. (2018). Contribution of bank webpages to the development of young adults' financial competence about mortgages. *Empirische Pädagogik, 32*(3/4), 434–459. https://doi.org/10.1186/s40461-019-0085-z

Fürstenau, B., & Hommel, M. (2019). Developing financial competence about mortgage loans by informal learning using banks' online calculators. *Empirical Research in Vocational Education and Training., 11*(10), 1–33. https://doi.org/10.1186/s40461-019-0085-z

Gärling, T., Kirchler, E., Lewis, A., & van Raaij, F. (2009). Psychology, financial decision making, and financial crises. *Psychological Science in the Public Interest, 10*(1), 1–47. https://doi.org/10.1177/1529100610378437

Geiger, J. M., Meretz, U., & Liening, A. (2016). Systematisierung deutschsprachiger Studien zur Kompetenzerfassung von financial literacy. *Zeitschrift für ökonomische Bildung, 5*, 72–93.

Grohs-Müller, S. (2018). *Jugendliche und ihr Umgang mit Geld. Eine empirische Studie zu Erfahrungen, Einstellungen und Verhaltensweisen von Schüler/inne/n am Ende der Sekundarstufe I* [Adolescents and their approach to money. An empirical study of students' experiences, attitudes, and behaviors at the end of lower secondary school]. Unpublished doctoral dissertation, Wirtschaftsuniversität Wien.

Grohs-Müller, S., & Greimel-Fuhrmann, B. (2018). Students' money attitudes and financial behaviour: A study on the relationship between two components of financial literacy. *Empirische Pädagogik, 32*(3/4), 369–386.

Haupt, M. (2022). Measuring financial literacy. The role of knowledge, skills, and attitudes. In G. Nicolini & B. J. Cude (Eds.), *The Routledge handbook of financial literacy* (pp. 79–95). Routledge.

Hommel, M., & Fürstenau, B. (2020). *Finanzkompetenz informell erwerben: Zusammenhänge mit Persönlichkeitsdimensionen, Geschlecht, numerischen Fähigkeiten und Risikoaversion* [Acquiring financial literacy informally: Associations with personality dimensions, gender, numerical ability, and risk aversion]. bwp@ Profil 6: Berufliches Lehren und Lernen: Grundlagen, Schwerpunkte und Impulse wirtschaftspädagogischer Forschung. 1–26.

Hommel, M., Fürstenau, B., Leopold, C., Ponce, H., & López, M. (2017). Beitrag von Banken-Webseiten zur Entwicklung der Finanzkompetenz ptentieller Darlehensnehmer/innen über Baufinanzierungen [Contribution of bank websites to the development of financial literacy of potential borrowers about construction financing]. In J. Seifried, S. Seeber, & B. Ziegler (Eds.), *Jahrbuch der berufs- und wirtschaftspädagogischen Forschung* (pp. 97–111) Barbara Budrich.

Houts, C. R., & Knoll, M. A. (2020). The financial knowledge scale: New analyses, findings, and development of a short form. *The Journal of Consumer Affairs, 54*(2), 775–800. https://doi.org/10.1111/joca.12288

Huston, S. J. (2010). Measuring financial literacy. *Journal of Consumer Affairs, 44*(2), 296–316. https://doi.org/10.1111/j.1745-6606.2010.01170.x

Kaiser, T., Lusardi, A., Menkhoff, L., & Urban, C. (2022a). Financial education affects financial knowledge and downstream behaviors. *Journal of Financial Economics, 145*(2), 255–272. https://doi.org/10.3386/w27057

Kaiser, T., & Menkhoff, L. (2017). Does financial education impact financial literacy and financial behavior, and if so, when? *World Bank Economic Review, 31*(3), 611–630. https://doi.org/10.2139/ssrn.2753510

Kaiser, T., & Menkhoff, L. (2020). Financial education in schools: A meta-analysis of experimental studies. *Economics of Education Review, 78*, 101930. https://doi.org/10.1016/j.econedurev.2019.101930

Kaiser, T., Menkhoff, L., & Oberrauch, L. (2022b). Is patience malleable via educational intervention? Evidence from field experiments. *CESifo working paper No. 10080.* https://doi.org/10.2139/ssrn.4279168

Kaminski, H., & Friebel, S. (2012). *Arbeitspapier "Finanzielle Allgemeinbildung als Bestandteil der ökonomischen Bildung"*. Institut für Ökonomische Bildung (IÖB).

Knoll, M. A., & Houts, C. R. (2012). The financial knowledge scale: An application of item response theory to the assessment of financial literacy. *The Journal of Consumer Affairs, 46*(3), 381–410. https://doi.org/10.1111/j.1745-6606.2012.01241.x

Kraitzek, A., & Förster, M. (2023). Measurement of financial competence—Designing a complex framework model for a complex assessment instrument. *Journal of Risk and Financial Management, 16*(4), 223. https://doi.org/10.3390/jrfm16040223

Lührmann, M., Serra-Garcia, M., & Winter, J. (2018). The impact of financial education on adolescents' intertemporal choices. *American Economic Journal: Economic Policy, 10*(3), 309–332. https://doi.org/10.1257/pol.20170012

Lusardi, A., & Mitchell, O. S. (2011). Financial literacy around the world: An overview. *Journal of Pension Economics & Finance, 10*(4), 497–508. https://doi.org/10.1017/S1474747211000448

Mania, E., & Tröster, M. (2015). Kompetenzmodell Finanzielle Grundbildung. Umgang mit Geld als Thema der Basisbildung. *Magazin erwachsenenbildung.at, 25*, 1. https://doi.org/10.25656/01:10955

Morrison, H. B. (2007). Snowball sampling: A review of the method and its potential use in evaluating psychotherapies. *Clinical Psychology Review, 27*(2), 268–274.

Nicolini, G. (2022). Assessment methodologies in financial literacy: Best practices and guidelines. In G. Nicolini & B. J. Cude (Eds.), *The Routledge Handbook of Financial Literacy* (pp. 110–123). Routledge.

Noctor, M., Stoney, S., & Stradling, R. (1992). Financial literacy: A discussion of concepts and competences of financial literacy and opportunities for its introduction into young people's learning (Report prepared for the National Westminster Bank). National Foundation for Education Research.).

Noy, C. (2008). Sampling knowledge: The hermeneutics of snowball sampling in qualitative research. *International Journal of Social Research Methodology, 11*(4), 327–344. https://doi.org/10.1080/13645570701401305

Oberrauch, L., & Kaiser, T. (2022). Cognitive ability, financial literacy, and narrow bracketing in time-preference elicitation. *Journal of Behavioral and Experimental Economics, 98*, 101844. https://doi.org/10.1016/j.socec.2022.101844

OECD/INFE (2011). Measuring Financial Literacy: Core Questionnaire in Measuring Financial Literacy: Questionnaire and Guidance Notes for conducting an Internationally Comparable Survey of Financial literacy. OECD, Paris.

OECD. (2013). *PISA 2012 assessment and analytical framework: Mathematics, reading, science, problem solving and financial literacy*. OECD Publishing.

OECD. (2014). *PISA 2012 results in focus. What 15-years-olds know and what they can do with what they know*. OECD Publishing.

OECD (2016). *OECD/INFE International Survey of Adult Financial Literacy Competencies*. OECD Publishing, Paris, www.oecd.org/ daf/fin/financial-education/OECD-INFE-International-Survey-of-Adult-FInancial-Literacy-Competencies.pdf (19.06.2025).

OECD. (2017). *G20/OECD INFE report on adult financial literacy in G20 countries*. OECD Publishing.

OECD. (2022). *Financial competence framework for adults in the European Union*. OECD Publishing.

Pan, L., Tlili, A., Li, J., Jiang, F., Shi, G., Yu, H., & Yang, J. (2021). How to implement game-based learning in a smart classroom? A model based on a systematic literature review and delphi method. *Frontiers in Psychology, 12*, 749–837. https://doi.org/10.3389/fpsyg.2021.749837

Retzmann, T., & Seeber, G. (2016). Financial education in general education schools: A competence model. In C. Aprea, E. Wuttke, K. Breuer, N. Keng Koh, P. Davies, & B. Greimel-Fuhrmann (Eds.), *International handbook of financial literacy* (pp. 9–24). Springer.

Rudeloff, M. (2019). Der Einfluss informeller Lerngelegenheiten auf die Finanzkompetenz von Lernenden am Ende der Sekundarstufe I [The impact of informal learning opportunities on learners' financial literacy at the end of lower secondary school.] [Doctoral dissertation, Georg-August-Universität Göttingen]. Springer.

Schürkmann, S. (2017). *FILS: Financial Literacy Study. Validierung und Analyse einer schüler-orientierten financial literacy* [Validation and analysis of student-centered financial literacy]. Doctoral dissertation, Universität Siegen, DeGruyter.

Seeber, G., & Retzmann, T. (2017). Financial Literacy – Finanzielle (Grund-)Bildung – Ökonomische Bildung. *Vierteljahrshefte zur Wirtschaftsforschung, 86*(3), 69–80. https://doi.org/10.3790/vjh.86.3.69

Sekścińska, K., & Markiewicz, Ł. (2020). Financial decision making and individual dispositions. In T. Zaleskiewicz & J. Traczyk (Eds.), *Psychological perspectives on financial decision making* (pp. 135–166). Springer. https://doi.org/10.1007/978-3-030-45500-2_7

Shavelson, R. J. (2010). On the measurement of competency. *Empirical Research in Vocational Education and Training, 2*, 41–63. https://doi.org/10.25656/01:5235

Silgoner, M., Greimel-Fuhrmann, B., & Weber, R. (2015). Financial literacy gaps of the Austrian population. *Monetary Policy & the Economy Q, 2*, 35–51.

Walstad, W. B., & Rebeck, K. (2017). The test of financial literacy: Development and measurement characteristics. *The Journal of Economic Education, 48*(2), 113–122. https://doi.org/10.1080/00220485.2017.1285739

Walstad, W., & Wagner, J. (2022). Required or voluntary financial education and saving behaviors. *The Journal of Economic Education, 54*, 17–37. https://doi.org/10.1080/00220485.2022.2144573

Weinert, F. E. (2001). Concept of competence: A conceptual clarification. In D. S. Rychen & L. H. Salganik (Eds.), *Defining and selecting key competencies* (pp. 45–65). Hogrefe & Huber Publishers.

Wuttke, E., & Aprea, C. (2018). A situational judgement approach for measuring young adults' financial literacy. *Empirische Pädagogik, 32*(3/4), 272–292.

Zaleskiewicz, T., & Traczyk, J. (2020). Emotions and financial decision making. In T. Zaleskiewicz & J. Traczyk (Eds.), *Psychological perspectives on financial decision making* (pp. 107–133). Springer. https://doi.org/10.1007/978-3-030-45500-2_6

Open Access This chapter is licensed under the terms of the Creative Commons Attribution 4.0 International License (http://creativecommons.org/licenses/by/4.0/), which permits use, sharing, adaptation, distribution and reproduction in any medium or format, as long as you give appropriate credit to the original author(s) and the source, provide a link to the Creative Commons license and indicate if changes were made.

The images or other third party material in this chapter are included in the chapter's Creative Commons license, unless indicated otherwise in a credit line to the material. If material is not included in the chapter's Creative Commons license and your intended use is not permitted by statutory regulation or exceeds the permitted use, you will need to obtain permission directly from the copyright holder.

Chapter 3
Financial Literacy Frameworks: A Scoping Review and Critical Appraisal

Carmela Aprea, Clara Vonhof, Nicole Ackermann, Bärbel Fürstenau, Ronja Baginski, and Manuel Vogler

Abstract The growing interest in financial literacy and related concepts such as financial capability or financial competence has led to the need for a common understanding of what financial literacy education should entail and to coordinate activities in policy and practice accordingly. One tool for achieving such a coordination are financial literacy frameworks. In this chapter, we describe the rationale, methodology and results of a scoping review that we conducted to identify and analyse existing financial literacy frameworks. Our principal aim is to provide a structured overview and description of those frameworks by focusing on the following research questions: (1) How can existing financial literacy frameworks be characterised in terms of developers, publication year, type of publication and target groups? (2) What is the conceptual and, where indicated, theoretical basis of those frameworks and which methodologies were used to develop them? (3) Which components (e.g. content, goals) do they entail? As we also intend to reveal potential areas of improvement for existing financial literacy frameworks as well as avenues

---

C. Aprea (✉) · C. Vonhof · R. Baginski
Business and Economics Education - Instructional Systems Design
and Evaluation & Mannheim Institute for Financial Education (MIFE),
University of Mannheim, Mannheim, Germany
e-mail: carmela.aprea@uni-mannheim.de; clara.vonhof@uni-mannheim.de; ronja.baginski@uni-mannheim.de; manuel.vogler@hs-rm.de

N. Ackermann
Vocational Education with a Focus on Didactics, Department for Research on Educational Sciences, Zurich University of Teacher Education, Zurich, Switzerland
e-mail: nicole.ackermann@phzh.ch

B. Fürstenau
Business Education and Management Training, Faculty of Business and Economics,
TU Dresden, Dresden, Germany
e-mail: baerbel.fuerstenau@tu-dresden.de

M. Vogler
Competence & Career Center, University of Applied Sciences Rhein-Main,
Wiesbaden, Germany
e-mail: manuel.vogler@hs-rm.de

© The Author(s) 2026
M. Förster, M. Hommel (eds.), *Conceptualisation and Measurement of Financial Competence*, SpringerBriefs in Education,
https://doi.org/10.1007/978-3-031-95690-4_3

for further reflection and research, we undertook a critical appraisal of those frameworks by addressing the following an additional research question: (4) What are the strengths and weaknesses of those frameworks? Our findings will help practitioners to better understand which frameworks might be adequate to guide their design and assessment decisions, policy makers to better judge which kind of orientation can be expected from existing frameworks and where further development is needed, and, last, but not least, researchers generate new ideas for where additional investigations are indicated.

Keywords Financial literacy · Financial competence · Financial capability · Framework · Scoping review

3.1 Introduction

As outlined in Chap. 1 of this SpringerBrief, financial literacy has gained momentum not only in research but also in educational policy and practice (Aprea et al., 2016; Lusardi & Mitchell, 2023; OECD, 2005, 2013, 2014; Walstad & Rebeck, 2017). This growing interest has, in turn, led to the need for a common understanding of what financial literacy education should entail to coordinate the various activities such as the development, implementation and monitoring of a financial education strategy, the design of educational programmes or learning materials, and the conceptualisation of financial literacy assessments. One tool for achieving such a coordination are financial literacy frameworks, with many of them having been developed in the last decades either by academics (e.g. Aprea & Wuttke, 2016; Davies, 2015; Kraitzek & Förster, 2023; Reifner, 2003; Schlösser et al., 2011) or by policy organisations, including national and inter- or supranational organisations (e.g. EU & OECD, 2022) as well as special interest advocacy groups (e.g. CEE & JumpStart, 2021). Financial literacy frameworks ensure that learning, instruction and assessment can be aligned, which is pivotal from an educational point of view (e.g. Goldman & Pellegrino, 2015; Pellegrino, 2006). Therefore, those frameworks have similar functions to educational standards and can be developed for different target groups (e.g. adolescents, adults) or school levels of the educational system (e.g. primary or secondary schools). Unlike educational standards, however, they do not necessarily have to be legitimised and adopted by a specifically authorised body but can in principle be developed by any person or institution. Hence, financial literacy frameworks may differ according to who developed them, when and where they are published, and for whom they are designed.

Another relevant feature of financial literacy frameworks is their conceptual background, i.e. which concept they use, possibly by referring to one or more theoretical perspectives. As already indicated in Chap. 2, typical concepts are financial literacy, financial competence and financial capability. Furthermore, financial literacy frameworks might have been developed in various ways, i.e. analytically (e.g. based on one or more theories or by means of literature reviews), empirically (e.g.

by interviewing experts or psychometric modelling and validation), or as a combination of these development methodologies. As a result of their conceptual background, theoretical underpinning and development methodology, financial literacy frameworks may consist of different components or elements that form their building blocks. Usually, one of these building blocks covers content areas, such as earning, spending or saving money. Moreover, further components such as goal statements or qualification levels may be included.

With these considerations in mind, the principal aim of this chapter is to provide a structured overview and description of existing financial literacy frameworks, focusing on the following research questions:

RQ1: How could the existing financial literacy frameworks be characterised in terms of developers, publication year, type of publication and target groups?
RQ2: What is the conceptual and, where indicated, theoretical basis of the existing financial literacy frameworks and which methodologies were used to develop them?
RQ3: Which components do the existing financial literacy frameworks entail?

To answer these questions, we conducted a scoping review to identify and analyse existing financial literacy frameworks. Given that our main research aim is exploratory and descriptive in nature, this type of research synthesis can be considered appropriate, as will be explained in the methodology section of this chapter. However, as we also intend to reveal potential areas of improvement for existing financial literacy frameworks as well as avenues for further reflection and research, we undertook an initial formative evaluation or critical appraisal of these frameworks, i.e. we wanted to provide first answers to the following research question:

RQ4: What are the strengths and weaknesses of existing financial literacy frameworks?

The chapter is structured as follows: In the next section, we specify how we proceeded in searching, analysing, synthesising and formatively evaluating the financial literacy frameworks. Subsequently, we present our results with reference to our research aims and questions. Finally, we summarise our findings, discuss possible limitations of our study and draw conclusions for further research and development activities.

3.2 Methodology

3.2.1 Rationale for Conducting a Scoping Review

As mentioned above, we conducted a scoping review, sometimes also called scoping study, which is a relatively new type of knowledge synthesis developed to 'map' the relevant literature in a particular area of interest (e.g. Arksey & O'Malley, 2005).

We consider this type of review to be suitable for our research aims for the following reasons:

- In contrast to systematic reviews, which are usually applied for quite narrowly defined goals (e.g. explaining the influencing factors of a certain phenomenon or for evaluating the effectiveness of a specific intervention), scoping reviews pursue much broader and generic purposes, such as structuring a certain field or identifying the main characteristics of a given topic (e.g. Peters et al., 2020; Tricco et al., 2018). As financial literacy is a relatively new research area that is not yet conceptually saturated (e.g. Aprea et al., 2016; Lusardi & Mitchell, 2023), we considered this openness of scoping reviews to be favourable.
- Given that scoping reviews are primarily explorative and not evaluative in nature, they are not limited to peer-reviewed journal articles but allow for inclusion of a wide array of different types of literature, such as grey literature (e.g. Thomas et al., 2020). Grey literature refers to documents produced by individuals or organisations and published as well as distributed outside the usual academic channels. Those documents may include reports, working papers, government documents, white papers, and similar materials. From our prior knowledge of the field, we can state that some of the most influential financial literacy frameworks (e.g. those developed and published by the OECD) belong to this type of literature.
- Finally, compared to other, more open-ended types of reviews (e.g. narrative reviews), scoping reviews have the advantage that an elaborated methodology already exists for them, namely the PRISMA extension guidelines for scoping reviews (Liberati et al., 2009; Tricco et al., 2018), which could be used for our purposes.

In the remainder of this section, we describe how we applied these guidelines to collect, analyse and formatively evaluate existing financial literacy frameworks. We first outline the search and selection strategy we followed and then outline how we extracted data and analysed the identified frameworks to answer the research questions above.

3.2.2 *Search and Selection Strategy to Identify Existing Financial Literacy Frameworks*

To identify existing financial literacy frameworks, we searched the relevant educational and economics databases, including EBSCO, ECONBIZ, Web of Science, ERIC and OECD iLibrary. As we wanted to include sources in English and German language, we also used Pedocs, Fachportal Pädagogik and FIS Bildung Literaturdatenbank as additional databases. The following search strings were applied on titles, abstracts and keywords:

- In English: (financ* OR economic) AND (literacy OR education OR competenc* OR capabilit* OR skill*) AND (framework OR model OR scheme OR standard)

- In German: (finanz* OR ökönom*) AND (literacy OR Bildung OR Kompetenz* OR Fähigkeit OR Fertigkeit) AND (framework OR model* OR schema OR standard*).

In accordance with the scoping review approach, we did not limit the database search to specific publication types, as we assumed that grey literature would also provide important contributions.

The search period covered the years 2000–2023. Financial literacy became the subject of academic and political debate on a larger scale around the turn of the millennium, so this can be seen as a reasonable restriction, which is also applied in other reviews on financial literacy (e.g. Goyal & Kumar, 2020; Graña-Alvarez et al., 2022). The database search was conducted between April and September 2023. In addition, we conducted a snowball search by analysing the reference lists of the records already found and included frameworks that we already knew.

As depicted in Fig. 3.1, the database search yielded 1223 records complemented by another 26 records as result of snowballing and already known frameworks. The resulting 1249 records were registered in an Excel spreadsheet. After removing duplicates (n = 415), the inclusion and exclusion criteria outlined in Table 3.1 were

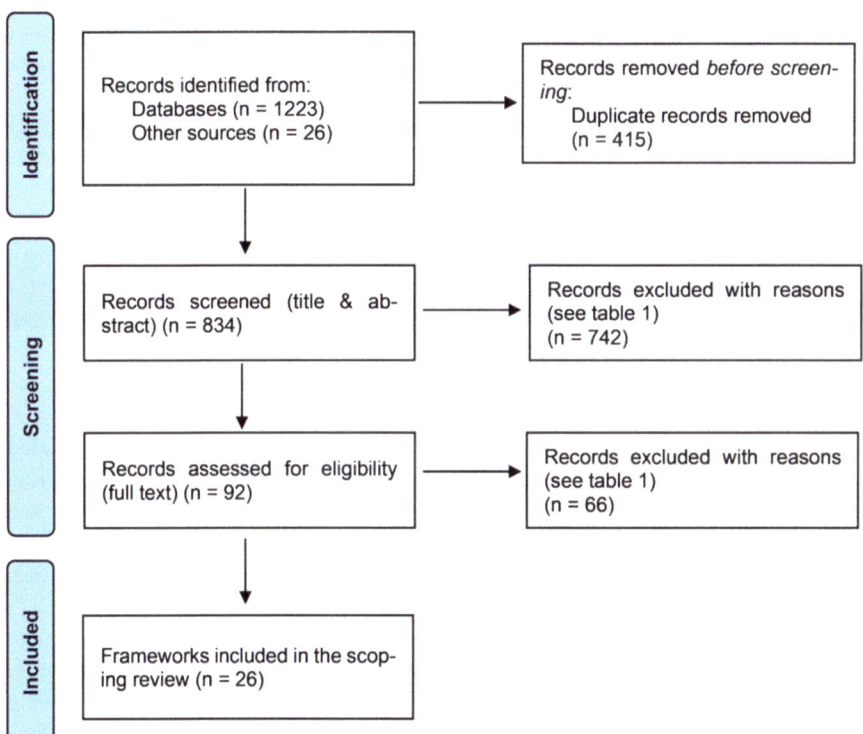

Fig. 3.1 PRISMA flow diagram of the search and filtration strategy for identifying available financial literacy frameworks

Table 3.1 Inclusion and exclusion criteria for the database search and the selection process

Key aspects	Inclusion criteria	Exclusion criteria
1. Language	English or German	Other languages
2. Adequacy for the research purpose	Frameworks developed to inform the promotion and/or assessment of financial literacy as well as the monitoring and/or evaluation of financial education programmes, especially in industrialised countries.	Frameworks from developing or emerging countries; frameworks for non-human agents; general papers about financial literacy; reports on financial literacy measurement without framework; overviews or summaries of studies on financial literacy; records where the term "framework" was wrongly assigned.
3. Target group covered by the frameworks	Frameworks targeted at people not working in the financial sector and covering a wide range of population groups (e.g. adults, young adults, children, private investors).	Frameworks targeted at professionals in the financial sector or at very specific communities (e.g. framework developed for a specific Amazonian municipality in Brazil).

applied to the title, abstract and full text of the remaining records. Since we searched in English and German, we excluded records in other languages. Moreover, we included records that describe frameworks that were developed to inform the promotion and/or assessment of financial literacy as well as the monitoring and/or evaluation of financial education programmes. Even though we included frameworks that are provided by supranational organisations such as the OECD, our focus is on industrialised countries, as the conditions in those countries significantly differ from developing or emerging countries. We have therefore excluded frameworks that were created specifically for developing or emerging countries. However, we included one study from China (Yuning, 2023) for two reasons: Firstly, China has risen to become the second largest economy in the world and has developed into a global production centre. Although the Chinese government classifies the country as a developing country for strategic reasons, this classification is currently being revised by international organisations such as the World Bank or the U.N. Development Program in view of China's economic indicators. Secondly, the study in question is based on a review, analysis and integration of frameworks that were predominantly developed in industrialised countries. In contrast, we excluded frameworks for non-human agents (e.g. frameworks developed for programming financial advising apps) as well as general papers on financial literacy (or related concepts), reports on financial literacy measurement that did not use a specific framework, papers containing overviews or summaries of financial literacy studies, and records that did not use the term "framework" appropriately.

Another group of inclusion and exclusion criteria relates to the question of who the frameworks were developed for. Given that financial literacy is targeted at the general population and not at professionals in the finance sector, we excluded frameworks that were developed for this latter group. Moreover, as we intend to cover substantial sub-groups of the general population, we also excluded frameworks developed for very small and specific communities.

Based on these inclusion and exclusion criteria, titles, abstracts and full texts were screened by at least two independent researchers, with divergent judgements being clarified discursively and with the involvement of another person. This resulted in a total of 26 frameworks to be included in the further data extraction and analysis procedures. For these frameworks, we also considered the websites of the developers to find additional material describing the respective framework. We found such material in case of the frameworks developed by Reifner (2003, 2011), Atkinson et al. (2006, 2007), Mania and Tröster (2015a, 2015b) as well as Schürkmann and Schuhen (2013), Schuhen and Schürkmann (2016) and Schürkmann (2017), respectively.

3.2.3 Data Extraction and Analysis of the Identified Financial Literacy Frameworks

The identified frameworks were added to a table (see Appendix A2) and analysed according to our research aims (i.e. overview, description and critical appraisal) and the four research questions (characteristics, conceptual/theoretical/methodological basis, components, strengths and weaknesses). Information related to RQ 1 is shown in the first column of Table A2 (Appendix). We extracted the names of the developers of the frameworks and categorised them as either academic or policy actors. In addition to the publication year, we also recorded the type of publication. Here, we distinguished between monographs, book chapters, journal articles, dissertations, working papers and policy reports. Moreover, we noted whether the frameworks were developed for children, adolescents, young adults, adults in general or specific groups such as private investors or MSME owners, as well as other information on the target audience (e.g. school level or country), where applicable. To answer RQ 2 (see column two of Table A2 (Appendix) we first analysed which concepts (i.e. financial literacy, financial competence or financial capability) the frameworks refer to and how these concepts are defined by the respective developers. Where this was evident, we also noted (a) what theoretical foundations the developers based their work on, and (b) what development methodology they used. Regarding RQ 3 we described the components of the frameworks in column three of Table A2 (Appendix). We grouped these components by using macro categories. The respective labels, assignment indications and examples are given in Table 3.2. These macro categories were basically derived inductively, but are, nevertheless, inspired by typical macro categories that we know from curriculum theory (e.g. Syomwene, 2020) and competence modelling approaches (e.g. Klieme et al., 2008; Klieme & Leutner, 2006; Weinert, 2001) as applied in other educational fields. In cases where single components of frameworks could not be assigned to any of these macro categories, we have introduced a generic category 'other components'.

As stated in the introduction, we wanted not only to provide an overview and describe the existing financial literacy frameworks but also carry out an initial formative evaluation to identify needs for improvement. In this regard and with the specific research interests of the AFin project in mind (Chap. 1), we were interested in determining the extent to which these frameworks cover a comprehensive conceptual understanding. We operationalised this aspect in two steps: We first

Table 3.2 Macro categories used to group the components of the identified financial literacy frameworks

Label	Assignment indication	Examples
Goal statements	A framework formulates goals and/or objectives that should be obtained.	Develop a basic understanding of key terms related to money, time and risk (e.g. products, product quality) (Reifner, 2003). People who are financially capable will make ends meet, keep track of one's finances and plan for predictable future expense (Atkinson et al., 2007).
Content areas	A framework lists contents or topics that are to be taught and learnt.	Earning income, Spending, Saving, Investing, Managing credit, Managing risk (CEE & Jumpstart, 2021)
Mental processes	A framework specifies cognitive processes that are involved in information processing and/or financial decision-making.	Financial decision making can be subdivided into 3 phases: (1) Planning of financial decisions; (2) Execution of financial decisions (3) Control of financial decisions (Aprea & Wuttke, 2016).
Psychological dispositions	A framework refers to different types of psychological dispositions that contribute to the intended outcome (i.e. financial literacy/competence/capability).	Financial competence entails cognitive dispositions such as knowledge, generic skills, intelligence and working memory as well as non-cognitive ones, i.e. interest, motivation/volition, risk preference, attitudes. Moral/ethics, emotions (Kraitzek & Förster, 2023).
Contexts	A framework designates different contexts, situations or perspectives in or under which an intended behaviour or goal is to be shown, a content used, or a process carried out.	Contexts refer to the situations in which the domain knowledge, skills and understandings are applied. They include: (1) Education and work; (2) Home and family; (3) Individual; (4) Societal (OECD, 2013).
Qualification levels	A framework distinguishes different levels of qualification.	Level 1: Basic understanding and developing confidence; Level 2: Developing competence and confidence; Level 3: Extending competence and confidence (Basic Skills Agency & Financial Services Authority, 2006)

examined whether the identified frameworks refer in some way to systemic aspects that are necessary for financial decision-making and the ability to make informed judgements, in addition to the individual or personal financial perspective. Second, we checked whether the frameworks include not only cognitive but also non-cognitive facets that can be considered important for the respective financial decisions. In addition to the breadth of the conceptual understanding, we also looked at the extent to which the identified frameworks reveal a link to the intended financial behaviours. We noted these judgments in the fourth column of Table 2 (Appendix).

However, as we sought to obtain a more general impression of the quality of the identified frameworks, we also noted any points that seemed particularly salient in terms of future research and development of financial literacy frameworks when analysing them in relation to research questions 1–3.

All analyses, categorisations and formative evaluation judgments were completed by at least two researchers. In the event of discrepancies, these were discussed within the larger team of authors to ensure communicative validation.

3.3 Results

3.3.1 Overview and Description of the Identified Financial Literacy Frameworks

3.3.1.1 Publication Years, Type of Publication, Developers and Target Groups of the Identified Financial Literacy Frameworks

The identified frameworks were published between 2003 and 2023. As Fig. 3.2 shows, there was an initial upswing in the mid-2010s, and ongoing development activities since then.

The outlets, where the 26 identified frameworks are published, include ten journal articles, nine policy reports, three book chapters, two dissertations, one monograph and one working paper. The timeline map in Fig. 3.3 depicts the development of the frameworks over time. Frameworks that have been further developed over time are linked with an arrow. Frameworks developed in an academic context are indicated by orange rectangles, those developed by policy organisations by blue ones.

Nine frameworks were developed by policy organisations, including the OECD, the European Union, as well as country specific institutions such as the Basic Skill Agency (2006) in the UK or the Council for Economic Education (CEE, 2013; CEE & Jumpstart, 2021) in the US (see Fig. 3.4). The remaining 17 frameworks were developed in an academic context. Seven of these latter frameworks come from a German-speaking context (Diehl, 2018; Kraitzek & Förster, 2023; Leumann et al., 2016; Mania & Tröster, 2015a, 2015b; Retzmann & Seeber, 2016; Rudeloff, 2019; Schürkmann & Schuhen, 2013), while the others stem from different countries such as Turkey or China.

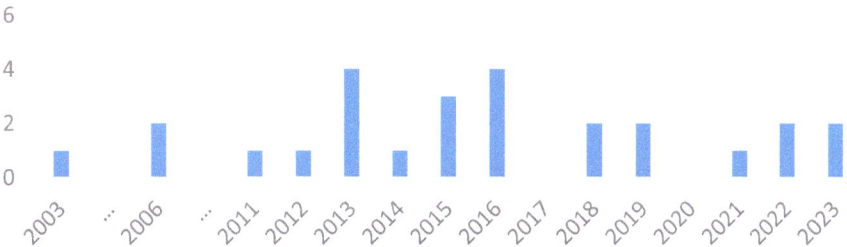

Fig. 3.2 Publication years of the identified financial literacy frameworks

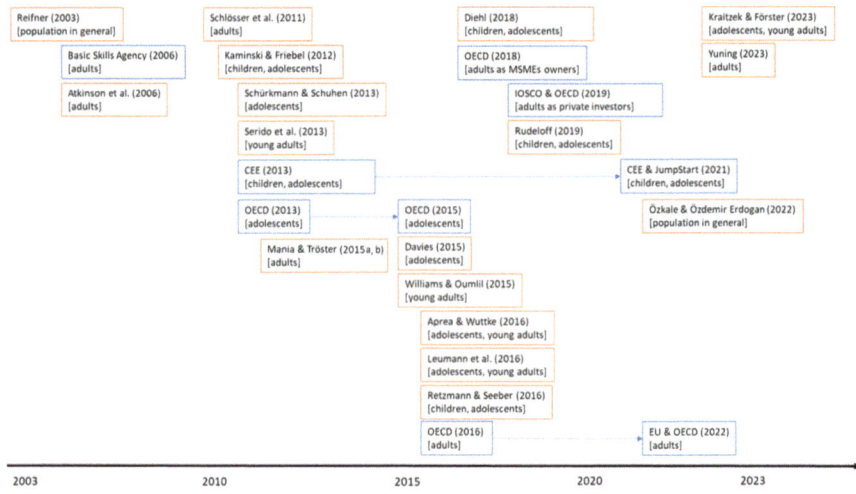

Fig. 3.3 Timeline map of financial literacy frameworks

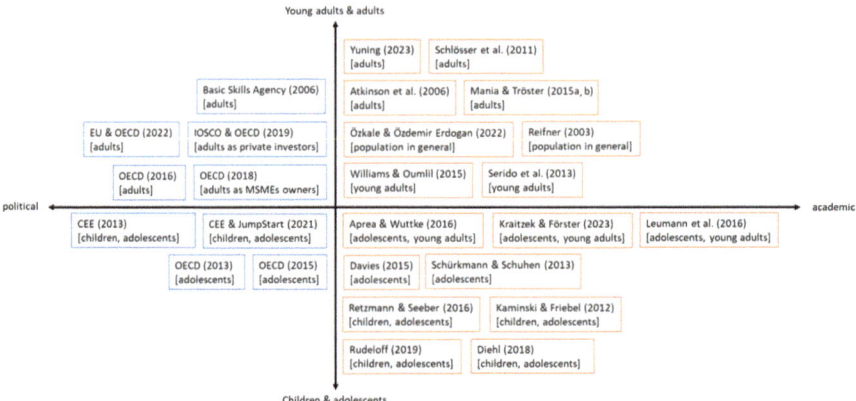

Fig. 3.4 Depicts the target groups (on y-axis) in relation to the type of publisher (on x-axis)

Most of the frameworks are targeted at the younger generations (see Fig. 3.4). Six frameworks focus on children and adolescents (CEE, 2013; CEE & Jumpstart, 2021; Diehl, 2018; Kaminski & Friebel, 2012; Retzmann & Seeber, 2016; Rudeloff, 2019), four only on adolescents (Davies, 2015; OECD, 2013; OECD, 2015; Schürkmann & Schuhen, 2013), another three on adolescents and young adults (Aprea & Wuttke, 2016; Kraitzek & Förster, 2023; Leumann et al., 2016), and two only on young adults (Serido et al., 2013; Williams & Oumlil, 2015), respectively. Six frameworks are designed for adults (Atkinson et al., 2007; Basic Skills Agency & Financial Services Authority., 2006; EU & OECD, 2022; OECD, 2016; Schlösser et al., 2011; Yuning, 2023), and an additional three frameworks address adults with specific needs and interests, i.e. adults with basic literacy needs (Mania & Tröster,

2015a, 2015b), private investors (IOSCO & OECD, 2019) and MSME owners (OECD, 2018). Two frameworks (Ozkale & Erdogan, 2022; Reifner, 2003, 2011) do not mention any specific target group but address the population in general.

3.3.1.2 Conceptual Background, Theoretical Foundation and Development Methodology of the Identified Financial Literacy Frameworks

Our analysis of the conceptual underpinnings of the identified frameworks shows that the term 'financial literacy' is used in particular in frameworks developed before 2013 (e.g. CEE, 2013; OECD, 2013), with some frameworks (e.g. Schlösser et al., 2011) treating 'financial literacy' and 'financial competence' as synonyms. Subsequently, the notion 'financial competence' or 'financial competencies' became more widespread, as is evident in the policy frameworks from the OECD but also in many frameworks from academic contexts, such as Schürkmann and Schuhen (2013), Mania and Tröster (2015a, 2015b), Leumann et al. (2016), Aprea and Wuttke (2016), Retzmann and Seeber (2016) or Kraitzek and Förster (2023), which explicitly refer to the term 'financial competence' or define financial literacy as a specific competence, respectively. As highlighted by Reifner (2011), an early adopter of the competence construct, this reference expresses the recognition that the current challenges related to financial markets and financial products require an empowerment of individuals that goes far beyond single pieces of knowledge. Instead, a more encompassing conceptualisation of the target construct is needed to ensure individual and collective financial well-being as well as financial inclusion. Another common feature of the competence-based frameworks is that they all focus on the ability to make appropriate financial decisions. Moreover, they underline the situated nature of financial decisions, as they do not only depend on individual dispositions but are also shaped by the affordances and constraints of the contexts and/or situations they are made in. This is a common feature that the competence-oriented frameworks seem to share with frameworks that refer to the concept of financial capability, which apparently occurs less frequently as only four identified frameworks (i.e. Atkinson et al., 2006, 2007; Basic Skills Agency & Financial Services Authority, 2006; Serido et al., 2013; Williams & Oumlil, 2015) adopt this concept. However, as will be discussed in the critical appraisal (see Sect. 3.2), the analysis of these frameworks showed that financial capability—except for the framework by Serido et al. (2013)—is not always clearly defined and/or differentiated from the other concepts.

Regardless of the specific concept used, it is noticeable that many frameworks developed in academic contexts highlight that financial literacy or competence should be conceptualised as part of a more encompassing educational area, with economic education being the most frequently mentioned point of reference (e.g. Retzmann & Seeber, 2016; Schlösser et al., 2011). In addition, two frameworks embed financial literacy into citizenship education (Davies, 2015) or mathematics education (Diehl, 2018), respectively. In contrast, the policy frameworks appear to consider financial literacy/competence/capability as a distinct domain or do not explicitly address this issue.

We also found that the identified frameworks are quite heterogeneous in terms of their theoretical foundation. Obviously, the competence-oriented frameworks that have been developed in academic contexts mostly refer to competence approaches from educational science (e.g. Klieme et al., 2008; Klieme & Leutner, 2006; Weinert, 2001), with this being the only line of argumentation that at least some of the identified frameworks share. Besides this, a wide variety of theoretical perspectives are mentioned. In addition to educational science, these mainly stem from economics and psychology and include normative (i.e. value-based) theories, such as Paulo Freire's (1970) 'Pedagogy of the Oppressed' or Roth's (1971) 'Pedagogical Anthropology', as well as descriptive ones, such as approaches from new institutional economics (e.g. Williamson, 2000) or psychological models of decision-making (e.g. Newell et al., 2022). However, as we will also discuss further in the critical appraisal section, the theories are not systematically elaborated in all cases but are sometimes mentioned in a rather bold manner.

With respect to the development process, we found that most developers used analytical methodologies to create their frameworks. These particularly include analogies to related domains (esp. economics education) as well as mostly narrative reviews of existing frameworks and/or other literature. Eight frameworks (Atkinson et al., 2006, 2007; CEE, 2013; CEE & Jumpstart, 2021; OECD, 2013, 2015; Mania and Tröster (2015a, 2015b); Leumann et al., 2016; EU & OECD, 2022) additionally used interviews, focus groups or workshops with experts or other stakeholders as an empirical methodology. However, only few developers (e.g. Aprea & Wuttke, 2016; Rudeloff, 2019; Schuhen & Schürkmann, 2016; Serido et al., 2013) have reported efforts to psychometrically analyse and validate their frameworks. In the case of the Basic Skills Agency and Financial Services Authority (2006), we did not find any description of how the framework was developed.

3.3.1.3 Components of the Identified Financial Literacy Frameworks

In reviewing the identified frameworks and summarising them in the table, we found that they differ significantly in terms of number and type of components they cover. Whereas some frameworks contain only one or two components (e.g. Davies, 2015; Serido et al., 2013; Yuning, 2023), others cover three or more. This applies especially to those developed by or in collaboration with political actors, such as the OECD or the CEE. In addition, we have found that the components in many frameworks are not neatly separated from each other, but are often intermingled, whereby different ways of structuring can be identified. For example, the Basic Skills Agency and Financial Services Authority (2006) framework mixes content areas with dispositions, Kaminski and Friebel (2012) connect contexts, goal statements and content areas, and Retzmann and Seeber (2016) combine contexts and goal statements. This situation constitutes the background for the following distinction and further analysis of the components.

Content areas is the component that is specified in most of the identified frameworks. Only six frameworks (Aprea & Wuttke, 2016; Atkinson et al., 2006, 2007; Kraitzek & Förster, 2023; Retzmann & Seeber, 2016; Serido et al., 2013; Yuning, 2023) do not explicitly mention this component. However, in our analysis we noticed that the identified frameworks substantially differ regarding the breadth and depth of the contents they cover as well as the way they are structured. There are frameworks that cover only a few areas with little or no further subdivision (e.g. Diehl, 2018; Schlösser et al., 2011), while others cover the content quite broadly, either by creating comprehensive content lists (e.g. Davies, 2015; Leumann et al., 2016) or by developing superordinate content categories that they then elaborate in further depth (e.g. CEE & Jumpstart, 2021; EU & OECD, 2022; OECD, 2015, 2016). Although the terminology for the contents varies widely in the different frameworks, contents relating to managing money in everyday life (e.g. payments or budgeting) as well as to saving and investing, borrowing and debt, and insurance and risk management appears to be included in most frameworks. In contrast, other contents such as information and counselling services, tax system or tax declaration are rarely mentioned. From a curriculum theoretical perspective (e.g. Tramm & Reetz, 2010), we noticed that the developers seem to have used different construction principles for the specification of the content areas, as they either refer to activity areas (e.g. budgeting, saving, borrowing) in some cases or to subject areas (e.g. types of payment, incentive systems, monetary policy) in others. These two principles are sometimes also mixed not only between, but also within the frameworks.

Goal statements are also quite widespread with 18 frameworks using them (Atkinson et al., 2006, 2007; CEE, 2013; CEE & Jumpstart, 2021; Diehl, 2018; EU & OECD, 2022; IOSCO & OECD, 2019; Kaminski & Friebel, 2012; Mania & Tröster, 2015a; OECD, 2015, 2016, 2018; Ozkale & Erdogan, 2022; Reifner, 2003; Retzmann & Seeber, 2016; Rudeloff, 2019; Schlösser et al., 2011; Williams & Oumlil, 2015; Yuning, 2023). However, as with the content component, we found that the frameworks differ with regard to how intensively goal statements are considered as well as to the way they are derived. While some frameworks only state exemplary goals (e.g. Diehl, 2018; Schlösser et al., 2011), others provide very comprehensive lists (e.g. EU & OECD, 2022). Most of the frameworks derive their goal statements by combining the content component with psychological dispositions (see next section) and formulate them as educational goals with a recognisable affinity to the Bloom et al. (1956) taxonomy or more recent elaborations thereof (Anderson et al., 2001). However, few frameworks use other construction principles to formulate goal descriptors, such as intended financial behaviours (Atkinson et al., 2006, 2007; Ozkale & Erdogan, 2022) or types of competences (e.g. Reifner, 2003). Moreover, Yuning (2023), who focuses exclusively on the goal component, expands the educational goals into economic and social ones.

Psychological dispositions are explicitly considered and specified in 12 frameworks. This applies to all frameworks developed by or with the involvement of the OECD (i.e. EU & OECD, 2022; IOSCO & OECD, 2019; OECD, 2015, 2016, 2018) as well as to those from the Basic Skills Agency and Financial Services Authority (2006), from Serido et al. (2013), Aprea and Wuttke (2016), Leumann et al. (2016),

Rudeloff (2019), Ozkale and Erdogan (2022), and Kraitzek and Förster (2023). Other than the content and the goal category, the disposition component is far more homogenous as all frameworks containing this component in some way or another seem to distinguish similar subcategories such as awareness, knowledge, skills, interest, motivation or confidence. In the case of the OECD frameworks, financial behaviour is also added. We will come back to this in the critical appraisal (see Sect. 3.2).

Mental processes are addressed in five frameworks, referring either to phases of information processing (OECD, 2013) or decision making (Aprea & Wuttke, 2016; CEE, 2013; CEE & Jumpstart, 2021; Kraitzek & Förster, 2023), while a context component is explicitly mentioned in four frameworks (Davies, 2015; Kaminski & Friebel, 2012; OECD, 2013; Retzmann & Seeber, 2016). In addition, four frameworks contain qualification levels, either defined as benchmarks for the school grades 4, 8, and 12, as in the case of the frameworks by the CEE (2013) and the CEE and Jumpstart (2021), respectively, or as different competence stages as in the Basic Skills Agency and Financial Services Authority (2006) framework and the OECD (2015) framework for adolescents.

We also made some interesting observations in the 'other components' category. Many frameworks emphasise the role of necessary prerequisites such as numeracy, reading and writing skills (e.g. Basic Skills Agency & Financial Services Authority, 2006; OECD, 2013; Ozkale & Erdogan, 2022). In addition, some frameworks (e.g. OECD, 2013, 2015, 2016; Ozkale & Erdogan, 2022) mention contextual prerequisites such as socio-economic background, national economic context, socialisation, access to information and education or access to money and financial products. Finally, Williams and Oumlil (2015) also include program design, implementation and delivery decisions as well as approaches to measure students' learning success and impact of the program into their framework.

3.3.2 Critical Appraisal of the Identified Financial Literacy Frameworks

In this section, we first describe our findings related to the extent to which the identified frameworks (a) cover a comprehensive understanding (i.e. individual and systemic aspects as well as cognitive and non-cognitive facets) and (b) reveal a link to the intended financial behaviours as noted in the fourth column of Table A2 (appendix). We then outline further observations that emerged during the analyses and that we found interesting for future research on and development of financial literacy frameworks.

Regarding the first issue, there seems to be a growing consensus that a more comprehensive understanding of the intended outcome of financial education is needed. From the 26 identified frameworks, we found that only six (CEE, 2013; Diehl, 2018; Mania & Tröster, 2015a; Schlösser et al., 2011; Williams & Oumlil, 2015) propagate a rather restricted understanding in that they only include individual and cognitive aspects, while the others have, at least to some extent, a broader notion. However, we found that it is quite rare that both systemic and non-cognitive aspects are considered at the same time. We also found that although at least one of these aspects is addressed in most of the frameworks, they are sometimes mentioned in a rather superficial way and are not always systematically integrated into the framework. Interestingly, though not surprisingly, frameworks that consider financial education as part of broader educational endeavours, such as economic or citizenship education (e.g. Davies, 2015; Retzmann & Seeber, 2016), in particular, seem to cover the systemic facet more broadly, while frameworks that explicitly rely on psychological approaches (e.g. Aprea & Wuttke, 2016; Kraitzek & Förster, 2023) seem to be more concerned with including non-cognitive aspects.

A similar picture appears with respect to the question whether the identified frameworks are linked to financial behaviour. Such a link is at least partially recognisable in nearly all frameworks, but they substantially differ in how this is established. Whereas only few frameworks consider financial behaviours or their mental correlates at the outset of their reasoning (e.g. Aprea & Wuttke, 2016; Atkinson et al., 2006, 2007), many frameworks start from other components, especially from content areas (e.g. Davies, 2015; Mania & Tröster, 2015a; Retzmann & Seeber, 2016), and then consider behaviour only as a possibility to apply knowledge. Some frameworks (e.g. Schlösser et al., 2011; Schürkmann & Schuhen, 2013) intermingle contents and behaviours. Interestingly, the OECD frameworks consider behaviour as a subcomponent of financial competence. However, this is contradictory to those competence theoretical accounts from educational science (e.g. Klieme et al., 2008; Klieme & Leutner, 2006; Weinert, 2001), which view behaviour as performance and thus as a manifestation and not as a part of competence. In any case, these observations add further conceptual ambiguities to those regarding the clarity of the three concepts financial literacy, financial capability and financial competence, which were already addressed in Sect. 3.1.2. Moreover, as our analyses in Sect. 3.1.3 show, there seems to be no consensus on which components belong to a framework and how these components should be related or arranged, a fact that further complicates the situation.

In Sect. 3.1.2, we also briefly mentioned that both the theoretical foundations and the methodologies for developing financial literacy frameworks require further consideration. With respect to the former, we have found that the theoretical foundations are generally rather weak and quite selective. Regarding the latter, analytical methodologies seem to dominate, while empirical validations of the frameworks are rare and, if they have been conducted at all, are mostly still in their very initial stages.

Overall, these observations suggest that developers should pay more attention to building their frameworks on a comprehensive and coherent conceptual and theoretical foundation. They should also subject their frameworks to empirical testing. Researchers, in turn, are called upon to provide such foundations as well as methodological guidelines that can support evidence-based financial education policy and practice. In doing so, they can draw on approaches, experiences and findings from other areas of education. However, as the goals of financial education are multi-faceted, theoretical accounts for future frameworks should also systematically incorporate knowledge from other disciplines, in particular economics, psychology and sociology.

In addition to these fundamental questions, we noticed two other points. Firstly, we were surprised by the fact that only four frameworks include qualification levels. As this is a key concern for interpreting the results of each competence assessment as well as for designing appropriate educational interventions for different subgroups, further development and research activities are needed in this regard. Secondly, we found it remarkable that digitalisation and sustainability are only considered in one framework, i.e. the one by the EU and OECD (2022). The same applies to social skills, which are also only explicitly mentioned in one framework (Reifner, 2003). Given the demands placed on financial decisions in the current economic and social contexts, we believe that these aspects should receive more attention.

3.4 Summary, Limitations and Conclusions

In this chapter, we described the rationale, methodology and results of a scoping review that we conducted to identify and analyse existing financial literacy frameworks. We identified 26 frameworks, which we characterised in terms of developers, publication year, type of publication and target groups (RQ1). We also looked at which concepts and possibly theories those frameworks are based on, and which methodologies were used to develop them (RQ2). In addition, we used inductively developed macro categories to indicate which components they contain (RQ3). Finally, we undertook a critical appraisal of the frameworks, i.e. we formatively evaluated their strengths and weaknesses (RQ4). This methodological approach enabled us to provide a structured overview and description of the identified financial literacy frameworks and to reveal potential areas of improvement as well as avenues for further development and research.

However, as any methodology, our approach also has some limitations. Although we have chosen and implemented our search strategy with the utmost care, we cannot completely rule out the possibility that we have overlooked important frameworks and/or that frameworks, which we excluded, could have provided relevant information. In addition, with a qualitative approach there is always the risk that, despite the best precautions, our analyses and judgments are still associated with a residual subjectivity, and it is possible that other researchers would have arrived at different categorisations and/or interpretations.

Despite these limitations, the findings presented in this chapter are equally relevant for educational practice and policy as well as for academia. Based on the overview, description and critical appraisal of the identified financial literacy frameworks, practitioners can better understand which framework might be adequate to guide their design and assessment decisions, policy makers can better judge which kind of orientation can be expected from existing frameworks and where further development is needed, and, last, but not least, researchers can generate new ideas where additional investigations are indicated.

3.5 Appendix

Table A2 Structured overview and description as well as critical appraisal of identified financial literacy frameworks in chronological order according to the methodology explained in Chap. 3

#	Overview and description			Critical appraisal
	Name (and type) of developer(s) Publication year Type of publication Target group (Country)	Conceptual foundation Development methodology	Components	Breath of conceptual understanding Link to financial behaviour
01	**Reifner** (academic) 2003, 2011 Monograph/Book chapter Population in general (no specific age group mentioned) (Germany)	**Financial competence** is defined as consumers' empowerment to use financial services adapted to their situation and needs, to represent their own interests, to ask questions and thus to play an active role in shaping the economy. Reference to models from new institutional economics as well as pedagogical anthropology and developmental theory, highlighting informed and responsible consumer behaviour. Development of the framework is based on literature review related to the financialization of everyday life in modern societies as well to the suitability of financial services products and their marketing methods.	**Goal statements related to 3 types of competences** I Subject competence, i.e. the ability to make judgements and act in a specific subject area. 1. Develop a basic understanding of key terms related to money, time and risk (e.g. products, product quality) II Self competence, i.e. the ability to act responsibly for oneself. 2. Recognise and reflect one's own situation, personal needs and interests and take these into account when dealing with money and financial services 3. Understand and plan as an active consumer III Social competence, i.e. the ability to act in a socially responsible way. 4. Present and represent one's own interests 5. Shape conversation with financial advisors 6. Elaborate and represent on group positions and interests **Content areas:** 1. consumer credit 2. maintaining a current account 3. home financing 4. insurance 5. investment/private pension provision 6. setting up a business 7. debt rescheduling	Comprehensive understanding is partially given: – Systemic aspects are only implicitly mentioned. – Non-cognitive (esp. social) aspects are somewhat covered. Link to financial behaviour is partially recognisable.

(continued)

Table A2 (continued)

#	Overview and description			Critical appraisal
	Name (and type) of developer(s) Publication year Type of publication Target group (Country)	Conceptual foundation Development methodology	Components	
02	**Basic Skills Agency & Financial Services Authority** (policy) 2006 Policy report Adults (UK)	**Financial capability** as key concept but no explicit concept definition and theoretical foundation mentioned. Development process mentioned as part of the national strategy, but not described further.	**3 types of psychological dispositions** I Financial knowledge and understanding: The ability to make sense of and manipulate money in its different forms, uses and functions. II Financial skills and competence: The ability to apply knowledge and understanding across a range of contexts including both predictable and unexpected situations. III Financial responsibility: The ability to appreciate the wider impact of financial decisions both on personal circumstances, the family and the broader community and to consider social and ethical issues. **9 content areas according to the 3 types of dispositions** I Financial knowledge and understanding 1. Different types of money/payments 2. Income generation 3. Income disposal II Financial skills and competence 4. Gathering financial information and record keeping 5. Financial planning – saving, spending, budgeting 6. Risk and return III Financial responsibility 7. Personal choices and the financial implications 8. Consumer rights, responsibilities, and sources of advice 9. Implications of finance **3 qualification levels** 1. Basic understanding and developing confidence 2. Developing competence and confidence 3. Extending competence and confidence **Further components** Underpinning literacy, language and numeracy skills	Breath of conceptual understanding Link to financial behaviour Comprehensive understanding is partially given: – Systemic aspects are only implicitly mentioned. – Non-cognitive aspects (esp. confidence) are mentioned, but not further specified. Link to financial behaviour is partially recognisable.

| 03 | **Atkinson et al.** (academic) 2006, 2007 Journal article Adults (UK) | **Financial capability** is considered as the ability to make informed judgements and take effective decisions regarding the use and management of money; no further theoretical foundation mentioned. Development of the model is based on a narrative review of literature related to the development and changes in financial markets and economic conditions. Additionally, focus group interviews with consumers and experts were conducted. The model underwent a first empirical validation by running a survey and conducting a cluster analysis to identify persons with specific competence profiles. | **Goal statements related to intended financial behaviours**
People who are financially capable will:
I Manage money:
• Make ends meet.
• Keep track of one's finances.
• Plan for predictable future expense.
II Plan ahead:
• Have some provision to cover a loss of income.
• Be able to meet a major expense without borrowing.
• Have made provision for anticipated major expenses.
• Make adequate provision for retirement.
III Choose financial products wisely:
• Shop around to get the best value financial products.
• Make sure they get the products most suitable for them.
• Make sure they know what is in the 'small print'.
IV Stay informed:
• Keep abreast of things likely to impact on their finances.
• Know key features of the products they hold.
• Are able and willing to deal with problems or complaints should they arise. | Comprehensive understanding is partially given:
– Systemic aspects are not mentioned.
– Non-cognitive (esp. volitional) aspects are somewhat covered.
Link to financial behaviour is recognisable. |

(continued)

Table A2 (continued)

#	Overview and description			Critical appraisal
	Name (and type) of developer(s) Publication year Type of publication Target group (Country)	Conceptual foundation Development methodology	Components	
04	**Schlösser et al.** (academic) 2011 Journal article Adults (Germany)	**Financial literacy and financial competence** are used interchangeably and are considered as part of the broader concept of economic education; no explicit concept definition or theoretical foundation provided. Development of the model is based on a narrative literature review of studies concerned with the purposes of financial literacy.	**4 core content areas with exemplary goal statements** I Building assets, involving sacrificing present consumption for future benefits. Additionally, understanding the risks, durations, and returns of most important and common financial products is crucial. II Dealing with debt, including comparing the pros and cons of taking out a loan, and understanding the basic practices of various lenders (such as banks, private credit brokers, and retailers). Additionally, knowledge of debt management, including over-indebtedness and the availability of counselling services, is important. Broader issues like national/international debt crises are also essential. III Insuring, including key concepts such as risks for individuals, their families, groups, and society along with social and individual insurance types, statistical foundations, and risk reduction through responsible individual behaviour. IV Dealing with money in everyday life, including keeping a personal budget book that entails income and expenses over a specific period, and the competence to manage a bank account (current account and credit card) for organizing financial transactions.	Breath of conceptual understanding Link to financial behaviour Restricted understanding is given: – Only individual aspects are covered. – Only cognitive aspects are covered. Link to financial behaviour is only partially recognisable, as the relationship to contents is not clear.

3 Financial Literacy Frameworks: A Scoping Review and Critical Appraisal

05	**Kaminski & Friebel** (academic) 2012 Working paper Children and adolescents (all school types) (Germany)	**Financial literacy** is viewed as the ability to use money wisely, to make rational use of different financial services and to analyse and participate in shaping the institutional contexts at a national and international level; no further theoretical foundation mentioned. The development of the framework is based on the authors prior work attempting to integrate financial literacy in the broader field of economic literacy and involving 3 perspectives: (1) Consumer perspective, (2) company perspective, and (3) economic policy perspective.	**Contexts, goal statements and content areas** I Consumer perspective: Acquire, process, and evaluate financial information to reduce information asymmetries in advisory and sales situations. • Dealing with credits and loans • Dealing with life risks • Asset accumulation and retirement planning • Money management • Procurement, processing and evaluation of financial information • Dealing with counselling and sales talks II Company perspective: Understand functions and interests of financial service providers, including potential conflicts of interest. • Tasks and objectives of financial service providers • Salaries of employees with financial service providers • Money creation • Incentive systems in sales III Economic policy perspective: Understand the role of the state and of international financial interconnections as well as the ability to shape institutional environments. • Monetary policy • Regulation (e.g. consumer protection) • Fiscal policy • Financial market regulation • Social security • International financial relations • Financial crises and their consequences	Comprehensive understanding is partially given: – Individual and systemic aspects are covered. – Only cognitive aspects are covered. Link to financial behaviour is only partially recognisable.

(continued)

Table A2 (continued)

#	Overview and description			Critical appraisal
	Name (and type) of developer(s) Publication year Type of publication Target group (Country)	Conceptual foundation Development methodology	Components	
06	**Council for Economic Education (CEE)** (policy) 2013 Policy report Children and adolescents (USA)	**Financial literacy** is viewed as the ability to make informed financial decisions and should be integrated in an economic perspective. Reference to rational choice theory is made. The development of the standards started through a conference and involved two committees: (1) Writing committee: Each writer drafted one standard based on expert input. (2) Review committee: Experts from academia, Federal Reserve and private sector reviewed the drafts of the writing committee.	**Content areas** 1. Earning Income 2. Buying Goods and Services 3. Saving 4. Using Credit 5. Financial Investing 6. Protecting and Insuring **Goal statements related to content areas** Learning outcomes are defined for the 6 content areas referring to what students at different grade levels should know and be able to do with that knowledge. **Exemplary mental processes (decision-making skills)** • Planning and goal setting • Making the decision • Assessing outcomes **Differentiation of qualification levels through grades 4, 8, 12**	Breath of conceptual understanding Link to financial behaviour Restricted understanding is given: – Only individual aspects are covered. – Only cognitive aspects are covered. Link to financial behaviour is recognisable, but only as application of knowledge.

07	**Schürkmann & Schuhen** (academic) 2013, 2016, 2017 Journal article/Book chapter/Dissertation Adolescents (students aged 14–17) (Germany)	**Financial literacy** is regarded as a competence and considered as the ability to make financial decisions and weight up risks- in financial service providers and their offers as well as the individual estimation and evaluation of rates, savings targets and pension amounts. The framework refers to competence approaches from educational science. The development of the framework is based on a critical review of available financial literacy frameworks. A first empirical validation of parts of the framework (construct validity) has been conducted.	**Content areas** 1. Debt 2. Asset accumulation 3. Insurance and taxes 4. Payment transactions 5. Monetary policy **Further components** Ability to use online calculators correctly for own information and provision is included as a further element of financial literacy.	Comprehensive understanding is partially given: – Individual and systemic aspects are covered, but focus is clearly on individual. – Non-cognitive (esp. attitudes towards money) aspects are somewhat covered. Link to financial behaviour is recognisable.
08	**Serido et al.** (academic) 2013 Journal article Young adults (esp. freshmen at university) (USA)	Conceptualization of **financial capability** as a developmental process, by which young adults acquire financial knowledge and behaviours needed to manage full-time adults' social roles and responsibilities. Framework refers to capability approach (Nussbaum, Sen). The development of the framework is based on a literature review of research on financial knowledge. The derived model is then empirically tested by examining co-occurring patterns of change in its components.	**Psychological dispositions** 1. Financial knowledge (divided into subjective and objective financial knowledge) 2. Financial attitude 3. Perceived behaviour control 4. Financial self-efficacy 5. Financial behaviour 6. Financial well-being 7. Overall well-being	Comprehensive understanding is partially given: – Individual and systemic aspects are covered, but focus is clearly on individual. – Non-cognitive (esp. volitional) aspects are somewhat covered. Link to financial behaviour is recognisable, but only as application of knowledge.

(continued)

Table A2 (continued)

#	Overview and description			Critical appraisal
	Name (and type) of developer(s) Publication year Type of publication Target group (Country)	Conceptual foundation Development methodology	Components	
09	**OECD** (policy) 2013 Policy report Adolescents (15-year-old students) (OECD member countries)	The OECD/INFE **financial literacy framework** is a supplement to the regular OECD PISA assessment; Financial Literacy is conceived as knowledge and understanding of financial concepts and risks, and the skills, motivation and confidence to apply such knowledge and understanding in order to make effective decisions across a range of financial contexts, to improve the financial well-being of individuals and society, and to enable participation in economic life. Reference to Bloom's taxonomy is made. The development process combines analysis of existing financial literacy frameworks of OECD member states with expert interviews and subsequent application of the framework in assessment practice.	**Content areas:** Comprises the areas of knowledge and understanding that must be drawn upon to perform a particular task. 1. Money and transactions 2. Planning and managing finances 3. Risk and reward 4. Financial landscape **Mental processes:** Relate to cognitive processes (mental strategies) used to describe students' ability to recognise and apply concepts relevant to the domain, and to understand, analyse, reason about, evaluate and suggest solutions. 1. Identify financial information 2. Analyse information in a financial context 3. Evaluate financial issues 4. Apply financial knowledge and understanding **Contexts:** Refer to the situations in which the domain knowledge, skills and understandings are applied. 1. Education and work 2. Home and family 3. Individual 4. Societal **Further components** 1. Access to information and education 2. Access to money and financial products 3. Attitudes towards and confidence about financial matter 4. Spending and saving behaviour 5. Reading comprehension and numeracy	Breath of conceptual understanding Link to financial behaviour Comprehensive understanding is partially given: – Individual and systemic aspects are covered, but focus is clearly on individual. – Non-cognitive factors are mentioned but their inclusion is not systematic. Link to financial behaviour is partially recognisable, especially through the context category, but the relationship to other categories is not clear.

10	Mania & Tröster (academic) 2014, 2015 Journal articles Adults with basic literacy needs (Germany)	(Basic) financial literacy refers to the necessary basic skills to address existentially basic and directly practical requirements of everyday behaviour and the conduct of life in monetary matters. It is equally important as and closely related to traditional basic literacies (reading, writing and calculating), and is a prerequisite for empowerment and social inclusion. References to Situated Learning, to the concept of Paulo Freire, to participation approaches as well as to competence approaches from educational science are made. The development of the framework includes interviews with different experts (e.g. debt counsellors and trainers) as well as with representatives of the target group, focusing on their opinions regarding learning needs and learning conceptions. Along with the theoretical considerations, the results of these interviews were used to develop a first draft of the model, which was then repeatedly discussed and adapted in the research team.	**Content areas** 1. Income 2. Money and payment transactions 3. Spending and buying 4. Budgeting 5. Borrowing money and debts 6. Provision and insurance **Goal statements related to different types of knowledge** 1. Knowing and understanding facts and relationships (declarative knowledge), and knowing how to perform tasks (procedural knowledge) 2. Understanding which materials require thorough or selective reading and identifying the documents, from which information needs to be extracted 3. Knowing how to take notes, articulate thoughts, and complete forms or documents 4. Calculating, estimating, or approximating values and managing numerical quantities and figures	Restricted understanding is given: – Only individual aspects are covered. – Only cognitive aspects are covered. Link to financial behaviour is recognisable.

(continued)

Table A2 (continued)

#	Overview and description			Critical appraisal
	Name (and type) of developer(s) Publication year Type of publication Target group (Country)	Conceptual foundation Development methodology	Components	
11	**Davies** (academic) 2015 Journal article Adolescents (secondary level school education)	Expanded approach to **financial literacy** which, alongside personal financial responsibility, also extends to citizens' understanding of the financial sector (and by implication the rationale for regulation) and government finances; Link to citizenship education with a commitment to value education (e.g. related to ethics/fairness and sustainability); Distinction between short-term and long-term financial choices is made. References to curriculum theory are made. The development of the framework is based on a narrative literature review and critical evaluation of existing conceptualisations and measurements of financial literacy and a needs analysis concerning the current state of democracies.	**Content areas related to short-term financial choices** 1. Income 2. Spending 3. Liquidity 4. Borrowing and saving **Content areas related to long-term financial choices** 1. Wealth 2. Debt 3. Interest 4. Time preference 5. Inflation 6. Risk and uncertainty **Contexts: Individual, institutional and systemic perspective (with examples)** 1. Individual: citizens' personal financial responsibility Short-term: Budgeting weekly Long-term: Income and expenditure forecast 2. Financial services: citizens' understanding of the financial sector Short-term: The interest rate margin between lending and borrowing Long-term: Real and nominal interest rates 3. Government/country: citizens' understanding of the role of government Short-term: government budget Long-term: financial crises	Breath of conceptual understanding Link to financial behaviour Comprehensive understanding is partially given: – Individual and systemic aspects are covered. – Non-cognitive aspects are not considered. Link to financial behaviour is partially recognisable, especially through short-term and long-term choices, but it is not clear how this translates into contents.

| 12 | OECD (policy) 2015 Policy report Adolescents (aged 15–18) (OECD member countries) | The OECD/INFE core competencies framework on **financial literacy** for youth conceives financial literacy as a complex construct, including knowledge and skills as well as a wide range of attitudes and behaviours that are clearly influenced by external factors. The OECD core competencies framework on financial literacy for the youth builds on previous OECD/INFE outputs and considers feedback received from participants at a dedicated workshop on core competencies, from two OECD committees in charge of financial education, the Committee on Financial Markets (CMF) and the Insurance and Private Pensions Committee (IPPC). | **Content areas** I Money and transactions: Covers different forms and purposes of money, payment methods, income, and financial transactions as well as taking care of cash and other valuables, calculating value for money, and filing documents and receipts are included. (1) Money, income (2) Payments and purchases, prices (3) Financial records and contracts (4) Foreign currency II Planning and managing finances: Reflects the importance of planning and managing income and wealth over the short and long term. (1) Budgeting, managing income and expenditure (2) Saving (3) Longer-term planning (4) Credit III Risk and reward: Includes knowledge of the types of products that may help people to protect themselves from the consequences of negative outcomes. (1) Changing value (2) Identifying risks (3) Financial safety nets and insurance (4) Balancing risk and reward IV Financial landscape: Covers rights and responsibilities of consumers in the financial marketplace, and typical features of the general financial environment. (1) Regulation and consumer protection (2) Education, information and advice (3) Rights and responsibilities (4) Financial service providers (5) Scams and fraud (6) Taxes and public spending, external influences **Psychological dispositions** • Awareness, knowledge and understanding • Confidence, motivation and attitudes • Skills and behaviour **Goal statements related to content and dispositions** Learning outcomes are defined by crossing content areas with psychological dispositions. | Comprehensive understanding is partially given: – Individual and systemic aspects are covered, but focus is clearly on individual. – Non-cognitive factors are considered. Link to financial behaviour is recognisable but the conceptual foundation is unclear. |

(continued)

Table A2 (continued)

#	Overview and description				Critical appraisal
	Name (and type) of developer(s) / Publication year / Type of publication / Target group (Country)	Conceptual foundation / Development methodology		Components	
				Qualification levels Foundational outcome 1: Competencies in this category may be expected of almost all young people. Foundational outcome 2 & 3: Competencies in this category represent more advances capabilities and may be expected of some young people. **Further components** Affecting factors: Socio-economic status, national context and access to a range of financial services.	Breath of conceptual understanding Link to financial behaviour
13	**Williams & Oumlil** (academic) 2015 Journal article Young adults (college students) (USA)	**Financial capability** is viewed as part of financial exclusion prevention; no further definition of the concept is given. Financial literacy and financial capability seem to be used interchangeably, no further theoretical foundation mentioned. The development of the framework is based on financial literacy literature mainly from economics, suggesting deficiencies in consumers' financial knowledge, across the age divide. The authors then use their previous consumer education-based models as a foundation.		**Content areas** 1. Credit / debt management, budgeting / money management 2. Managing student loans, understanding consumer behaviour 3. Long-term financial decision-making, short-term financial decision-making 4. Financial markets, investments **Goal statements related to intended financial behaviours** 1. Awareness of risky & responsible credit behaviour, financial market awareness 2. Enhanced budgeting acumen, awareness of financial products / services **Further components** Affecting factors: E.g. socio-economic factors, existing financial knowledge Program design, implementation and delivery: Establishing strategies, institutional conditions and marketing efforts to ensure program success Assessment and evaluation: Approaches to measure students' learning success and impact of the program	Restricted understanding is given: – Only individual aspects are covered. – Only cognitive aspects are covered. Link to financial behaviour is not recognisable.

| 14 | **Aprea & Wuttke** (academic) 2016 Book chapter Adolescents and young adults (Germany) | **Financial literacy** is a potential that enables a person to effectively plan, execute, and control financial decisions. This potential is based on individual dispositions and is contingent on situational characteristics. The framework refers to competence approaches from educational science as well as psychological action-regulation and decision-making theories. The development process includes a narrative literature review and critical evaluation of existing conceptualisations and assessments of financial literacy, analogical reasoning from other educational domains as well as a first empirical validation of the framework. A systematic methodology is proposed. | **Mental processes** 1. Planning of financial decisions 2. Execution of financial decisions 2.1. Collecting product information 2.2. Conducting product selection 2.3. Concluding contract 3. Control of financial decisions **Psychological dispositions** Knowledge, skills, motivations, interests, attitudes, and values | Comprehensive understanding is partially given: – Systemic aspects considered, but only implicitly. – Non-cognitive aspects are considered. Link to financial behaviour is recognisable. |

(continued)

Table A2 (continued)

#	Overview and description			Critical appraisal
	Name (and type) of developer(s) Publication year Type of publication Target group (Country)	Conceptual foundation Development methodology	Components	
15	**Retzmann & Seeber** (academic) 2016 Book chapter Children and adolescents (all school types) (Germany)	**Financial competence** is defined as the sum of an individual's cognitive judgement, decision-making and planning abilities, their practical and technical skills for implementing decisions and plans, including the use of electronic media, and their motivational, volitional and social disposition with regard to liquid funds, recent and future income and material and nonmaterial assets for themselves, as a trustee for other people, and as a social or political representative for the general public, in efficiently and responsibly generating and implementing such assets to achieve the best possible effect on the short, medium and/or long-term well-being of the people concerned. The framework refers to competence approaches from educational science. The development of the framework is mainly based on an adaption of existing competence models for economic education.	**Contexts and goal statements** I Decision-making and rationality: Make rational financial decisions by considering constraints, anticipating consequences, and evaluating options to maintain or improve their financial well-being responsibly. Incl.: (1) Analysing situations; (2) Evaluating different possible actions;(3) Shaping possible actions. II Relationship and interaction with others: Describe economic relationships as exchanges benefiting both parties, analyse interests, evaluate consequences, identify cooperation advantages, troubleshoot cooperation issues, and analyse formal and informal rules governing economic interactions. Incl.: (1) Analysing constellations of interests; (2) Analysing, evaluating and shaping cooperations. III Order and system: Transition from an active participants viewpoint to an observer's perspective regarding rules, order and system. Incl.: (1) Analysing markets; (2) Analysing economic systems and orders; (3) Judging political regulations economically. **Further components** The role of necessary prerequisites such as numeracy, reading and writing skills, metacognitive skills as well as media and ICT skills is highlighted.	Breath of conceptual understanding Link to financial behaviour Comprehensive understanding is partially given: – Individual and systemic aspects are covered. – Non-cognitive factors are mentioned but their inclusion is not systematic. Link to financial behaviour is partially recognisable.

| 16 | Leumann et al. (academic) 2016 Book chapter Adolescents and young adults (European countries) | **Financial literacy** is considered as a holistic concept, covering not only cognitive facets but also attitudes and motivational aspects. In addition, the role of the eco-systems that surround financial decision makers are highlighted. The development process contained a review and categorisation of existing financial literacy conceptions as well as an interview study with 40 key stakeholders (i.e. financial education experts, VET teachers, and VET students) from six European countries. | **Content areas** 1. Planning and managing financial matters 2. Saving money/building assets 3. Spending money 4. Borrowing money/raising a credit/financing methods 5. Retirement planning 6. Prevent (over-)indebtedness 7. Knowing information and counselling services in the context of money and financial affairs 8. Earning/taking money 9. Comparing/contracting insurances 10. Monetary, financial and social security system and policy **Psychological dispositions** 1. Knowledge and skills 2. Interest and awareness for (personal) financial matters 3. Attitudes and values towards money and socio-economic/political issues (e.g. willingness to participate as a citizen, interest in solidarity and distributional justice) 4. Volitions (e.g. discipline, self-control. Delay of gratification) | Comprehensive understanding is given: – Individual and systemic aspects are covered. – Cognitive and non-cognitive aspects are covered. Link to financial behaviour is recognisable. |

(continued)

Table A2 (continued)

#	Overview and description			Critical appraisal
	Name (and type) of developer(s) Publication year Type of publication Target group (Country)	Conceptual foundation Development methodology	Components	Breath of conceptual understanding Link to financial behaviour
17	**OECD** (policy) 2016 Policy report Adults (aged over 18) (OECD member countries)	The OECD/INFE core competencies framework on **financial literacy** for adults highlights a range of financial literacy outcomes that may be considered to be universally relevant or important for financial well-being in everyday life. It describes the types of knowledge that adults aged 18 or over could benefit from, what they should be capable of doing and behaviours that may help to sustain or improve financial wellbeing, as well as the attitudes and confidence that will support this process. The framework development builds on previous OECD/INFE outputs and complements the OECD/INFE core competencies framework on financial literacy for youth.	**Content areas** I Money and transactions: This area covers different forms and purposes of money and its uses, income generation and management, comparison shopping, payments, and the importance of financial records and contracts. This includes: (1) Money and currencies (2) Income (3) Payments, prices and purchases (4) Financial records and contracts II Planning and managing: This area incorporates day to day financial planning, as well as longer term planning. This includes: (1) Budgeting (2) Managing income and expenditure (3) Saving (4) Investing (5) Longer-term planning and asset building (6) Retirement (7) Credit (8) Debt and debt management III Risk and reward: This area covers risk assessment, financial safety, and managing risk and reward, including understanding risks from financial products and other factors affecting personal and household financial well-being. This includes: (1) Identifying risks (2) Financial safety nets and insurance (3) Balancing risk and reward	Comprehensive understanding is partially given: – Individual and systemic aspects are covered, but focus is clearly on individual. – Non-cognitive factors are considered. Link to financial behaviour is recognisable but the conceptual foundation is unclear.

IV Financial landscape: This area includes regulation, consumer protection, education, and awareness of financial products, scams, taxes, and other factors affecting personal financial security of well-being. This includes: (1) Regulation and consumer protection (2) Rights and responsibilities (3) Education, information and advice (4) Financial products and services (5) Scams and fraud (6) Taxes and public spending (7) External influences

Psychological dispositions

- Awareness, knowledge and understanding: information already acquired by individuals
- Skills and behaviour: competencies related to actions
- Confidence, motivation and attitudes: internal, psychological mechanisms that may support or hinder decisions, behaviours and well-being

Goal statements related to content and dispositions

Learning outcomes are defined by crossing content areas with psychological dispositions.

Further components

Affecting factors: socio-economic status, national context and access to a range of financial services.

(continued)

Table A2 (continued)

#	Overview and description			Critical appraisal
	Name (and type) of developer(s) Publication year Type of publication Target group (Country)	Conceptual foundation Development methodology	Components	
18	**OECD** (policy) 2018 Policy report Adults, esp. MSMEs owners and potential entrepreneurs (OECD member countries)	The OECD/INFE core competencies framework on **financial literacy** for MSMEs defines financial literacy as financial knowledge and skills that owners and managers of MSMEs or potential entrepreneurs benefit from, the behaviours that may help to improve the management of the business finances, as well as the attitudes that support this process. The framework development builds on previous OECD/INFE outputs and complements the OECD/INFE core competencies framework on financial literacy for adults.	**Content areas** I Choice and use of financial services: This area covers business financing and payment/deposit services. These include: (1) Basic payment and deposit services; (2) Financing the business II Financial and business management and planning: This area covers short-term financial management and long-term planning, as well as different legal requirements and maintaining records. These include: (1) Registration, taxes and other legal requirements (2) Keeping records and accounting (3) Short-term financial management (4) Planning beyond the short term III Risk and insurance: This area covers personal and business risk and insurance. These include: (1) Personal risk and insurance (2) Business risk and insurance IV Financial landscape: This area covers external influences and financial protection and guidance. These include: (1) External influences (2) Financial protection for MSMEs (3) Financial information, education and advice **Psychological dispositions** a) Awareness, knowledge and understanding b) Skills and behaviour c) Attitudes **Goal statements related to content and dispositions** Learning outcomes are defined by crossing content areas with psychological dispositions. **Further components** Main stages of development of the firm (or life stages) 1. Basic/informal: Pre-requisites to formally setting up a business 2. Starting up/becoming formal: Start formal business 3. Growing: Managing business beyond the start-up phase and making it grow 4. Closing: Sale, liquidation, succession or bankruptcy of a business	Breath of conceptual understanding Link to financial behaviour Comprehensive understanding is given: – Individual and systemic aspects are covered. – Non-cognitive factors are considered. Link to financial behaviour is recognisable but the conceptual foundation is unclear.

| 19 | **Diehl** (academic) 2018 Dissertation Children and adolescents (all school types) (Germany) | **Financial literacy** is described as the combination of asset accumulation, dealing with debt, dealing with insurance, and the daily handling of money with the aim to embed financial literacy into mathematics education. The development process includes a narrative literature review of financial literacy conceptions and a connection with national mathematics standards. Based on one part of the framework, an exemplary lesson is developed and tested. | **Content areas with related exemplary goal statements**
I Asset accumulation: Being able to plan and manage financial matters to be financially liquid throughout life, including retirement planning.
– Name pros and cons of different investment forms
– Explain the compound interest effect
II Dealing with debt: Understanding reasons for debt and possibilities to avoid borrowing as well as dealing with financial products and their features.
– Name pros and cons of different types of credit
– Calculation of the loan interest rate
III Dealing with insurance: recognising life risks depending on the stages of life and insuring them accordingly.
– Identify (necessary and recommendable) insurances for different life stages
– Name pros and cons for private insurance
IV Daily handling of money: Understanding topics around the cash flow (income as well as expenditure) of a household.
– Know possible uses of a current account
– Plan short and long-term expenditure using a budget | Restricted understanding is given:
– Only individual aspects are covered.
– Only cognitive aspects are covered.
Link to financial behaviour is only partially recognisable. |

(continued)

Table A2 (continued)

#	Overview and description		Critical appraisal
	Name (and type) of developer(s) / Publication year / Type of publication / Target group (Country)	Conceptual foundation / Development methodology	Breath of conceptual understanding / Link to financial behaviour
		Components	Content areas
20	IOSCO & OECD (policy) / 2019 / Policy report / Adults, esp. private investors (OECD member countries)	**Financial literacy** is considered as competency containing knowledge, attitudes and behaviours that retail investors should ideally exhibit, to make informed investment decisions. The work builds on previous OECD/INFE & IOSCO outputs and was developed within a working group. The development process included desktop research to identify competencies relevant to investing, a survey distributed to all members to prioritize competencies and a draft revision with the chairperson and circulation between all members.	**Content areas** I Basic investing principles and concepts: the broad underlying principles of investing. II Investment product attributes: key features such as product structure and fees as well as the potential risks of various investment products. III Buying/selling process of investment products: the competencies applicable during the process of selecting investment products, financial service providers and platforms for buying and selling investment products. IV Owning investment holdings: the competencies applicable to monitoring and managing investments. V Investor rights and responsibilities: investor rights and responsibilities and investor protection measures such as complaint and redress procedures. VI Behavioural biases related to investing: the emotional or cognitive biases that may affect investors when making investment decisions. VII Investment scams and frauds: the common features of investment scams and the ability to avoid being a victim of scams and frauds.	Comprehensive understanding is partially given: – Individual and systemic aspects are covered, but focus is clearly on individual. – Non-cognitive factors are considered. Link to financial behaviour is recognisable but the conceptual foundation is unclear.

3 Financial Literacy Frameworks: A Scoping Review and Critical Appraisal

			Psychological dispositions a) Awareness and knowledge: information acquired by a retail investor such as the fees, features and risks of common investment products. b) Skills and behaviours: actions, or the ability to act, in a manner that achieves positive outcomes, using the behaviours that would most likely lead to financial well-being e.g., evaluating the real return on investments before selecting an investment product. c) Attitudes, confidence and motivations: the internal, psychological mechanisms that may hinder/support informed decision-making and financial well-being, e.g. retail investors' belief that the past performance of an investment is an indication of future returns. **Goal statements related to content and dispositions** Learning outcomes are defined by crossing content areas with psychological dispositions.	
21	**Rudeloff** (academic) 2019 Dissertation Children and adolescents (lower secondary school level) (Germany)	**Financial literacy** is considered a multidimensional construct that cannot be reduced to consumer perspective but should also incorporate the one of the responsible economic citizens. The framework refers to competence approaches from educational science. Development process includes review of selected existing frameworks as well as qualitative and quantitative validation studies.	**Content areas** 1. Money and transaction 2. Saving 3. Loans 4. Insurances 5. Monetary policy **Goal statements** • Reproducing, remembering • Simple application • Analyse, elaborate, validate • Evaluate, reflect, criticise **Psychological dispositions** a) Types of knowledge (declarative procedural, conditional) b) Motivations and interest c) Emotions d) Attitudes e) Self-efficacy expectations	Comprehensive understanding is partially given: – Individual and systemic aspects are covered, but focus is clearly on individual. – Non-cognitive factors are considered. Link to financial behaviour is only partially recognisable.

(continued)

Table A2 (continued)

#	Overview and description			Critical appraisal
	Name (and type) of developer(s) Publication year Type of publication Target group (Country)	Conceptual foundation Development methodology	Components	
22	**Council for Economic Education (CEE) & Jumpstart** (policy) 2021 Policy report Children and adolescents (USA)	Further development of the 2013 **financial literacy** standards by sharpening focus on decision making and including current topics such as behavioral finance, higher education financial planning, identity theft, financial technology, mobile payments, cryptocurrency, and alternative financial services that were not prevalent when earlier standards were published. The development process included 5 steps: (1) Draft prepared by writing committee; (2) Feedback from educator review committee (consisting of teachers); (3) Draft revisions; (4) Review through broad cross-section of experts (5) Equity and bias review by independent consulting firm.	**Content areas** 1. Earning income 2. Spending 3. Saving 4. Investing 5. Managing credit 6. Managing risk **Goal statements related to content areas** Learning outcomes are defined for the 6 content areas referring to what students at different grade levels should know and be able to do with that knowledge. **Exemplary mental processes (decision-making skills)** • Planning and goal setting • Making the decision • Assessing outcomes **Differentiation of qualification levels through grades 4, 8, 12**	Breath of conceptual understanding Link to financial behaviour Restricted understanding is given: – Only individual aspects are covered. – Only cognitive aspects are covered. Link to financial behaviour is recognisable, but only as application of knowledge.

| 23 | Özkale & Özdemir Erdogan (academic) 2022 Journal article Population in general (no specific age group mentioned) (Turkey) | **Financial literacy** is viewed as a wide-ranging competency encompassing knowledge, skills, behaviours and affecting factors. The development process included a narrative review and thematic analysis of existing financial literacy conceptualisations. | **Psychological dispositions and content areas** Financial knowledge: Basic concepts of finance, mathematical knowledge required for finance, local and global financial developments and realities, and risk-reward situations. (1) Fundamental element of finance (2) Mathematical knowledge (3) Economic rationales (4) Risk and Reward (5) Expected and unexpected situations Skills: Understanding of the meaning of a situation and the reasoning related to it, as well as communication, and the use of technology. (1) Numeracy (2) Financial reasoning (3) Problem-solving (4) Communicating (5) Using technology **Goal statements related to intended (financial) behaviours** Behaviours: Demonstrate financial behaviour through budgeting, investment opportunities, financial choices/ advice, having financial responsibility, and obtaining financial independence. (1) Financial management and planning (2) Selecting the optimum opportunity (3) Using financial skills in various contexts (4) Getting proper advice (5) Providing financial assurance and financial security (6) Transferring knowledge to everyday life (7) Financial access and financial independence (8) Qualifying financial behaviours **Further components** Affecting factors: Personal factors and socialization | Comprehensive understanding is partially given: – Individual and systemic aspects are covered, but focus is clearly on individual. – Only cognitive factors are included. Link to financial behaviour is recognisable, but only as application of knowledge and skills. |

(continued)

Table A2 (continued)

#	Overview and description			Critical appraisal
	Name (and type) of developer(s) Publication year Type of publication Target group (Country)	Conceptual foundation Development methodology	Components	Breath of conceptual understanding Link to financial behaviour
24	**EU & OECD** (policy) 2022 Policy report Adults (EU countries)	**Financial competence** is viewed as a combination of financial awareness, knowledge, skills, attitudes and behaviours necessary to make sound financial decisions and ultimately achieve individual financial well-being. The framework focuses on competences pertaining to personal finance. The development of the framework builds on previous outputs from the OECD/INFE (e.g. core competencies framework on financial literacy for adults) and the EU (e.g. DigiComp). Based on these, the development process included two steps: (1) Development of the framework with a dedicated subgroup of the EU Government Expert Group on Retail Financial Services (GEGRFS) (2) Technical discussion with experts to explore usability of the draft	**Content areas** I Money and transactions 1. Money and currencies 2. Income 3. Prices, purchases and payments 4. Financial records and contracts II Planning and managing finances 1. budgeting 2. Managing income and expenditure 3. Saving 4. Investing 5. Longer-term planning and asset building 6. Retirement 7. Credit 8. Debt and debt management III Risk and reward 1. Identifying risks 2. Financial safety nets and insurance 3. Balancing risk and reward IV Financial landscape 1. Regulation and consumer protection 2. Rights and responsibilities 3. Financial education, information and advice 4. Financial products and services 5. Scams and fraud 6. Tax and public spending 7. External influences	Comprehensive understanding is partially given: – Individual and systemic aspects are covered, but focus is clearly on individual. – Non-cognitive factors are considered. Link to financial behaviour is recognisable but the conceptual foundation is unclear.

			Psychological dispositions a) Awareness, knowledge and understanding b) Skills and behaviour c) Confidence, motivation and attitudes **Goal statements related to content and dispositions** Learning outcomes are defined by crossing content areas with psychological dispositions. **Further components** Integration of cross-cutting dimensions into the different content areas a) Digital financial competences b) Sustainable finance competences c) Financial resilience	
25	**Kraitzek & Förster** (academic) 2023 Journal article Adolescents and young adults (students aged 16–20) (Germany)	**Financial competence is defined as** the sum of (domain-specific) financial knowledge and skills, abilities, motivation, attitudes, and the confidence to apply and execute such knowledge and skills in order to deal with financially relevant situations or issues appropriately. The framework refers to competence approaches from educational science as well as to psychological models of problem solving. The development process includes a narrative literature review and critical evaluation of existing conceptualisations and assessments of financial literacy, analogical reasoning from other educational domains as well as a first empirical validation of the framework. A systematic methodology is proposed.	**Psychological dispositions** I. Cognitive Knowledge, generic skills, intelligence, working memory II. Non-cognitive: Interest, motivation/volition, risk preference, attitudes. Moral/ethics, emotions **Mental processes** 1. Perception/awareness 2. Appraisal 3. Analysis/synthesis 4. Decision making 5. Reflection & reorganizing	Comprehensive understanding is partially given: – Systemic aspects are not considered. – Non-cognitive aspects are considered. Link to financial behaviour is recognisable.

(continued)

Table A2 (continued)

#	Overview and description			Critical appraisal
	Name (and type) of developer(s) Publication year Type of publication Target group (Country)	Conceptual foundation Development methodology	Components	Breath of conceptual understanding Link to financial behaviour
26	**Yuning** (academic) 2023 Journal article Adults (China)	The **financial literacy** framework contains key perspectives, which further describe and differentiate educational objectives related to financial education. The key perspectives are deduced from 34 financial literacy and financial education definitions contained in the national curricula in different countries.	**Goal statements** I Political and economic concerns • Enhance the national economic growth • Apply governance approach • Building political orientation of individual • Maintaining financial stability of the nation II Human capital • Enhance job competitiveness • To be prepared for an unpredictable future • Enhance the national economic growth III Personal financial sustainability • Enhance personal financial well-being • Enhance financial socialization of individual • Enhance mental-well-being • Improve the efficiency of personal financial management and prepare for the future • Enhance capability for consumer protection and risk tolerance of individual IV Social relation and inclusion • Enhance the financial and social inclusion • Enhance the awareness of the social responsibility of individual V Differences in personal development • Enhance the equity of education VI Behavioural transformation • Enhance rational financial decision-making for efficient financial behaviour VII Functional literacy • Ensure comprehensive understanding on financial knowledge VIII Critical pedagogy • Cultivate critical reflection and creative action-taking on various financial situations	Comprehensive understanding is partially given: – Individual and systemic aspects are included. – Non-cognitive aspects are not explicitly considered. Link to financial behaviour is partially recognisable.

References

Anderson, L. W., Krathwohl, D. R., Airasian, P. W., Cruikshank, K. A., Mayer, R. E., Pintrich, P. R., Raths, J., & Wittrock, M. C. (2001). *A taxonomy for learning, teaching, and assessing: A revision of Bloom's taxonomy of educational objectives*. Longman.

Aprea, C., & Wuttke, E. (2016). Financial literacy of adolescents and young adults: Setting the course for a competence-oriented assessment instrument. In C. Aprea, E. Wuttke, K. Breuer, N. K. Koh, P. Davies, B. Greimel-Fuhrmann, & J. S. Lopus (Eds.), *International handbook of financial literacy* (pp. 397–414). Springer. https://doi.org/10.1007/978-981-10-0360-8_27

Aprea, C., Wuttke, E., Breuer, K., Koh, N. K., Davies, P., Greimel-Fuhrmann, B., & Lopus, J. S. (Eds.). (2016). *International handbook of financial literacy*. Springer. https://doi.org/10.1007/978-981-10-0360-8

Arksey, H., & O'Malley, L. (2005). Scoping studies: Towards a methodological framework. *International Journal of Social Research Methodology: Theory & Practice, 8*(1), 19–32. https://doi.org/10.1080/1364557032000119616

Atkinson, A., McKay, S., Collard, S., & Kempson, E. (2007). Levels of financial capability in the UK. *Public Money & Management, 27*(1), 29–36. https://doi.org/10.1111/j.1467-9302.2007.00552.x

Atkinson, A., McKay, S., Kempson, E., & Collard, S. (2006). *Levels of financial capability in the UK: Results of a baseline survey*. https://www.bristol.ac.uk/media-library/sites/geography/migrated/documents/pfrc0602.pdf.

Basic Skills Agency & Financial Services Authority. (2006). *Adult financial capability framework* (2nd ed.). https://learningandwork.org.uk/resources/research-and-reports/adult-financial-capability-framework/

Bloom, B. S., Engelhart, M. D., Furst, E. J., Hill, W. H., & Krathwohl, D. R. (1956). *Taxonomy of educational objectives: The classification of educational goals*. David McKay Company.

CEE. (2013). *National standards for financial literacy*. Council for Economic Education. https://www.councilforeconed.org/wp-content/uploads/2013/02/national-standards-for-financial-literacy.pdf

CEE, & Jump$tart. (2021). *National standards for personal financial education*. Council for Economic Education & Jump$tart Coalition for Personal Financial Literacy. https://www.councilforeconed.org/wp-content/uploads/2021/10/2021-National-Standards-for-Personal-Financial-Education.pdf

Davies, P. (2015). Toward a framework for financial literacy in the context of democracy. *Journal of Curriculum Studies, 47*(2), 300–316. https://doi.org/10.1080/00220272.2014.934717

Diehl, S. (2018). *Finanzielle Allgemeinbildung und Mathematik: Konzeptualisierung der Bildungsstandards für das Fach "Finanzen", implementiert in den Fachbereich "Mathematik"*. Unpublished doctoral dissertation, Universität Vechta.

European Union/OECD. (2022). *Financial competence framework for adults in the European Union*. https://www.oecd.org/finance/financial-competence-framework-for-adults-in-the-European-Union.htm

Freire, P. (1970). *Pedagogy of the oppressed*. Seabury Press.

Goldman, S. R., & Pellegrino, J. W. (2015). Research on learning and instruction. *Policy Insights From the Behavioral and Brain Sciences, 2*(1), 33–41. https://doi.org/10.1177/2372732215601866

Goyal, K., & Kumar, S. (2020). Financial literacy: A systematic review and bibliometric analysis. *International Journal of Consumer Studies, 45*(1), 80–105. https://doi.org/10.1111/ijcs.12605

Graña-Alvarez, R., Lopez-Valeiras, E., Gonzalez-Loureiro, M., & Coronado, F. (2022). Financial literacy in SMEs: A systematic literature review and a framework for further inquiry. *Journal of Small Business Management, 62*(1), 331–380. https://doi.org/10.1080/00472778.2022.205117

IOSCO, & OECD. (2019). *Core competencies framework on financial literacy for investors*. https://www.iosco.org/library/pubdocs/pdf/IOSCOPD639.pdf.

Kaminski, H., & Friebel, S. (2012). *Finanzielle Allgemeinbildung als Bestandteil der ökonomischen Bildung (working paper)*. Universität Oldenburg, Institut für Ökonomische Bildung. https://www.ioeb.de/files/ioeb/publications/documents/Kaminski_Friebel%202012_Arbeitspapier_Finanzielle_Allgemeinbildung.pdf

Klieme, E., Hartig, J., & Rauch, D. (2008). The concept of competence in educational contexts. In J. Hartig, E. Klieme, & D. Leutner (Eds.), *Assessment of competencies in educational contexts* (pp. 3–22). Hogrefe.

Klieme, E., & Leutner, D. (2006). Kompetenzmodelle zur Erfassung individueller Lernergebnisse und zur Bilanzierung von Bildungsprozessen. Beschreibung eines neu eingerichteten Schwerpunktprogramms der DFG. *Zeitschrift für Pädagogik, 52*(6), 876–903. https://doi.org/10.25656/01:4493

Kraitzek, A., & Förster, M. (2023). Measurement of financial competence—Designing a complex framework model for a complex assessment instrument. *Journal of Risk and Financial Management, 16*(4), 223. https://doi.org/10.3390/jrfm16040223

Leumann, S., Heumann, M., Syed, F., & Aprea, C. (2016). Towards a comprehensive financial literacy framework: Voices from stakeholders in European vocational education and training. In E. Wuttke, J. Seifried, & S. Schumann (Eds.), *Economic competence and financial literacy of young adults: Status and challenges* (pp. 19–40). Barbara Budrich). https://doi.org/10.2307/j.ctvbkk29d.4

Liberati, A., Altman, D. G., Tetzlaff, J., Mulrow, C., Gøtzsche, P. C., Ioannidis, J. P., Clarke, M., Devereaux, P., Kleijnen, J., & Moher, D. (2009). The PRISMA statement for reporting systematic reviews and meta-analyses of studies that evaluate health care interventions: explanation and elaboration. *Journal of Clinical Epidemiology, 62*(10), e1–e34. https://doi.org/10.1016/j.jclinepi.2009.06.006

Lusardi, A., & Mitchell, O. S. (2023). The importance of financial literacy: Opening a new field. *The Journal of Economic Perspectives, 37*(4), 137–154. https://doi.org/10.1257/jep.37.4.137

Mania, E., & Tröster, M. (2015a). Kompetenzmodell finanzielle Grundbildung. Umgang mit Geld als Thema der Basisbildung. *Magazin Erwachsenenbildung, 25*, 10955. https://doi.org/10.25656/01:10955

Mania, E., & Tröster, M. (2015b). Finanzielle Grundbildung - Ein Kompetenzmodell entsteht. *Hessische Blätter für Volksbildung, 64*, 136–145. https://doi.org/10.3278/HBV1402W

Newell, B. R., Lagnado, D. A., & Shanks, D. R. (2022). *Straight choices: The psychology of decision making* (3rd ed.). Psychology Press. https://doi.org/10.4324/9781003289890

OECD. (2005). Recommendation on principles and good practices for financial education and awareness: Recommendation of the council. www.oecd.org/finance/financial-education/35108560.pdf.

OECD. (2013). Financial literacy framework. In *PISA 2012 assessment and analytical framework: mathematics, reading, science, problem solving and financial literacy* (pp. 139–166). OECD Publishing. https://doi.org/10.1787/9789264190511-7-en

OECD. (2014). *PISA 2012 results: Students and money (Volume VI): Financial Literacy skills for the 21st century*. OECD Publishing. https://doi.org/10.1787/9789264208094-en

OECD. (2015). *OECD/INFE Core competencies framework on financial literacy for youth*. https://web-archive.oecd.org/temp/2024-06-18/370303-core-competencies-frameworks-for-financial-literacy.htm.

OECD. (2016). *G20/OECD INFE Core competencies framework on financial literacy for adults*. https://web-archive.oecd.org/temp/2024-06-18/370303-core-competencies-frameworks-for-financial-literacy.htm.

OECD. (2018). *OECD/INFE core competencies framework on financial literacy for MSMEs*. Organisation for Economic Co-operation and Development (OECD).

Ozkale, A., & Erdogan, E. O. (2022). Review of financial literacy models for educational studies. *HAYEF Journal of Education, 19*(1), 61–70. https://doi.org/10.5152/hayef.2022.21050

Pellegrino, J. W. (2006). *Rethinking and redesigning curriculum, instruction and assessment: What contemporary research and theory suggests*. National Center on Education and the Economy for the New Commission on the Skills of the American Workforce. https://www.researchgate. net/publication/237136880_Rethinking_and_Redesigning_Curriculum_Instruction_and_ Assessment_What_Contemporary_Research_and_Theory_Suggests

Peters, M. D., Marnie, C., Tricco, A. C., Pollock, D., Munn, Z., Alexander, L., McInerney, P., Godfrey, C. M., & Khalil, H. (2020). Updated methodological guidance for the conduct of scoping reviews. *JBI Evidence Synthesis, 18*(10), 2119–2126. https://doi.org/10.11124/jbies-20-00167

Reifner, U. (2003). *Finanzielle Allgemeinbildung: Bildung als Mittel der Armutsprävention in der Kreditgesellschaft*. NOMOS Verlag. https://doi.org/10.5771/9783845258652

Reifner, U. (2011). Finanzielle Allgemeinbildung und ökonomische Bildung. In T. Retzmann (Ed.), *Finanzielle Bildung in der Schule: Mündige Verbraucher durch Konsumentenbildung* (pp. 9–30). Wochenschau Verlag*.

Retzmann, T., & Seeber, G. (2016). Financial education in general education schools: A competence model. In C. Aprea, E. Wuttke, K. Breuer, N. K. Koh, P. Davies, B. Greimel-Fuhrmann, & J. S. Lopus (Eds.), *International handbook of financial literacy*. https://doi.org/10.1007/978-981-10-0360-8_2

Roth, H. (1971). *Pädagogische Anthropologie. Band II: Entwicklung und Erziehung Grundlagen einer Entwicklungspädagogik*. Schroedel Verlag.

Rudeloff, M. (2019). *Der Einfluss informeller Lerngelegenheiten auf die Finanzkompetenz von Lernenden am Ende der Sekundarstufe I*. Springer. https://doi.org/10.1007/978-3-658-25131-4

Schlösser, H. J., Neubauer, M., & Tzanova, P. (2011). Finanzielle Bildung. *Aus Politik und Zeitgeschichte (APuZ), 12*, 21–27. https://www.bpb.de/shop/zeitschriften/apuz/33414/finanzielle-bildung/

Schuhen, M., & Schürkmann, S. (2016). Construct validity with structural equation modelling. In C. Aprea, E. Wuttke, K. Breuer, N. K. Koh, P. Davies, B. Greimel-Fuhrmann, & J. S. Lopus (Eds.), *International handbook of financial literacy* (pp. 383–396). Springer. https://doi.org/10.1007/978-981-10-0360-8_27

Schürkmann, S. (2017). *FILS: Financial literacy study*. De Gruyter Oldenbourg. https://doi.org/10.1515/9783110555622

Schürkmann, S., & Schuhen, M. (2013). Kompetenzmessung im Bereich Financial Literacy: Ergebnisse zum Umgang mit Online-Rechnern aus der FILS-Studie. *Zeitschrift für ökonomische Bildung, 1/2013*, 73–89. https://doi.org/10.7808/zfoeb.1.1.64

Serido, J., Shim, S., & Tang, C. (2013). A developmental model of financial capability. *International Journal of Behavioral Development, 37*(4), 287–297. https://doi.org/10.1177/0165025413479476

Syomwene, A. (2020). *Curriculum theory: Characteristics and functions*. European Journal of Education Studies. https://doi.org/10.46827/ejes.v0i0.2935

Thomas, A., Lubarsky, S., Varpio, L., et al. (2020). Scoping reviews in health professions education: challenges, considerations and lessons learned about epistemology and methodology. *Advances in Health Science Education, 25*, 989–1002. https://doi.org/10.1007/s10459-019-09932-2

Tramm, T., & Reetz, L. (2010). Berufliche Curriculumentwicklung zwischen Persönlichkeits-, Situations- und Wissenschaftsbezug. In R. Nickolaus, G. Pätzold, H. Reinisch, & T. Tramm (Eds.), *Handbuch Berufs- und Wirtschaftspädagogik* (pp. 220–226). Bad Heilbrunn.

Tricco, A. C., Lillie, E., Zarin, W., O'Brien, K. K., Colquhoun, H., Levac, D., Moher, D., Peters, M. D., Horsley, T., Weeks, L., Hempel, S., Akl, E. A., Chang, C., McGowan, J., Stewart, L., Hartling, L., Aldcroft, A., Wilson, M. G., Garritty, C., et al. (2018). PRISMA extension for scoping reviews (PRISMA-SCR): Checklist and explanation. *Annals of Internal Medicine, 169*(7), 467–473. https://doi.org/10.7326/m18-0850

Walstad, W. B., & Rebeck, K. (2017). The test of financial literacy: Development and measurement characteristics. *The Journal of Economic Education, 48*(2), 113–122. https://doi.org/10.1080/00220485.2017.1285739

Weinert, F. E. (2001). Concept of competence: A conceptual clarification. In D. S. Rychen & L. H. Salganik (Eds.), *Defining and selecting key competencies* (pp. 45–65). Hogrefe and Huber Publishers.

Williams, A. J., & Oumlil, B. (2015). College student financial capability: A framework for public policy, research and managerial action for financial exclusion prevention. *International Journal of Bank Marketing, 33*(5), 637–653. https://doi.org/10.1108/IJBM-06-2014-0081

Williamson, O. E. (2000). The new institutional economics: Taking stock, looking ahead. *Journal of Economic Literature, 38*(3), 595–613. http://www.jstor.org/stable/2565421

Yuning, T. (2023). A conceptual framework for financial education. *Citizenship Social and Economics Education, 22*(2), 65–84. https://doi.org/10.1177/14788047231180851

Open Access This chapter is licensed under the terms of the Creative Commons Attribution 4.0 International License (http://creativecommons.org/licenses/by/4.0/), which permits use, sharing, adaptation, distribution and reproduction in any medium or format, as long as you give appropriate credit to the original author(s) and the source, provide a link to the Creative Commons license and indicate if changes were made.

The images or other third party material in this chapter are included in the chapter's Creative Commons license, unless indicated otherwise in a credit line to the material. If material is not included in the chapter's Creative Commons license and your intended use is not permitted by statutory regulation or exceeds the permitted use, you will need to obtain permission directly from the copyright holder.

Chapter 4
Towards A Generic Financial Competence Process Model

Bärbel Fürstenau ⓘ, Nicole Ackermann ⓘ, Mandy Hommel ⓘ, Christin Siegfried ⓘ, and Manuel Förster ⓘ

Abstract The aim of this chapter is to introduce a generic financial competence process model that represents individual financial decision-making processes and the factors that potentially influence them. The development of the model is based on the conceptualisation of both competence in general and financial competence in particular as well as on existing competence process models. The model and its individual components are explained and illustrated using examples from the finance domain. The model can be used as a basis for the development of teaching and learning materials, for the design of teaching and learning environments and for the measurement of financial competence.

B. Fürstenau (✉)
Business Education and Management Training, Faculty of Business and Economics,
TU Dresden, Dresden, Germany
e-mail: baerbel.fuerstenau@tu-dresden.de

N. Ackermann
Vocational Education with a Focus on Didactics, Department for Research on Educational Sciences, Zurich University of Teacher Education, Zurich, Switzerland
e-mail: nicole.ackermann@phzh.ch

M. Hommel
Vocational Education, Faculty of Electrical Engineering, Media and Computer Science,
OTH Amberg-Weiden, Amberg and Weiden, Germany
e-mail: m.hommel@oth-aw.de

C. Siegfried
Business Education for the Vocational Teaching Profession, Faculty of Economics and Social Sciences, University of Potsdam, Potsdam, Germany
e-mail: christin.siegfried@uni-potsdam.de

M. Förster
Business and Economic Education, School of Social Sciences and Technology,
Technical University of Munich, Munich, Germany
e-mail: manuel.foerster@tum.de

© The Author(s) 2026
M. Förster, M. Hommel (eds.), *Conceptualisation and Measurement of Financial Competence*, SpringerBriefs in Education,
https://doi.org/10.1007/978-3-031-95690-4_4

Keywords Competence · Financial competence · Financial competence process model · Financial decision-making

4.1 Introduction

The development of a generic financial competence process model requires clarification of the terms "competence" and specifically "financial competence". In addition, the type and purpose of the model to be developed needs to be specified. To meet these requirements, we can draw on the two previous chapters of this SpringerBrief (Chaps. 2 and 3) in which we discuss the vagueness and heterogeneity of terms (e.g. financial competence, financial literacy, financial capability etc.), definitions, and conceptual backgrounds as they appear in either studies or financial competence frameworks. In this chapter, we expand the results gained so far in the following respects:

1. We relate definitions of competence in general and of financial competence to each other to sharpen our understanding of the term financial competence. In doing so, it becomes clear that competence in general and financial competence share central components, and that financial competence can be regarded as competence in a specific domain, in our case finance.
2. By dealing with the definitions of competence in general, we identify central components of competence which we in turn use as the basis for our working definition of financial competence.
3. Likewise, we refer to models of competence in general to develop our model of financial competence. Consequently, we suggest a financial competence model that draws on existing foundations.

Our model is intended as a process model that aims to capture components relevant in the course of individual financial decision-making. Our model can then be used as basis for fostering financial competence by designing learning material and learning environments. Furthermore, it can serve as a basis for measuring financial competence. We keep our model generic which means that, depending on its purpose in educational, learning or measurement settings, all components could be further specified.

In the following, we will firstly clarify the concept of competence and specifically our understanding of financial competence (Sect. 4.2). Secondly, and building on this, we will look at how models of competence in general can be designed, then propose our generic process model of financial competence and explain its individual components (Sect. 4.3). Thirdly, we illustrate the model with some examples for financial decision-making processes (Sect. 4.4). Finally, we summarise our approach and draw conclusions (Sect. 4.5).

4.2 Defining Financial Competence

4.2.1 Conceptions of Competence

Many definitions and models of competence can be found in the relevant literature (e.g. Klieme et al., 2008). Nevertheless, competence has remained rather vague in meaning (e.g. Weinert, 2001) which becomes—inter alia—obvious by the use of different terms (e.g. competence, ability, literacy etc.). The variety of meanings can be explained by the fact that the definitions were developed from different perspectives or with different intentions, or referring to different theoretical backgrounds, e.g. general cognitive competencies vs. specialized cognitive competencies, objective vs. subjective competence, competence vs. performance, or competence as only cognition vs. competence including cognition and other dispositions such as interest or motivation as well as context (e.g. Weinert, 2001). For the development of our model, it is necessary to be aware of at least two lines of argumentation, namely (1) the competence-performance dichotomy, and (2) the width of components covered by competence.

Starting from the competence-performance dichotomy, we can refer to linguistic research by Chomsky (1980) who prominently used the distinction between competence and performance in the context of acquiring a mother tongue. According to this approach, competence is an internal disposition whereas performance is a behaviour visible from the outside. Competence and performance are interlinked in that competencies are used during performance. In case of language learning, for example, competencies (e.g. linguistic principles, rules) are used to understand and form sentences (Weinert, 2001, p. 48).

Likewise, in psychological research, the differentiation between competence and performance is well established. Blömeke, Gustafsson and Shavelson (2015, pp. 5–7), for example, explain that differentiating between competence and performance mirrors the dichotomy between the behavioural tradition stemming from organisational psychology and the dispositional tradition stemming from empirical pedagogy. In the behavioural tradition, competence is seen *as* performance, i.e. the observable behaviour of a person in a specific situation. The focus lies on situational tasks and situational performance, not on the underlying dispositions (e.g., knowledge, skills, motivation) leading to this performance. The reason is that dispositions may change during the in-situation performance. In the dispositional tradition, competence is seen *as* the internal resources of a person required to perform in a specific situation or—in other words—a prerequisite to successfully complete tasks or meet demands (e.g. Aprea & Wuttke, 2016). The focus, then, lies on the composition of these dispositions (e.g., cognitive resources, motivational resources) and on the prediction of situational performance by these dispositions. Thus, behaviour can be used as criterion to validate dispositions as measures of competence. The underlying assumption following the dispositional approach is a unidirectional relation between disposition (= competence) and performance, i.e. competence leads to performance or is a prerequisite of performance. However, this disregards the option of a "bi-directional relation between competence and performance […], such that cognitive competence or competencies not only guide performance but also are shaped by it" (Sophian, 1997, p. 281).

Independent of the respective position, researchers share the opinion that competence is related to tasks to be completed or demands to be met. Therefore, competence requires the interaction between the individual and the environment in the course of which both internal dispositions (= competence) and external behaviour (= performance) are necessary (e.g. Rychen & Salganik, 2002). Following this line, Rychen and Salganik (2002) define competence as the "ability to meet a complex demand successfully or carry out a complex activity or task" (2002, p. 5). Blömeke, Gustafsson, and Shavelson (2015) claim that competence is seen as closely tied to demands and as manifested by action. Since competence and tasks are tied to each other, and the completion of tasks requires action, some authors, for example in the context of the OECD, consider performance as part of competence (see the critical appraisal Section in Chap. 3 of this SpringerBrief).

Continuing with the width of components covered by competence, in a narrow sense and following, for example, Chomsky (1980) competence is only internal and only cognition. Also, in a narrow sense and following the behavioural tradition, competence is only external and thus only behaviour that is observable. The question, then, arises which and how many dispositions play a role when people cope with tasks or demands. Closely related to this question is the question of whether dispositions, specifically cognition, are general or related to a specific content area. Researchers such as White (1959) are of the opinion that since competence can be related to action, not only cognition but also motivation as action tendency is relevant (Weinert, 2001, p. 49). Likewise, Rychen and Salganik (2002) in their OECD discussion paper on "Definition and Selection of Competencies: Theoretical and Conceptual Foundations" (DeSeCo) proclaim that competence is not only cognition. Instead, emotional, motivational, social, and behavioural components must be regarded as relevant parts of competence (Rychen & Salganik, 2002, p. 6). In addition, they claim that the structure and development of competence are influenced by the context, such as the social and cultural context (Rychen & Salganik, 2002, p. 6). This notion of competence is compatible with Weinert's (2001) concept of "action competence" which "includes all those cognitive, motivational, and social prerequisites necessary and/or available for successful learning and action" (p. 21). According to Weinert (2001) the concept of "action competence" is relevant when it comes to conditions for successfully meeting tasks or for successful actions in specific fields. Concerning the specificity of (cognitive) dispositions, both general cognitive dispositions respectively competencies (e.g. intelligence, memory capacity) and domain-specific ones (e.g. specialised skills and routines to play chess) are to be taken into account (Weinert, 2001). This, in turn, means that competencies that are specific for completing tasks in a domain can be learned (Klieme et al., 2008).

Following the positions outlined above, we can draw an intermediate conclusion about the characteristics of competence (see also Aprea & Wuttke, 2016; Blömeke, Gustafsson, & Shavelson, 2015; Rychen & Salganik, 2002):

- Competence is related to (real-world) situations, tasks or demands.
- Competence is an interaction between an individual and the environment in which both dispositions and performance play a role.
- Competence comprises several dispositions, such as cognitive, conative, affective, and motivational.
- Competence might be influenced by the social and cultural context.
- Competence can be developed by learning.

4.2.2 Conceptions of Financial Competence

To define financial competence, we draw on definitions of both financial competence and financial literacy (see Chap. 2 in this SpringerBrief). The term financial literacy seems to have been more common in literature before 2013. Since then, the term financial competence has gained momentum. This might be explained by the fact that the challenges of financial markets and the complexity of financial products require more than knowledge pieces but instead complex knowledge as well as several dispositions and the ability to effectively utilise dispositions when coping with demands of specific financial situations (see Chap. 3 in this SpringerBrief). Therefore, we suggest a competence-oriented understanding of financial literacy (e.g. Kraitzek & Förster, 2023) according to which financial literacy can be regarded as a competence that shares the characteristics of competence in general mentioned above.

The term financial literacy can be found in literature since the 1990s (Schagen & Lines, 1996; Świecka, 2019, p. 1; Cude, 2022, p. 5). Since then, various definitions have been developed. Those definitions differ in manifold ways, among others in the number of components covered. For instance, definitions focus on one or more individual components, i.e. mainly knowledge, or application of knowledge and behaviour. Other definitions add context factors (e.g. economic conditions). Overviews of definitions are provided, e.g. by Hung et al. (2009), Faulkner (2015); Bedi et al. (2019), Świecka (2019), or Cude (2022) (see also Chap. 2 in this SpringerBrief).

Narrower views define financial literacy as financial knowledge that results in informed financial decisions (e.g. Schagen & Lines, 1996 referring to Noctor et al., 1992). Consequently, financial knowledge and application of financial knowledge are the two relevant, but not necessarily related components of financial literacy. The U.S. President's Advisory Council on Financial Literacy (PACFL) defines financial literacy as "the ability to use knowledge and skills to manage financial resources effectively for a lifetime of financial well-being" (Cude, 2022, p. 5). Thus, the PACFL expands knowledge by adding the component of skills, by emphasizing the ability to manage financial resources, and by the ultimate target of achieving financial well-being. Huston (2010) introduces a conceptualisation of financial literacy composed of a knowledge and an application component. Consequently, financial literacy is more than just knowledge (p. 307). In addition, she suggests that financial literacy can be influenced by financial education and that personal financial behaviour is influenced by other factors, e.g. economic conditions or time preferences (p. 308). Furthermore, Huston (2010) compared different definitions of financial literacy and concluded that some focus primarily on ability, others primarily on knowledge, and that some state a desired outcome, e.g. financial well-being (p. 303). Based on their empirical study regarding household management, Hilgert et al. (2003) set financial knowledge and decision-making (as application of knowledge) into a causal relationship meaning that financial knowledge will lead to effective financial management practices (Malik, 2024).

Even broader and more comprehensive views of financial competence respectively financial literacy have been developed by researchers following a competence-oriented view towards financial literacy. Aprea and Wuttke (2016), for example, define "financial literacy as the potential that enables a person to effectively plan, execute, and control financial decisions. As such, it is based on the availability of individual dispositions—that is knowledge and skills, motivations and interests, attitudes and values—and contingent on situational characteristics" (p. 402). In addition, researchers working for international non-profit organisations, first and foremost for the Organization for Economic Cooperation and Development (OECD) and the International Network on Financial Education (INFE) have developed comprehensive definitions of financial literacy. Their views differ from those of, for example, Aprea and Wuttke (2016) in that they see performance or behaviour as component of competence whereas the latter authors prefer the dispositional approach (see also Chap. 3 in this SpringerBrief).

In general, these comprehensive views share the idea that financial competence is seen as more than financial knowledge and the application of this knowledge. For example, Atkinson and Messy (2012) define financial literacy as "a combination of awareness, knowledge, skill, attitude and behaviour necessary to make sound financial decisions and ultimately achieve individual financial wellbeing" (p. 14). This definition relates to a survey instrument developed by the OECD/INFE meant to measure financial literacy (OECD/INFE, 2023). The OECD (2013) defines financial literacy as "knowledge and understanding of financial concepts and risks, and the skills, motivation and confidence to apply such knowledge and understanding in order to make effective decisions across a range of financial contexts, to improve the financial well-being of individuals and society, and to enable participation in economic life" (OECD, 2013, p. 144). In their financial literacy framework targeting adults, the EU and OECD (2022) define that "financial literacy refers to a combination of financial awareness, knowledge, skills, attitudes and behaviours necessary to make sound financial decisions and ultimately achieve individual financial well-being" (EU & OECD, 2022, p. 5).

Based on the few examples, it becomes obvious that the OECD provides several comparatively similar definitions of financial literacy. The definitions have been developed with the aim to promote a shared understanding among relevant stakeholders (e.g. Member States, national authorities and educational institutions), to support coordinated efforts to improve financial well-being (e.g. EU & OECD, 2022, p. 5), and to lay foundations for assessment of financial literacy (e.g. Atkinson & Messy, 2012, p. 14).

Looking at the OECD definitions, several components of financial literacy and some inconsistencies across definitions can be identified:

- Knowledge and understanding: Both components refer to cognition. However, while some definitions include knowledge and understanding, others only name knowledge.
- Awareness: This component seems to be associated with cognitive psychological processes. It addresses a person's consciousness of his or her environment and the resulting implications for action. Whether awareness, knowledge and skills are jointly mentioned or not varies across definitions.
- Skills: This component refers to generic cognitive processes, such as accessing, comparing and contrasting information.
- Behaviour: This component may be interpreted as a form of action, such as goal setting, or evaluating different options to invest money. In some definitions, skills and behaviours are mentioned in combination. The term behaviour remains somewhat fuzzy across definitions. On the one hand, the difference between skills and behaviour remains unclear. On the other hand, behaviour is seen as both a prerequisite and a consequence of decision-making.
- Attitude, motivation and confidence: These components are associated with non-cognitive psychological processes that may support or hinder decision-making. Some definitions comprise just attitude, others motivation and confidence, and yet others a combination of the three.
- Application of knowledge and understanding: Application of knowledge and understanding is considered to be necessary while making effective, i.e. informed and responsible, decisions. Application is not explicitly mentioned in all definitions. In some definitions decision-making is seen as application of knowledge. In others, the application of knowledge follows decision-making. Furthermore, application of knowledge overlaps with behaviour and skills.

In addition to these components, the definitions specify the ultimate objective of financial literacy, which is to make effective or sound financial decisions. Furthermore, the desired consequences of such effective decisions are included, such as improving the financial well-being of both individuals and the society and enabling peoples' participation in economic life.

Concluding from the definitions of financial literacy respectively financial competence and those of general competence, we can further characterise our understanding of the central term:

- Financial competence is related to (real-world) situations, tasks or demands.
- Financial competence is an interaction between an individual and the environment in which both dispositions and performance play a role.
- Financial competence comprises both several dispositions, be they cognitive or non-cognitive, e.g. knowledge, understanding, awareness, attitude, motivation, confidence, values, and performance, i.e. observable financial behaviour. Therefore, financial competence is neither only dispositions nor just performance.
- Financial competence, specifically performance, has consequences, such as changing financial well-being or enabling participation in economic life.

- Financial competence might be influenced by conditions, such as the social and cultural context, economic conditions, or time preferences.
- Financial competence can be developed by learning.

4.3 Modelling Financial Competence

4.3.1 General Competence Models

Starting from the definitions and characteristics of financial competence, we aim to model financial competence. For that purpose, we consider both a general model of competence and a model of person-environment-interaction. Knowing that many other models exist, we have selected the two models since they match the above-mentioned characteristics of financial competence and can therefore serve as the basis for the development of our generic financial competence process model. A well-known general competence model is that of Blömeke, Gustafsson, and Shavelson (2015). The authors consider competence as a continuum, meaning that there are processes, such as perception and interpretation of a situation as well as decision-making, that mediate between dispositions and performance (Blömeke, Gustafsson, & Shavelson, 2015, p. 8; see Fig. 4.1). According to this perception-interpretation-decision-making (PID) model of competence, multiple transitions between dispositions and performance are possible (Blömeke, König, et al., 2015, p. 310).

As for the person-environment-interaction model, we consider the one developed by Becker et al. (1987). According to this model, action and decision-making processes are regarded as an interaction between a person and his or her environment (see Fig. 4.2). Such a process starts when a person experiences himself or herself in a certain situation and perceives the situation as relevant. This situation is

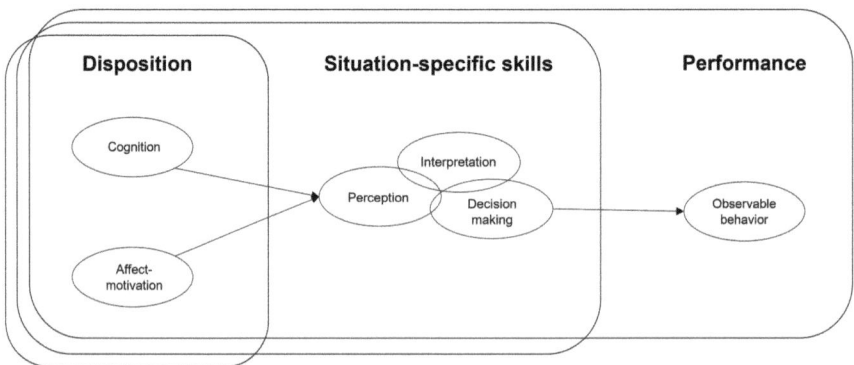

Fig. 4.1 Modelling competence as continuum (Blömeke, Gustafsson, & Shavelson, 2015, p. 9)

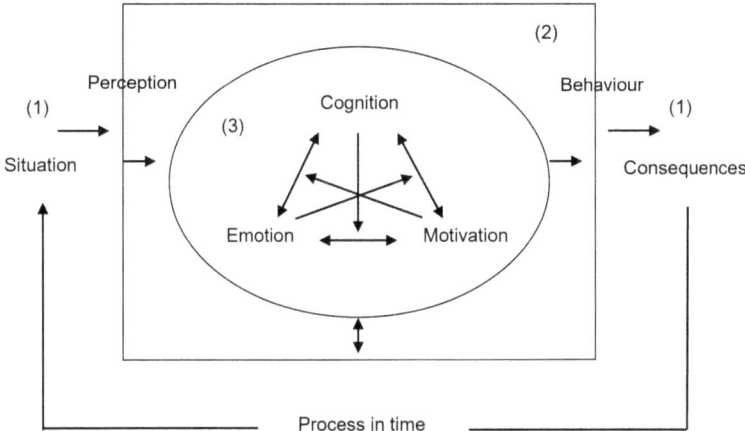

Fig. 4.2 Structure of the psycho-physical system in the person-environment-interaction (slightly modified version of Becker et al., 1987, p. 433); Note: (1): socio-physical context, (2) psycho-physical organism (person); (3) psychological inner world (person)

constituted by observable physical and social circumstances and by what the person is conscious of. In the course of perception, the person structures the situation, i.e. some details move into the foreground, others into the background. This process is influenced by cognitive and non-cognitive state variables, and by perceptual traits (developed by experiences or customs) (see for state and trait variables e.g. Steyer et al., 1999). Then, the perceived situation is processed internally, influenced by cognitive and non-cognitive state variables and their multiple interactions (psychological components of the inner world of a person). In addition, the physical system of a person interacts with his or her psychological components. The perceived and internally processed aspects of the situation are finally transformed into observable behaviour which in turn changes the initial situation. The whole process is embedded in a socio-physical context that comprises, for example, political, societal, social, or institutional conditions.

The two models are compatible though their focus is different. Both models conceptualize competence as a process or continuum including dispositions as well as performance. In addition, both relate competence to real-world situations. However, whereas the model of Blömeke, Gustafsson, and Shavelson (2015) focuses on processes bridging dispositions and performance, the one of Becker et al. (1987) focuses on the complete person-environment-interaction, specifying the internal processes triggered by a situation and resulting in action.

Against the background of the models presented above, we can further clarify the characteristics of financial competence (Sect. 4.2.2), in that we agree with Blömeke, Gustafsson, and Shavelson (2015) and support the idea of conceptualising competence as a continuum assuming an internal process mediating between dispositions and performance, i.e. a PID process. Consequently, for our purpose, we recommend overcoming the dichotomy of conceptualising competence as either performance or dispositions. Instead, we integrate both dispositions and performance in our generic financial competence process model.

4.3.2 A Generic Financial Competence Process Model

4.3.2.1 Overview of the Model

A person finds himself or herself in a financially relevant situation where a financial task has to be completed, or a financial decision has to be made (see Fig. 4.3). The person perceives aspects of the situation, interprets these perceived aspects and consequently makes a decision. During this internal process (PID = perception, interpretation, decision-making), not only the activated cognitive, but also the activated non-cognitive state variables (e.g. motivation and emotion) play a role. The state variables interact with each other in multiple ways. In addition, the PID process is influenced by multiple cognitive and non-cognitive dispositions (trait variables). Consequently, the PID process leads to a result, and the person performs accordingly. The performance, in turn, changes the initial situation, and leads to consequences for financial well-being. The interaction between person and situation is embedded in different kinds of contexts, such as the personal context (e.g. sociodemographics), the social context (e.g. family and friends), and the systemic context (e.g. culture, society, or economy).

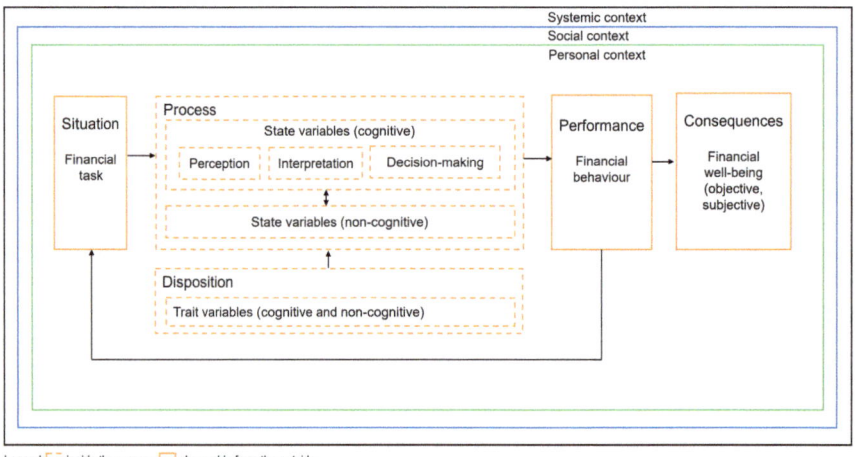

Fig. 4.3 A generic financial competence process model

4.3.2.2 Description of the Model's Components

The components of the model are explained in the following:

Context "Contexts refer to the situations in which the domain knowledge, skills and understandings are applied, ranging from the personal to the global" (OECD, 2013, p. 146). In our model, we differentiate the following contexts:

- Personal context. The personal context refers to a person's socio-demographic characteristics, e.g. age and gender.
- Social context. The social context refers to a person's social environment, e.g. family, friends and peers.
- Systemic context. The systemic context refers to the economic, societal and ecological system, e.g. cultural values, social norms, natural resources, economic prosperity.

Situation The situation is constituted by the characteristics of the task the person has to complete in interaction with the person's activated physical and psychological conditions and embedded in different contexts. The task's content is located in the financial domain, and its level may range from simple to complex.

Process "Processes describe the mental strategies or approaches that are called upon to negotiate the material" (OECD, 2013, p. 146). Cognitive and non-cognitive state variables are activated and interrelated in the process. However, not all components have to be equally conscious for the individual at any point in time: some components can come to the fore, others move to the background (Becker et al., 1987). In addition, the process is influenced by cognitive and non-cognitive trait variables (dispositions).

Cognitive State Variables Cognition is understood as content and processes of cognitive activity. In our model, we focus on cognitive state variables such as PID (perception, interpretation, decision-making):

- Perception. The person perceives aspects of this situation, i.e. how the task is presented, and which physical and social conditions are given. Situation and perception are closely interlinked. The perception of the situation is starting point of the process.
- Interpretation. The person interprets the perceived aspects of the situation by comparing the new information with existing knowledge, i.e. either recognising that the situation can be regarded as similar to already known situations or as a (partly) new one.
- Decision-making. The person's decision-making comprises different phases, such as setting goals, searching for information, weighing up options, planning actions, making decisions. A different number of phases can be run through dependent on the task's type and complexity, and the individual's capacity or

(deliberate) decision. Moreover, algorithms and heuristics can be applied in decision-making. Decision-making can be incomplete and deficient.

Non-cognitive State Variables Non-cognitive state variables refer to the affective components activated in the PID process, such as motivation or emotion. Motivation can be understood as goals or as motives that lead to a willingness to act. Emotions refer to how the quality of the state of the psycho-physical system is currently experienced, i.e. whether people feel happy or angry.

Dispositions Dispositions are (persistent) cognitive (e.g. knowledge, skills) and non-cognitive traits (e.g. motivation, volition, values, risk-preferences), which are bound to the person's characteristics and are not affected by the situation (Steyer et al., 1999).

Performance Performance is the observable financial behaviour preceded by the internal process. Performance means that a person takes action, which causes the initial situation to change. It might also be the case that the person, as a result of the internal process, does not act at all. If a person does not take action, the initial situation does not change, unless it is self-dynamic or changes due to changes in external conditions. It has to be noted that a person can also show behaviour before the final decision is made. This intermediate financial behaviour can, for example, refer to calculations necessary for decision-making.

Consequences The consequence of the performance (financial behaviour) or non-performance is financial well-being. Financial well-being encompasses objective aspects (e.g. availability of financial resources to cope with negative financial shocks) and subjective aspects (e.g. feelings about one's financial situation). Financial well-being can have different levels ranging from serious financial ill-being to very high financial well-being.

4.4 Illustrating the Generic Financial Competence Process Model

4.4.1 Financing Daily Mobility Between Work and Home

As an example, you can imagine that a person starts a new job in a different location that is further away from home than the old one. Consequently, he or she finds himself or herself in a financially relevant situation that requests him or her to consider how to finance mobility to travel back and forth to work. The person perceives the situation as relevant for his or her professional future [*perception* of *situation* with task or demand]. Then, he or she compares the new situation with the existing one and realises that the distance between home and work is now greater than before, and that the destination cannot be reached by bike or public transportation. The person is aware of the fact that the situation is not familiar and needs a new solution. At the same time, the person realises that he or she cannot afford to buy a car [*interpretation*]. As part of the decision-making process, the person sets himself or herself the goal of getting to work on time every day by car. He or she finds out information about buying a car and alternative financing options, such as leasing or car subscribing. He or she calculates and compares all options and comes to the decision to lease a small car since subscribing leads to higher monthly costs at least at first glance [*decision-making/cognitive state variables*]. The person overlooks the fact that a car subscription does not include any hidden costs for transfer, down payment or final instalment, which would be the case with leasing. Besides these cognitive factors, motivational and emotional factors play a role in this process. For example, motivationally, the goal of good and time-saving accessibility of the workplace takes centre stage. However, the person may feel uncomfortable because a car, or at least its purchase, could reduce the disposable monthly income too much and harms the climate, too. In addition, the person feels stressed and insecure about the "correct" decision on how to finance a car [*non-cognitive state variables*]. The entire process is also influenced by trait variables, e.g. basic numeric skills, the attitude towards green mobility or car driving anxiety [*disposition/cognitive and non-cognitive trait variables*]. The whole process might be influenced by different contexts. The nationality of the person might ease or hinder buying, leasing, or subscribing. In addition, the comparatively young age and limited driving experience of the person might cause high insurance amounts [*personal context*]. The family might represent sustainable values and urge the person not to drive a car, if possible [*social context*]. Due to potential oil and gas shortages, prices for fuel might be very high [*economic context*]. Ultimately, the person leases a small car [*performance/ financial behaviour*]. This changes the initial situation, as a car is now available [*new situation*]. However, the leasing model has negative consequences for financial well-being, as the household income is objectively reduced too much, and the person will soon need to borrow money or take out a loan [*consequences/financial well-being*]. After a while, this upcoming new financial situation might initiate another process possibly resulting in deciding in favour of car sharing.

4.4.2 Purchase of a Family Home and Decisions About a Mortgage Loan

Potential buyers of a family home are faced with the *complex task* of deciding on the purchase and the sound financing of a property. Aspects of the *situation* could be that a family wants to buy a home in order to leave the now far too small, rented apartment. A suitable home has been found. Characteristics of the home are location, age of the property, price, additional costs associated with the purchase (e.g. ancillary costs, potential modernisation costs) etc. Now the financing has to be considered. The situational aspects are *perceived* as relevant and *interpreted* by comparing them with existing knowledge and experiences. Consequently, the *decision-making process* of buying the house and, associated with it, of taking a mortgage loan starts. The family considers and compares possible finance options for a loan, the amount of equity that can be used for the purchase, interest levels as well as the amount of free monthly income for the loan repayment, and finally *decides* in favour of one option. *Non-cognitive state variables* (emotion and motivation) influence the PID process, such as the strength of the desire for homeownership and the motivation to invest in own property instead of continue renting a home. *Other dispositions*, like risk awareness as a *trait*, can also influence the process. The *performance*, e.g. signing the contract for a mortgage loan, is the result of the PID process. This may lead to subjective or objective *financial well-being* (in a positive or negative sense) since it influences the homebuyer's free monthly income after annuity payment. In addition, it changes the initial situation since now the homebuyers are new homeowners. The whole process is framed by the *personal context* of the potential homebuyers (e.g. their age, employment status), the *social context* (family status, number and age of children, and others) as well as the *systemic context* (e.g. desirable way of living in society, possibilities of debt financing).

4.4.3 Spontaneous Purchase of Trainers (Sneakers)

If we take an example that requires less cognitive involvement but instead represents a frequently recurring situation, impulse purchases such as the spontaneous purchase of trainers can be mentioned. Impulse purchases are often characterised by a high level of emotional involvement, while cognitive control is significantly lower. A person may find himself or herself in a department store or on the internet, looking at various trainers offers [*situation without specific task*]. Since the person is addicted to trainers, the situation is *perceived* as relevant and possibly *interpreted* as a potential buying situation—the latter based on prior experiences. Here, for example, the *systemic context* determines how large the range of shoes is and how it is advertised (e.g. differences between developing and industrialised countries). Furthermore, the financial situation, but also the current life circumstances (e.g. parents vs. single; potential expectancies of peers), play a significant role in determining which impulse purchases one is susceptible to [*personal and social context*]. The (cognitive) *decision-making process* for such an impulse purchase is less comprehensive than in the previous examples and is often abbreviated. The *perception* of the situation is often influenced by specific characteristics designed by the seller (positioning of the goods, special discounts, presentation, buy now pay later offers), so that the buyer becomes aware of the shoes and the offer. The person makes a spontaneous decision. Here, heuristics are often applied that shorten the decision-making process based on certain rules. Consequently, the product is bought that has received sufficiently good ratings from other customers, that is below a subjective anchor price or in the middle of the price range. Even with impulse buying, *cognitive state and trait variables* are usually needed. For example, prices may be estimated and compared [*cognitive state variables, process steps*], so that here, too, a basic numeracy or knowledge of prices of shoes [*cognitive trait variables*] is helpful. In addition, factors such as delay of gratification or impulse control, which target the handling of emotional impulses [*cognitive state variables*], become relevant. Beliefs and attitudes [*non-cognitive trait variables*] are also of great importance, since these influence heuristics to a high degree. If the buyer is generally convinced that branded products are always better than no-name products, then he or she will also buy certain brands. The current emotional mood [*non-cognitive state variables*] also plays an important role. If the buyer is a student who has just received a positive result on an exam, then he or she is in a good mood and perhaps more willing to buy the shoe and reward himself or herself. In this context, cognitive and non-cognitive dispositions as well as personal and socio-economic and social contexts interact. For example, the social environment in which a person moves and in which status symbols play a major or minor role, can influence his or her purchase decision. The shoe purchase [*performance*] can then turn out to have different *consequences* for *financial well-being* as a result of evaluation processes. It is possible that the buyer regrets the purchase and now associates the shoes with guilt depending on his or her now even tighter financial situation.

4.5 Summary and Conclusion

The aim of the article was to develop a generic but at the same time holistic process model for the financial competence of individuals and to clarify the basis for its development. It is generic, since all its components can be specified—dependent on the purpose of use. It is holistic, as it considers different state and trait variables of the person, but also the environment or different contexts and the interaction of all these variables. It is a process model insofar as 1) the person interacts with the environment, and this can be seen as a process in time including interactions between the person and the environment and 2) a decision-making process with several phases takes place within the individual. This model complements previous content and level models of financial literacy and those that relate to individual or just a few selected variables. The model is based on definitions of competence and financial competence as well as a selected competence model and a person-environment-interaction model. Together with Blömeke, Gustafsson, and Shavelson (2015), we endeavour to overcome the dichotomy between dispositions and performance. Consequently, we understand competence as a continuum in which a PID (perception-interpretation-decision-making) process mediates between dispositions and performance. In this respect, both competence and performance are considered in relation to a financial task and are also embedded in different contexts.

The generic model can be extended and refined in different aspects, e.g. by specifying the individual variables. For example, cognitive dispositions (traits) maybe specified as knowledge, intelligence, or working memory capacity, non-cognitive dispositions (traits) as general interest in financial matters, attitude towards money, or risk preferences (Kraitzek & Förster, 2023). Another option for refinement is that variables interact in multiple ways. For example, in the decision-making process cognitive and non-cognitive state variables interact, state and trait variables interact, or context and personal variables interact. Furthermore, the integration of feedback loops is an option for refinement. For example, performance may have an influence on trait variables and not only on the initial situation. Or delayed effects of financial well-being may influence the person and the situation. Those refinements were not included or are at least not explicitly mentioned and displayed.

Dependent on the purpose of use and research interest, different specifications may be applicable and justifiable for the model's specifications and refinement. For example, if researchers or educators are interested in just cognition, only the cognitive factors can be regarded. If researchers or educators are interested in the interaction of emotion and cognition, they can specifically assess or foster this interaction. If researchers or educators are interested in measuring or fostering financial competence holistically—just as we are—all components and their respective specifications should be regarded.

To sum up: The model can be used to foster awareness of the multitude of components relevant in financial decision-making, and further to support and align learning, instruction, and assessment.

Acknowledgments We express our heartfelt thanks to the participants of the AFin-Meetings (Chap. 1) for many inspiring and fruitful discussions which substantially helped us in developing the suggested generic financial competence process model.

References

Aprea, C., & Wuttke, E. (2016). Financial literacy of adolescents and young adults: Setting the course for a competence-oriented assessment instrument. In C. Aprea, E. Wuttke, K. Breuer, N. K. Koh, P. Davies, B. Greimel-Fuhrmann, & J. S. Lopus (Eds.), *International handbook of financial literacy* (pp. 397–414). Springer. https://doi.org/10.1007/978-981-10-0360-8_27

Atkinson, A., & Messy, F. (2012). Measuring financial literacy: Results of the OECD/International Network on Financial Education (INFE) Pilot Study. In *OECD working papers on finance, insurance and private pensions, No. 15*. OECD Publishing. https://doi.org/10.1787/5k9csfs90fr4-en

Becker, D., Oldenbürger, H.-A., & Piehl, J. (1987). Motivation und emotion. In G. Lüer (Ed.), *Allgemeine Experimentelle Psychologie* (pp. 431–470). Hogrefe.

Bedi, H. S., Karn, A. K., Kaur, G. P., & Duggal, R. (2019). Financial literacy – A bibliometric analysis. *Our Heritage, 67*(10), 1042–1054.

Blömeke, S., Gustafsson, J.-E., & Shavelson, R. J. (2015). Beyond dichotomies: Competence viewed as a continuum. *Zeitschrift für Psychologie, 223*(1), 3–13. https://doi.org/10.1027/2151-2604/a000194

Blömeke, S., König, J., Suhl, U., Hoth, J., & Döhrmann, M. (2015). Wie situationsbezogen ist die Kompetenz von Lehrkräften? Zur Generalisierbarkeit der Ergebnisse von videobasierten Performanztests [To what extent is teacher competence situation-related? On the generalizability of the results of video-based performance tests]. *Zeitschrift für Pädagogik, 61*(3), 310–327. https://doi.org/10.25656/01:15350

Chomsky, N. (1980). Rules and representations. *The Behavioral and Brain Sciences, 3*, 1–61.

Cude, B. J. (2022). Defining financial literacy. In G. Nicolini & B. J. Cude (Eds.), *The Routledge handbook of financial literacy* (pp. 5–17). Routledge.

EU & OECD. (2022). *Financial competence framework for adults in the European Union*. European Commission, Organisation for Economic Co-operation and Development (OECD). https://www.oecd.org/finance/financial-competence-framework-for-adults-in-the-European-Union.htm

Faulkner, A. E. (2015). A systematic review of financial literacy as a termed concept: More questions than answers. *Journal of Business & Finance Librarianship, 20*(1–2), 7–26. https://doi.org/10.1080/08963568.2015.982446

Hilgert, M. A., Hogarth, J. M., & Beverly, S. G. (2003). Household financial management: The connection between knowledge and behavior. *Federal Reserve Bulletin, 89*, 309–322.

Hung, A. A., Parker, A. M., & Yoong, J. K. (2009). Defining and measuring financial literacy. *RAND Labor and Population working paper series*, WR-708. https://doi.org/10.2139/ssrn.1498674.

Huston, S. J. (2010). Measuring financial literacy. *Journal of Consumer Affairs, 44*(2), 296–316. https://doi.org/10.1111/j.1745-6606.2010.01170.x

Klieme, E., Hartig, J., & Rauch, D. (2008). The concept of competence in educational contexts. In J. Hartig, E. Klieme, & D. Leutner (Eds.), *Assessment of competencies in educational contexts* (pp. 3–22). Hogrefe.

Kraitzek, A., & Förster, M. (2023). Measurement of financial competence—Designing a complex framework model for a complex assessment instrument. *Journal of Risk and Financial Management, 16*(223), 1–28. https://doi.org/10.3390/jrfm16040223

Malik, A. (2024). *Visual design of financial information*. Dissertation, TU Dresden.

Noctor, M., Stoney, S., & Stradling, R. (1992). *Financial literacy: A discussion of concepts and competences of financial literacy and opportunities for its introduction into young people's learning*. National Foundation for Educational Research.

OECD. (2013). PISA 2012 financial literacy framework. In *PISA 2012 assessment and analytical framework* (pp. 139–165). Organisation for Economic Co-operation and Development (OECD). https://www.oecd.org/pisa/pisaproducts/46962580.pdf

OECD/INFE (2023). *International survey of adult financial literacy*. Organisation for Economic Co-operation and Development (OECD).

Rychen, D. S. & Salganik, L. H. (2002). DeSeCo Symposium – Discussion Paper Jan 15–02. https://www.deseco.ch/bfs/deseco/en/index/04.parsys.29226.downloadList.67777.DownloadFile.tmp/2002.desecodiscpaperjan15.pdf. Accessed 12 May 2024.

Schagen, S., & Lines, N. (1996). *Financial literacy in adult. Life. A report to the NatWest Group Charitable Trust*. National Foundation for Educational Research.

Sophian, C. (1997). Beyond competence: The significance of performance for conceptual development. *Cognitive Development, 12*, 281–303. https://doi.org/10.1016/S0885-2014(97)90001-0

Steyer, R., Schmitt, M., & Eid, M. (1999). Latent state–trait theory and research in personality and individual differences. *European Journal of Personality, 13*(5), 389–408. https://doi.org/10.1002/(SICI)1099-0984(199909/10)13:5<389::AID-PER361>3.0.CO;2-A

Świecka, B. (2019). A theoretical framework for financial literacy and financial education. In B. Świecka, A. Grzesiuk, D. Korczak, & O. Wyszkowska-Kaniewska (Eds.), *Financial literacy and financial education. Theory and survey* (pp. 1–12). de Gruyter.

Weinert, F. E. (2001). Definitions of the concept of "competence". In D. S. Rychen & L. H. Salganik (Eds.), *Defining and selection key competencies* (pp. 45–65). Hogefe und Huber.

White, R. H. (1959). Motivation reconsidered: The concept of competence. *Psychological Review, 66*, 297–333. https://doi.org/10.1037/h0040934

Open Access This chapter is licensed under the terms of the Creative Commons Attribution 4.0 International License (http://creativecommons.org/licenses/by/4.0/), which permits use, sharing, adaptation, distribution and reproduction in any medium or format, as long as you give appropriate credit to the original author(s) and the source, provide a link to the Creative Commons license and indicate if changes were made.

The images or other third party material in this chapter are included in the chapter's Creative Commons license, unless indicated otherwise in a credit line to the material. If material is not included in the chapter's Creative Commons license and your intended use is not permitted by statutory regulation or exceeds the permitted use, you will need to obtain permission directly from the copyright holder.

Chapter 5
Complexity in the Measurement of Financial Competence

William B. Walstad ⓘ, Andreas Kraitzek ⓘ, Carlo Di Chiacchio, Sabrina Greco, and Manuel Förster ⓘ

Abstract This chapter explores the complexity of measuring financial competence, emphasizing the construct's cognitive and non-cognitive facets. Financial competence, a multi-dimensional construct, encompasses not only knowledge about personal finance but also the attitudes, personal financial preferences, decision-making processes, and behaviours, that influence financial outcomes. The chapter reviews various measurement instruments used in research about personal financial education, detailing how these instruments assess the cognitive and non-cognitive dimensions of financial competence. It highlights the challenges posed by the diversity of financial constructs, as well as the variability in how these constructs are defined, measured, and applied across different demographic groups. The chapter underscores the difficulties in comparing and generalising results from different studies by examining what part of financial competence and its related components is measured, how it is measured, and who is measured. The review also emphasizes the need for more comprehensive tools that simultaneously assess cognitive knowledge and non-cognitive factors, such as financial behaviours and attitudes, to better capture the full scope of financial competence. This work aims to guide future research and improve the effectiveness of financial education by offering a clearer understanding of measurement complexities and promoting the development of more holistic assessment instruments.

W. B. Walstad (✉)
Economics, University of Nebraska–Lincoln, Lincoln, NE, USA
e-mail: wwalstad1@unl.edu

A. Kraitzek · M. Förster
Business and Economic Education, School of Social Sciences and Technology, Technical University of Munich, Munich, Germany
e-mail: andreas.kraitzek@tum.de; manuel.foerster@tum.de

C. Di Chiacchio · S. Greco
International Studies, National Institute for the Evaluation of the Educational System, INVALSI, Rome, Italy
e-mail: carlo.dichiacchio@invalsi.it; sabrina.greco@invalsi.it

© The Author(s) 2026
M. Förster, M. Hommel (eds.), *Conceptualisation and Measurement of Financial Competence*, SpringerBriefs in Education,
https://doi.org/10.1007/978-3-031-95690-4_5

Keywords Assessment of financial competence · Financial literacy · Measurement approaches · Questionnaire

5.1 Introduction

Measurement instruments are essential for conducting empirical research and providing effective education in personal finance. From the perspective of research, assume that a study investigates the hypothesized relationship between two financial variables. The evidence to evaluate the hypothesis comes from a statistical analysis of the data, which in turn relies on the reliable and valid measurement of the two financial variables of interest. Measurement instruments are also important for financial education as educators need to know what their subjects understand about personal finance and what they can do with that understanding. This information, too, is best obtained by reliable and valid measures from each subject.

This chapter discusses measurements in personal finance related to financial competence. The topic, however, is quite complex as financial literacy understood as a financial competence is a multi-dimensional construct with different aspects and interrelated parts contributing to its whole (Cude, 2022; Huston, 2010; Kraitzek & Förster, 2023; OECD, 2014). In the following we use the term financial competence instead of financial literacy relying on the understanding of financial competence as presented in Chap. 4. Of course, there are understandings of financial literacy that align well with an understanding of financial competence (e.g. OECD, 2014), but there are also some understandings where financial literacy encompasses significantly less than our understanding of a more comprehensive financial competence (see also Chaps. 2–4). As explained in previous chapters of this SpringerBrief, financial competence has both cognitive and non-cognitive dimensions that influence its formation. These cognitive and non-cognitive dimensions then affect how decisions are made and if actions are taken. Given this multi-dimensionality and the decision-making process, the measurement of financial competence is more likely to focus on its cognitive and non-cognitive dimensions, and their subparts, instead of the whole of the construct.

This chapter advances understanding of financial competence as a construct by reviewing measurement instruments used in research studies to assess financial competence and the relation to its cognitive and non-cognitive dimensions as well as their subparts. The review also covers many content areas in personal finance associated with financial competence, such as money management, saving, investing, credit, debt, risk, and insurance (Atkinson & Messy, 2012; CEE, 2021; Hilgert et al., 2003). The number of research studies in personal finance is voluminous and constantly growing (Braunstein & Welch, 2002; Gomes et al., 2021; Lusardi & Mitchell, 2014). In that respect, this review cannot give a definitive list of all instruments and items that are in existence for the assessment of personal financial competence. Instead, it offers an illustrative selection of available instruments measuring various aspects of financial competence. It presents findings for each instrument in a comprehensive and detailed table.

The following content provides an explanation of the framework used for discussing the measurement of financial competence. It is structured to address three major questions. The first asks *what is measured* to offer perspective on the wide range of constructs related to financial competence that have been used or investigated in prior studies. The second reflects on *how it is measured* to explain the different approaches to the construction and implementation of various measurement instruments related to financial competence. The third looks at *who is measured* to show that the use of instruments will often vary by group when considering aspects of financial competence.

The main conclusion is that the empirical study of financial competence is complex as each study has unique *what*, *how*, and *who* characteristics. These differences make it challenging to summarize or generalise findings across instruments used to assess the various aspects of financial competence. The purpose of this review is to provide information about current instruments to help practitioners and researchers in personal finance understand this complexity. This information should be a useful guide for choosing the most appropriate instrument for future studies given this complexity and interest in developing new instruments. The Table A3 in the supplementary material to this chapter presents a detailed description of a broad sample of available instruments used to assess different aspects of financial competence.

5.2 What Is Measured?

Numerous constructs related to financial competence have been developed and used to study topics in personal finance. Consider the following list of financial constructs related to different aspects of financial competence that have been used in research studies (see also Chap. 2 in this SpringerBrief for further details): financial literacy (Förster et al., 2017; Lusardi & Mitchell, 2007); financial knowledge (Dare et al., 2020; Houts & Knoll, 2020); financial well-being (CFPB, 2015; Gutter & Copur, 2011); financial capability (Xiao & O'Neill, 2016); financial competence (Bateman et al., 2014; Kershaw & Webber, 2008); financial behaviours (Allgood & Walstad, 2016; Kaiser & Menkhoff, 2017); financial decision-making (Agarwal et al., 2007; Aprea & Wuttke, 2016); financial satisfaction (Archuleta et al., 2013; Joo & Grable, 2004); financial stress (Friedline et al., 2021); financial anxiety (Shapiro & Burchell, 2012); financial confidence (Parker et al., 2012; Tokar Asaad, 2015); financial risk (Bannier & Neubert, 2016; Charness & Gneezy, 2012); financial numeracy (Lusardi, 2012); financial disposition (De Winne, 2021); and financial advice (Calcagno & Monticone, 2015; Collins, 2012; Kramer, 2016). What this list of financial constructs and studies suggests is that any of a person's cognitive or non-cognitive characteristics may be the focus of a study as they are thought to affect financial actions and behaviours.

Furthermore, each financial construct related to aspects of financial competence may be refined or re-defined to apply to a specific topic in personal finance. Instruments designed to measure financial literacy may be restricted to study a particular type and content such as credit, debt, or insurance literacy (Courchane et al., 2008; Lin et al., 2019; Lusardi & Tufano, 2015). Similarly, studies of financial behaviours may be limited to a specific type such as saving or investing (Babiarz & Robb, 2014; Gallery et al., 2011; Jappelli & Padula, 2013; van Rooij et al., 2011a). Likewise, studies of financial attitudes can be conducted on specific financial transactions such as mortgages or other consumer purchases (Cox et al., 2014). Also, measures of financial decision-making could focus on retirement or budgeting decisions (Antonides et al., 2011; Lusardi & Mitchell, 2017; van Rooij et al., 2011b). Other instruments may use a broader approach and assess aspects of financial competence across a range of content areas (Aprea & Wuttke, 2016; OECD, 2014).

The general point is that differences in the financial construct, the instruments used to measure them, and the personal finance topics studied make it difficult to sort and categorize research studies into homogeneous groups. Each study, even if it assesses the same or a similar financial construct, may differ based on the respective construct's definition, how it is measured, and the other variables and conditions under which the research is conducted. Even when there are commonalities among studies based on similar financial constructs, similar measurement procedures, and similar personal finance topics, there can still be subtle differences and nuances in measurement (Walstad & Allgood, 2022).

Consequently, the first step in measuring a financial construct requires a definition to understand *what* exactly is to be measured. The definitions of financial constructs, however, can be limited and vary by study, as is exemplified in the discussion of the construct *financial literacy* in several reviews (Huston, 2010; Remund, 2010; Stolper & Walter, 2017; also see Chap. 2 in this SpringerBrief). For example, Remund (2010) identified five different types of *conceptual* definitions for financial literacy (knowledge, communication skill, management aptitude, decision-making, and planning) across the set of research studies he reviewed. He then combined the different types to make a recommended conceptual definition: "Financial literacy is a measure of the degree to which one understands key financial concepts and possesses the ability and confidence to manage personal finances through appropriate, short-term decision making and sound, long range financial planning, while mindful of life events and changing economic condition" (Remund, 2010, p. 284). As another example, for the 2012 implementation of financial literacy assessment in the Programme for International Student Assessment (PISA), the OECD defined financial literacy as "knowledge and understanding of financial concepts and risks, and the skills, motivation and confidence to apply such knowledge and understanding in order to make effective decisions across a range of financial contexts, to improve the financial well-being of individuals and society, and to enable participation in economic life." (OECD, 2014, p. 33).

The juxtaposition of these two definitions shows that while they are similar in some respects (e.g., decision-making, understanding financial concepts) they differ significantly in other respects (e.g., focus on well-being, including life events or economic environments). The same problem often applies to definitions of other financial constructs. They can appear to be similar based on a general descriptor but differ in particulars of the definition. Given this problem, a clear definition of a financial construct to be assessed is a minimal requirement for valid and transparent measurement in personal finance. Additionally, providing a clear definition helps with the subsequent construction of the items and helps readers of the study to decide if the constructs, the measurements, and the results are comparable.

A full understanding of what has been measured related to financial competence is essential for understanding the value of a study and interpreting its results. Although the complexity of a definition adds richness to research in personal finance and allows it to address different topics, at the same time it makes it difficult to compare results across studies and summarise the findings. Caution, therefore, should be exercised when drawing conclusions across studies of the same financial construct as what is being measured by one study is likely to be different in some nuanced or unique ways from what is being measured by another study, even if the two studies are supposedly measuring a common financial construct.

5.3 How Is It Measured?

After deciding what to measure, the next question to answer is *how* is it measured. As previously discussed, financial competence is a multi-dimensional construct, with cognitive and non-cognitive dimensions and related subparts. The two dimensions of a financial construct, however, are not mutually exclusive. They can overlap and interact with each other and thus both can affect the financial construct (OECD, 2014). Definitions of the financial construct will describe in theory what it is supposed to be measured, but the challenging task for instrument developers is to operationalise the definition (Ouachani et al., 2021).

A cognitive financial construct is often assessed with objective test measures as they focus on measuring individuals' knowledge or understanding of personal finance content or topics. Consider financial literacy as a financial construct to be measured. It has been assessed with just a few objective test items (Lusardi & Mitchell, 2014) covering a few personal finance topics and also with a large set of items covering a wide range of personal finance content (OECD, 2014; Walstad & Rebeck, 2017). In the latter case, a content framework or guideline specifies what people should know and understand about the assessed financial topics (Bosshardt & Walstad, 2014; OECD, 2005).

The number of items included in an instrument depends on whether the purpose of the study is to create a general financial literacy index or to generate a profile describing financial literacy scores on different concepts and topics. Time and other constraints on data collection also limit the number of items tested, so each instrument only includes a representative sample of the possible content that could be assessed. The format for test items is often multiple-choice, true-false, or a combination, so that responses can be scored as correct or incorrect. Statistical analysis is conducted with the test data using classical test theory or item response theory to assess test reliability and validity (Gignac & Ooi, 2021; Ranyard et al., 2019). Alternative assessment methods, i.e., test formats other than standardised multiple-choice or true-false items, are only used occasionally. And if they are used, they are more likely to be implemented for the investigation of non-cognitive components of financial competence. Andersen et al. (2008), for example, used Multiple Price Lists (MPL) and pay-off tables to experimentally assess individuals' risk-aversion and time preferences in financially relevant matters. As another example, Hastings and Mitchell (2020) conducted a game-like experiment to investigate whether peoples' impatience and their ability to delay gratification influence investment decisions and financial planning.

Subjective measures of the cognitive dimensions of a financial construct such as financial literacy ask people to evaluate their perceived level of knowledge or competence in understanding or managing financial matters. Subjective assessment of a financial construct is mainly measured by Likert scale items. For example, the U.S. National Financial Capability Study (Lin et al., 2022) used a single item asking respondents to evaluate their own overall financial knowledge. In the OECD/INFE toolkit (OECD, 2022) respondents need to evaluate their perceived knowledge in comparison with other adults living in the same country. Other studies asked respondents to self-evaluate how they feel about their ability in financial matters and their overall knowledge (Morris et al., 2022; Robb & Woodyard, 2011). It is also possible to gain insights into the influence of subjective and objective financial literacy on financial behaviours from a combined analysis of responses from a self-assessment with the individual scores from an objective test (Allgood & Walstad, 2016; Bannier & Neubert, 2016; Warmath & Zimmerman, 2019).

Subjective measures also are used as measures of non-cognitive dimensions of a financial construct by using them to collect data on attitudes, motivations, and behaviours (OECD, 2019). Usually, attitudes or motivations are measured by Likert scales rating individuals' level of agreement or disagreement with specific statements (Barry, 2014; Bocchialini et al., 2022; Grohs-Müller & Greimel-Fuhrmann, 2018).

Financial behaviours can be treated either as outcome variables or as process variables like attitudes and motivations. Moreover, behaviours may be considered a structural part of attitudes along with cognitive and affective components. For example, a qualitative index of saving behaviour developed in several studies asked respondents to indicate whether individual/family income is equal or greater or lower than expenses (Harris et al., 2002; Mahdzan & Tabiani, 2013). Other studies have asked individuals to evaluate specific behaviours, either saving or spending, by using an agreement/disagreement scale or asking about either the frequency or the likelihood to behave in a specific way (OECD, 2017; OECD, 2020; OECD, 2022).

Another approach to measurement is to assess the response process when making a financial decision. For example, a Situation Judgment Test (SJT) can be used to make a financial problem as realistic as possible and meaningful for respondents (Aprea & Wuttke, 2016; Wuttke & Aprea, 2018). In shaping the situation and the response options, it is possible to investigate cognitive and non-cognitive dimensions linked to financial decision-making. To solve an SJT, respondents may choose their most likely response option (usually a behaviour) from a list of other behaviour responses. Or they may indicate, for each response option, the likelihood that respondents would behave in that way. Therefore, the main advantage of using an SJT is to evaluate the response process rather than evaluate the correctness of the choice.

Answering the question of how to measure a financial construct is challenging. It requires more than selecting an instrument and then conducting a psychometric analysis on the data. Instruments developed for one purpose may not work well for another purpose. Instruments may not be sufficiently realistic to capture the desired financial outcome, whether the outcome be knowledge, attitude, or behaviour. It may also be important to understand the context or nuances in which the instruments are administered to subjects. Studies may also benefit from further analysis beyond the quantitative perspective that provide a better understanding of how individuals formed their responses or made their decisions.

5.4 Who Is Measured?

Since 2000, there has been growing recognition that financial education should start as early as possible in schools and continue throughout life (CEE, 2021; OECD, 2005). In this way, children and adolescents can learn the basic knowledge and develop financial skills that contribute to financial competence (Kaiser & Menkhoff, 2019). The rationale for this line of research is that financial education will improve young peoples' financial competence and better prepare them for their financial future as independent adults. Such educational approaches are necessary as evidence indicates that young people's levels of financial literacy are consistently lower than those of other demographic groups (Cordero et al., 2022). Given this rationale, it should not be surprising that many studies have focused on youth and their financial literacy (CFPB, 2019; Dare et al., 2020; Förster et al., 2017; OECD, 2014; Walstad et al., 2017).

College or university students are a special group that falls between youth and adults. They are emerging adults who may or may not have full financial responsibility for their livelihood and financial decisions. They may also face unique financial issues related to part-time work, paying for educational loans, handling credit card debt and other financial matters. In this respect, their financial situation differs from full-time employed adults (Archuleta et al., 2013; Aydin & Selcuk, 2019; Gutter & Copur, 2011).

Most research studies in personal finance have focused on adults for the basic reason that adults make all types of financial decisions throughout their lifetime (Agarwal et al., 2007; Gomes et al., 2021). Poor financial decisions can have severe consequences for meeting worthy financial goals related to money management, saving, investing, and other financial activities. Although for some financial decisions, adults can receive financial advice from professionals, such advice can be costly, and in the end, personal responsibility for the decision and its positive or negative outcomes remains with the adults.

Given these circumstances, it should not be surprising that researchers have looked at aspects of financial competence, such as financial literacy and financial education, as ways for adults to improve their downstream financial behaviours (Kaiser et al., 2022; Kaiser & Menkhoff, 2017). Furthermore, adults are not all the same and should not be considered a homogenous group. Their responses to financial issues or matters may differ based on demographics such as age, income, occupations, and other demographic characteristics (Lusardi & Mitchell, 2014; Walstad et al., 2017).

What should also be understood is that adults are more likely to be assessed on their non-cognitive responses to a financial construct than are youth. This occurs as there are somewhat fewer restrictions for collecting non-cognitive data from adults than from youth. Additionally, with adults, there can be a progression in learning experiences with the management of money and the handling of personal finances that occur over time. For example, studies of adults have been conducted on attitudes toward money (Barry, 2014) and risk tolerance (Weber et al., 2002). Other adult studies have investigated emotional components related to financial competence, such as financial well-being (CFPB, 2015, 2017) and perceived level of stress (Heo et al., 2020).

Responding to the question of who is measured frames not only the target population to study, but also the kind of intervention. Elementary and secondary students are mainly assessed for their knowledge of basic financial concepts. In this case, their education can lay a knowledge foundation for financial competence later in life. College students need more refined education to fit their particular financial situations. Financial education for adults will also vary based on their financial circumstances and their stage in life as adults. In general, financial education for younger and older adults will emphasise both the cognitive and non-cognitive dimensions of financial competence.

5.5 Application and Extension

The measurement of financial competence is complex as it will vary based on what cognitive or non-cognitive dimensions are to be measured, how the measurement will be conducted, and who the target group is for a study. Answers to the *what*, *how*, and *who* questions will shape the characteristics of each research investigation. These factors make each study unique and contribute to the diversity of studies. This uniqueness and diversity are evident in the Appendix Table A3 summarising the features of 31 studies.

The process for selecting studies for the table was informed by the systematisation of concepts (Chap. 2 of this SpringerBrief), a review of existing frameworks discussing personal finance (Chap. 3) and the development of a conceptual definition of financial competence as prepared for this brief (Chap. 4). It became clear from this initial review that most published studies and frameworks concerning personal finance often differentiate between cognitive dimensions (e.g., financial knowledge, financial understanding, financial comprehension) and non-cognitive dimensions (e.g., financial attitudes, financial risk taking, financial confidence). That cognitive and non-cognitive distinction was also consistent with our description of financial competence as a multidimensional construct and our theoretical framework model (Chap. 4).

The selection of the 31 studies to include in the table came from a review of existing instruments in published research studies as found in relevant scientific databases (e.g., Google Scholar, Web of Science), literature reviews (e.g., Lusardi & Mitchell, 2014) and meta-analyses (e.g., Kaiser & Menkhoff, 2017). Due to the large body of research, it was not possible to include a fully comprehensive review of all existing instruments. Therefore, we tried to find illustrative examples for the operationalisation of each construct of financial competence and its various subparts. We tried to include at least one study for each construct in order to give an example of how to assess the construct with a respective instrument. Each study included in the table was then analysed to answer the *what*, *how*, and *who* questions that structure this chapter. Answers to the *what* question focused on (1) how the respective construct was named and (2) whether a definition of the construct was provided. Additional information was sought to determine (3) whether the financial constructs studied were perceived as cognitive, non-cognitive or mixed. Furthermore, (4) the study's content was investigated. Answers to the *how* question are based on study details about the (5) assessment format, (6) sample size and (7) number of items. Also included is information on (8) unique measurement features and psychometric properties along with (9) information about the respective construct's interrelations to other variables, e.g., sociodemographic criteria. Answers to the *who* question focused on (10) the main target group for the administered instrument. All results from the summaries and data reported in the table's columns should be self-explanatory. Further information can be obtained from an actual copy of the study.

Several general characteristics of the studies reported in the table should be noted. First, the results show that financial knowledge and its measurement are often a common denominator for conducting studies related to financial competence. This finding is in line with the findings in Chap. 2 in this SpringerBrief and it is also consistent with the general conception that financial knowledge is the basis for financial competence, in the sense that individuals cannot show competent financial behaviour without some meaningful level of financial knowledge or understanding. The only substantive difference across studies is how this assessment of financial knowledge is framed (as specific financial knowledge, as general financial understanding, or as a universal financial skill).

Second, whether clear definitions of the main financial construct are supplied varies by study. Some studies provide a clear definition of the financial construct to be measured in general (e.g., Aprea & Wuttke, 2016; Stolper & Walter, 2017), whereas others do not. Some studies do not provide a definition for a financial construct related to a financial competence construct but do define a related latent variable (e.g., attitude towards money, Tang, 1992, 1995; risk attitude, Weber et al., 2002). Due to this inconsistency, it is often difficult to determine whether the studies offer a clear conception of the assessed construct, and whether it is cognitive, non-cognitive or mixed. Furthermore, some of the definitions are broad and cover more than one content area or topic (e.g., Heo et al., 2020; Archuleta et al., 2013 on financial stress).

5.6 Limitations and Conclusion

The focus of this review was primarily on personal finance, thereby excluding broader economic behaviours that could provide additional insights into financial literacy and competence. Furthermore, alternative assessment methods such as serious games or behavioural economic experiments, which could offer innovative perspectives on financial behaviours, remain underrepresented in this review. Finally, the approach used in selecting financial constructs for investigation may limit the scope of the research and overlook emergent constructs that could be highly relevant.

Although measurement in personal finance is an expanding field of study, it faces significant challenges in terms of integration and standardization across various financial constructs and demographics. The development of a comprehensive framework for assessing financial competence as suggested throughout the AFin project (Chap. 1) could address these challenges by providing clearer guidelines and a unified structure for future instruments and practical applications.

The analysis of measurement instruments in personal finance as discussed in this chapter highlights the ongoing complexity and diversity of approaches in personal finance. Despite extensive research and the development of numerous tests and other instruments, a holistic measure that encapsulates the multi-dimensionality of financial competence, and its related subparts, has yet to be created. Of course, it may not measure in a single instrument such a broad construct as financial competence with its interrelated cognitive and non-cognitive influences. Instead, researchers predominantly rely on specific instruments to measure other financial constructs that are related to and part of financial competence. Although this more restrictive approach to instruments and measurement does provide valuable research insights, it does not provide a comprehensive understanding of financial competence.

The field of personal finance and its related financial constructs is vast. Extensive research conducted over the years has produced numerous definitions and operationalisations of financial constructs, making it challenging to compare and generalise results across similar, and yet unique studies. Additionally, the diversity of target groups, that includes adults and youth further segmented by sociodemographic factors such as age, income, and gender, adds another layer of complexity. This segmentation also makes it hard to draw broad conclusions from the data, as variations in financial competence are influenced by these demographic distinctions.

Going forward, the definition of a financial construct plays a crucial role in the advancement of research. It is relatively easy to define a financial construct in narrow and limited terms and develop measures of it. It is significantly more challenging to define a more comprehensive financial construct such as financial competence and operationalise with a measurement instrument. If that assessment work can be done so that it produces a reliable and valid instrument, or even several instruments, it can provide a more integrated and wholistic understanding of the relationship between financial competency and financial behaviours. This work can offer a pathway toward more cohesive and comprehensive assessments in the field.

It can also be seen that the focus of the measurement instruments is on measuring the respective level of competence and its sub-constructs. This makes sense, of course, as this is also a decisive criterion from a diagnostic point of view. From a learning psychology perspective, however, diagnostic information about the solution process would be highly relevant, as this would provide an insight into which process steps the test subjects are unable to perform or only perform incorrectly. This also becomes clear in our competency model in Chap. 4. However, this process component is largely ignored in the existing instruments. Instead, the instruments are outcome-orientated rather than process-orientated, which highlights the need for new instruments that allow conclusions to be drawn about the steps involved in the solution process.

Appendix

Table A3 Summary of studies featuring measurement instruments for the assessment of constructs related to financial competence

Author/s (Year)	Name of the construct	Definition of the construct	Cognitive, non-cognitive, or mixed	Target group	Sample size of study	Contents assessed	Item format	Number of items	Measurements features/ psychometric properties/ dimensionality (if applicable)	Additional constructs assessed in the study/relationship to other variables	Comments
relation to the 3-question-structure of the article	what	what	what	who	who/how	what	how	how	how	how	
(mostly) cognitive dispositions of personal finance											
Chen and Volpe (1998)	personal financial literacy / knowledge	no explicit definition is given; according to the authors, personal finance consists of financial literacy on general (finance) knowledge, savings and borrowing, insurance, and investment (p. 109)	not specified	college students; age 18 to 40+	N = 924	general knowledge, savings and borrowing, insurance, investment,	single choice, ranking	52 items: 9 for general personal finance knowledge; 9 for savings and borrowings; 6 for insurance; 12 for investments; 8 for personal finance opinions, decisions and education; 8 for sociodemographic variables	C-Alpha: 0.85	Education (academic disciplines, class rank); Demographic characteristics (gender, race, nationality); Experience (years of work experience, years of age); Income	The survey is used in a pilot study to refine the instrument.
Knoll and Houts (2012)	knowledge ("Financial Knowledge Scale")	no explicit definition of financial knowledge is given; the authors distinguish between knowledge and skills and behaviors but do not provide an explanation of what they consider the differences (p. 385)	not specified	not specified	N = 6001 data was taken from several large-scale US surveys (ALP, HRS, NS-NFCS) including multiple overlapping item-sets;	interest, inflation, time value of money, investing, diversification of risk, housing, debt management, retirement savings, life insurance, annuities	multiple choice, true/false-questions	20 questions for final test instrument	each item set was checked for dimensionality prior to IRT analyses (p. 396) instrument was IRT-scaled with a 2PL model marginal reliability (TIF): 0.85	gender, age, income, self-reported financial knowledge, math ability, economics, behavioral variables (save enough to cover 3 months of expenses, consultation of financial planners, having savings account)	

	financial literacy / knowledge and understanding								
Lusardi and Mitchell (2009)	financial literacy / knowledge and understanding	The researchers define *financial literacy* as the knowledge and understanding of basic financial concepts and principles, such as compound interest, inflation, risk diversification, and the functioning of financial markets. It also includes more advanced financial knowledge, such as the difference between stocks and bonds, asset pricing, and the relationship between bond prices and interest rates. (p. 7 – p. 9)	not explicitly specified, but discussed for the measures (p. 17, footnote 16)	adults, (age 18+)	N = 989	Basic FL questions: 1) Numeracy 2) Compound Interest 3) Inflation 4) Time Value of money 5) Inflation / Money illusion Sophisticated FL questions: 1) Stock Market Functioning 2) Knowledge of Mutual Funds 3) Interest rate/Bond Prices Link 4) Safer: Company Stock or Mutual Fund 5) Riskier: Stocks or Bonds 6) Long Period Returns 7) Highest Fluctuation/ Volatility 8) Risk Diversification	single choice, (Note: variations of the content items were introduced by randomly reversing the question word order for some items (p. 9) self-assessment of peoples' understanding of economics (1 item, 7-point rating scale)	5 items ("basic") 8 items ("sophisticated") 1 item self-assessment of understanding of economics	capacity to handle basic financial literacy concepts and advanced financial knowledge; factor loadings range from 0.167 to 0.442 (basic questions) and from 0.099 to 0.325 (sophisticated questions)	socioeconomic variables (age, sex, marital status, race/ ethnicity, income) self-assessment of peoples' understanding of economics retirement readiness, economics lessons in school or at work; education level;	Data from the American Life Panel (ALP) is used.
Lusardi and Mitchell (2011)	financial literacy / knowledge and understanding	no explicit definition is provided; the researchers see the construct of *financial literacy* as the understanding of three economic concepts: interest compounding, inflation, and risk diversification. They measured financial literacy by designing questions that evaluated individuals' ability to carry out elementary calculations related to these concepts. (p. 499)	not specified	Age 50 + they were thoroughly tested in other data sets using respondents from different age groups and time periods.	age 50+ -> N = 1200 + other age groups -> not in the text	"The Big Three": (1) Understanding of interest compounding (2) Understanding of inflation (3) Understanding of risk diversification	single choice (Note: question wording was randomly inverted to evaluate measurement errors such as guessing. p. 501)	3 items	"Across the board, these variables do a good job of characterizing peoples' levels of financial knowledge; moreover, they strongly correlate with financial behaviors"	gender, age, education, demographics, socioeconomic variables;	The questions were used in many different panels, e.g., US Health and Retirement study (HRS) 2004, National Longitudinal Survey of Youth (NLSY), 2007–2008, ALP 2008, Financial Capability Study (FINRA) 2010. The questions were included in many different household surveys around the world allowing for comparison between countries (c.f., Stolper & Walter, 2017)

(continued)

Table A3 (continued)

Author/s (Year)	Name of the construct	Definition of the construct	Cognitive, non-cognitive, or mixed	Target group	Sample size of study	Contents assessed	Item format	Number of items	Measurements features/ psychometric properties/ dimensionality (if applicable)	Additional constructs assessed in the study/relationship to other variables	Comments
Mandell (2008)	financial literacy / knowledge, behavior	no explicit definition is provided; However, the author mentions that *financial literacy* is measured by the JumpStart survey, which is described as a measure of problem-solving ability rather than possession of a body of time-limited financial facts. The researchers also mention that financial literacy includes *skills* such as knowing how to approach a problem and how to research it, which are important for making personal financial decisions (p. 29).	not specified	American high school seniors + American college students	For the 2008 survey: N = 5150 high school seniors; N = 1030 college students	High School instrument: four key areas and their major sub-categories 1) income 2) money management 3) saving and interest 4) spending and credit College Instrument 1) income 2) money management 3) saving and interest 4) spending and credit + behavioral questions (e.g., credit card use, incurrence of debt, checking account balance, incidence of insufficient funds, tax preparation)	multiple choice; "Wherever possible, questions were put into age- and life cycle-appropriate "case-studies" to make them relevant to the students" (p. 10)	High school: 49 questions with the first 31 on financial literacy College: 56 questions with the first 31 on financial literacy + additional behavioral questions	/	Background (Parents' income; highest level of parents' education; sex/ gender; race; region; age); Aspirations (educational plans; occupation; expected fulltime income; college entrance score); Money management education (classes, semester); Money management experience (credit card use, atm use, auto use, bank account, ….); Financial Behavior (debt, cc use, no. of cc, payment behavior, etc.)	Instrument got used for the various surveys of the JumpStart Coalition; the questionnaires used are displayed in the appendices of the 2008 publication;

OECD (2013, 2014) Financial Literacy module for the Programme of International Student Assessment (PISA)	financial literacy; knowledge and understanding; skills; processes; contexts; motivation and confidence; problem-solving;	"Financial literacy is knowledge and understanding of financial concepts and risks, and the skills, motivation and confidence to apply such knowledge and understanding in order to make effective decisions across a range of financial contexts, to improve the financial well-being of individuals and society, and to enable participation in economic life." (p. 144)	Mixed	students, (age 15)	in 2012: 18 participating countries and economies (13 OECD, 5 partner);	Content 1) Money and Transactions 2) Planning and Managing finances 3) Risk and Reward 4) Financial Landscape Processes 1) Identify financial information 2) Analyze information in a financial context 3) Evaluate financial issues 4) Apply financial knowledge and understanding Contexts 1) Education and Work 2) Home and family 3) Individual 4) Societal Non-cognitive factors 1) access to information and education 2) access to money and financial products 3) attitudes towards and confidence about financial matters 4) spending and saving behavior	Paper-and-pencil tests (In a range of countries, an additional computer-based assessment) constructed-response (short answer) items; selected-response (multiple-choice) items; circling the answer ticking a box True/false-items calculations	40 items +5 questions on financial education practices (school questionnaire);	One-parameter item response model; (partial credit model was used in the case of items with more than two categories)	numeracy skills, reading and vocabulary, learning strategies, interest in and enjoyment of mathematics, instrumental motivation, self-efficacy, self-concept, mathematics anxiety, family background, career expectations, parental involvement in school, discussion of school related matters at home, computer availability and use, language background, migration background, learning time, extracurricular activities, educational aspirations, student motivation, attitudes towards learning	good basis for international comparison (Germany did not take part yet); The Financial Literacy module of the PISA assessment was first implemented in 2012 and then repeated in 2015, 2018, and 2022.

(continued)

Table A3 (continued)

Author/s (Year)	Name of the construct	Definition of the construct	Cognitive, non-cognitive, or mixed	Target group	Sample size of study	Contents assessed	Item format	Number of items	Measurements features/ psychometric properties/ dimensionality (if applicable)	Additional constructs assessed in the study/relationship to other variables	Comments
Stolper and Walter (2017) (Comprehensive overview, strong focus on "Big Three")	financial literacy; financial advice; financial behavior;	The researchers define *financial literacy* as "the ability to use knowledge and skills to manage one's financial resources effectively for lifetime financial security." Additionally, the researchers mention that financial literacy includes knowledge and understanding of financial concepts and risks, as well as the skills, motivation, and confidence to apply that knowledge in order to make effective financial decisions (p. 588)	not specified	/	N = 3565 (Panel on Household finances)	The "Big three": 1) individuals' numeracy and their ability to do simple calculations 2) inflation and money illusion 3) if familiar with the concept of risk diversification	2 x 5 possible responses 1 x 4 possible responses single choice	3 Items	Across the board, these variables do a good job of characterizing peoples' levels of financial knowledge; moreover, they strongly correlate with financial behaviors (Lusardi & Mitchell, 2011).	lower FL in transition and lower-income economies. Inconclusive evidence on the effect of financial advisory. professional status, income, wealth levels and the impact of financial socialization (family background, educational attainment of parents, and the educational attainment of neighbors)	Overview on FL studies using the "big three" and household surveys (pp. 591–594); Overview on household surveys asking about FL (pp. 603–606); Overview on studies investigating the link between FL and financial advice;
Walstad and Rebeck (2016a, 2016b, 2016c, 2017, 2018)	personal finance; financial literacy/knowledge; "Basic Finance Test" (BFT); "Test of Financial Knowledge" (TFK); "Test of Financial Literacy" (TFL);	no explicit definition is provided;	cognitive (knowledge, comprehension, application)	high school students (TFL); upper middle to lower high school students (TFK); upper elementary to lower middle school students (BFT)	BFT: N = 294 TFK: N = 181 TFL: N = 1218	1) Earning Income; 2) Buying Goods and Services; 3) Saving; 4) Using Credit; 5) Financial Investing; 6) Protecting and Insuring;	single choice (4 possible responses, 1 correct);	BFT: 35 items; TFK: 40 items; TFL: 45 items;	BFT: C-Alpha = 0.90 TFK: C-Alpha = 0.83 TFL: C-Alpha = 0.87 TFL-G: 3-dimensional structure everyday money management – insurance – banking) with good fit (Förster et al. 2018; Kraitzek et al. 2022); all test were scaled with a 4PL-IRT model;	instruction in personal finance; gender; grade level; race/ethnicity; verbal ability;	Tests are based on the National Standards for Financial Literacy (CEE, 2013); German versions: TFL-G by Förster et al. (2017); TFK-G by Kraitzek and Förster (2024)

Aprea and Wutke (2016); Wutke and Aprea (2018)	financial literacy; competence, knowledge and skills, motivation and interest, values, perceived importance of money and financial concerns; awareness of necessity to care for financial decisions; confidence to cope with financial demands; delay of gratification;	The authors defined the construct of *financial literacy* "as the potential that enables a person to effectively plan, execute, and control financial decisions. This potential is based on individual dispositions, including knowledge and skills, motivations and interests, attitudes, and values, and is contingent on situational characteristics." (Aprea & Wutke, 2016: p. 402; Wutke & Aprea, 2018: p. 274)	Mixed: cognitive (knowledge, skills, and abilities); non-cognitive (emotional, motivational, and volitional aspects, social values and norms)	2016: students (eighth & nineth grade, lower to middle secondary schools), age 14 to 17; 2018: students (higher secondary education; university; vocational schools) age 16 to 25; young adults in the process of starting their (professional) life and becoming responsible for their financial affairs;	2016: N = 198 (pilot study); 2018: N = 206	1) Evaluation of own income (four situations, four items each) 2) Planning expanses in agreement with own needs and possibilities (three situations, 2x4 and 1x6 items) 3) Drawing up a budget (four situations, four items each)	Situational Judgment Task (SJT); item generation and scaling based on standard procedures for the development of SJTs (Muck, 2013) (pp. 281–282); 2016: dichotomous items (1 = correct, 0 = wrong); Likert scale (1–4);	2016: 23 items (financial SJT): 10 multiple-choice 10 short-answer items 3 arithmetic; 4 self-report items (motivational and attitudinal aspects) 2018: 11 situations, 46 items;	2016: item difficulty between 0.30 and 0.80; item discrimination coefficients range from –0.08 to 0.53; 2018: factor analysis (3 factors): 1) Control of own financial situation, C-Alpha = 0.75; 2) Budgeting, C-Alpha = 0.57; 3) Sensitive handling of money, C-Alpha = 0.69;	age, gender, migration background, school affiliation; personal financial context; major socialization agents (parents, peers, school);

attitude towards money

Barry (2014)	attitude towards money;	"Attitude towards money is a mental and neutral state of readiness that arises and is structured by experience and learning processes and has a controlling and/or dynamic influence on an individual's reaction to certain stimuli. Three main classes of reactions are distinguished: cognitive, affective and behavioral." (p. 79–80; Translated by the authors)	non-cognitive	university students and students in vocational training; age 18 to 25;	N = 272	1) Reputation/Power 2) Financial planning 3) Quality through money 4) Significance of money 5) Avarice/Greed	Likert scales (1–7)	28 items: 8 items for reputation/power 7 items for financial planning 5 items for quality through money 4 items for significance of money 4 items for avarice / greed	Factor 1 C-Alpha = 0.85 Factor 2 C-Alpha = 0.88 Factor 3 C-Alpha = 0.77 Factor 4 C-Alpha = 0.79 Factor 5 C-Alpha = 0.70	attended courses in economics or finance; self-reported financial knowledge; numeracy; self-report on personal financial experience, saving and payment; demographics; monthly living expenses; self-reported German language proficiencies; (p. 151–152)	Questionnaire is based on the work of Yamauchi and Templer (1982), Furnham (1984) and Tang (1992)

(continued)

Table A3 (continued)

Author/s (Year)	Name of the construct	Definition of the construct	Cognitive, non-cognitive, or mixed	Target group	Sample size of study	Contents assessed	Item format	Number of items	Measurements features/ psychometric properties/ dimensionality (if applicable)	Additional constructs assessed in the study/relationship to other variables	Comments
Bocchialini et al. (2022); in combination with Bocchialini and Ronchini (2019)	attitude towards finance; **Note:** authors differentiate between *"attitude towards finance"* and *"financial attitude"*. According to them, the former explicitly considers a mutual relationship between emotions and beliefs.	The researchers defined the construct *"attitude towards finance"* as the combination of one's beliefs, feelings, and self-perception with finance, which determine the predisposition to respond favorably or unfavorably to a particular financial stimulus. The construct is characterized by three interlinked subcomponents: view of finance, emotional disposition towards finance, and perceived competence in finance. Each subcomponent can be characterized as positive, negative, or neutral, and the overall attitude profile of an individual depends on the combination of these subcomponents. (p. 15 – 17)	mixed: cognitive (beliefs); non-cognitive (feelings, self-perception and predisposition to respond)	university students (Economics); age 19 to 30+;	N = 466; convenience sample;	attitude towards finance measured via questionnaire developed by Bocchialini and Ronchini (2019): 1) View of finance; 2) Emotional disposition toward finance; 3) Perceived competence in finance; for the 2022 study, the questions were refined to suit the sample and the financial setting: 1) finance is a difficult and math-heavy subject 2) Use of financial education is useful in their daily professional lives 3) Gender of finance 4) financial skills are fixed or malleable 5) emotion when dealing with finance related issues 6) self-confidence in financial context Basis financial knowledge (Lusardi & Mitchell, 2011); Advanced financial knowledge (van Rooij et al. 2012);	Likert scales (1–5) (Bocchialini & Ronchini, 2019); refined for 2022-study: Likert scales (1–4);	30 items (Bocchialini & Ronchini, 2019): 11 for "View of finance" 7 for "Emot. disposition toward finance" 12 for "Perceived competence in finance"; 51 items (Bocchialini et al., 2022, p. 19): 30 items for "View" 9 items for "Emotion" 12 items for "Competence" 6 financial knowledge items: 3 basic 3 advanced;	/	gender; age; nationality (Italian vs. foreign); area/region of origin; level of university education; financial education attended; type of high school diploma; grades; cohabitation;	A significant positive correlation is found between financial knowledge and attitude toward finance. The direction of causality is found to be from attitude toward finance to financial knowledge, and this finding suggests that attitude toward finance can play an important role in financial education.

		"*Financial attitude*" refers to the combination of beliefs, feelings, and self-perception related to finance that determine an individual's predisposition to respond favorably or unfavorably to financial stimuli. It includes the cognitive and affective components of attitude towards finance. On the other hand, "*attitude towards finance*" is a broader construct that encompasses the view of finance, emotional disposition towards finance, and perceived competence in finance. It specifically focuses on an individual's beliefs, emotions, and self-efficacy related to finance. (p. 14)						
Grohs-Müller and Greimel-Fuhrmann (2018)	money attitudes;	no explicit definition is provided; The authors asses *money attitudes* as a two-component construct consisting of cognitive and non-cognitive elements (p. 44)	not explicitly specified (potentially mixed)	students of lower secondary education (eighth grade)	N = 1343	1) Happiness and power 2) Financial planning 3) Quality through money 4) Money-related fear and anxiety	Likert scales (1–5)	18 items: 5 items for happiness and power 5 items for financial planning 4 items for quality through money 4 items for money-related fear and anxiety	Factor analysis Factor 1 C-Alpha = 0.79 Factor 2 C-Alpha = 0.75 Factor 3 C-Alpha = 0.81 Factor 4 C-Alpha = 0.67	gender; school type; federal state (Austria); migration background; financial socialization (family, peers, school, advertising); parental financial education; interest; reasons for consumption;	Questionnaire is based on the work of Barry (2014), but was adapted for Austrian youth

(continued)

Table A3 (continued)

Author/s (Year)	Name of the construct	Definition of the construct	Cognitive, non-cognitive, or mixed	Target group	Sample size of study	Contents assessed	Item format	Number of items	Measurements features/ psychometric properties/ dimensionality (if applicable)	Additional constructs assessed in the study/relationship to other variables	Comments
Tang (1992)	attitude towards money; "Money Ethic Scale" (MES)	The researchers defined the construct as the *individual's perception and evaluation of money*, including their positive or negative attitudes towards money, their beliefs about the meaning and purpose of money, and their behaviors and values related to money. This construct was measured using the *Money Ethic Scale (MES)*, which consists of six factors: positive attitudes, negative attitudes, achievement, power, management of money, and self-esteem. These factors capture different aspects of individuals' attitudes towards money. (p. 197)	not specified in this publication; in Tang (1995, p. 810), the various components of the MES are described as "affective" (Good/Evil), "cognitive" (Achievement, Respect, Freedom/Power), and "behavioral" (Budget) => mixed	people of various professions (university students, personnel managers attending professional compensation seminars, workers of local schools, banks, churches, and other establishments); only subjects with full time work experience were included;	N = 249	1) Good (positive attitudes towards money) 2) Evil (negative attitudes towards money) 3) Achievement 4) Respect/Self-esteem 5) Budget 6) Freedom/Power	Likert scales (1–7)	30 items: 9 items for "Good" 6 items for "Evil" 4 items for "Achievement" 4 items for "Respect" 3 items for "Budget" 4 items for "Freedom/Power"	Factor analysis Factor 1 C-Alpha = 0.81 Factor 2 C-Alpha = 0.69 Factor 3 C-Alpha = 0.70 Factor 4 C-Alpha = 0.68 Factor 5 C-Alpha = 0.72 Factor 6 C-Alpha = 0.71 items with a factor loading of 0.40 or greater were selected for the final scale;	demographics (age, sex, income) personality; work-related variables (e.g.; job satisfaction)	Scale touches an ethical aspect of money

Tang (1995)	attitude towards money; "Money Ethic Scale" (MES) – Short scale	The researchers defined the construct as *people's general and positive attitudes toward money*. They developed a 12-item *Money Ethic Scale (MES)* to measure these attitudes. The scale includes factors such as Success (a cognitive component), Budget (a behavioral component), and Evil (an affective component). The researchers also found that positive attitudes toward money and negative attitudes toward money are not related to the same dimension or factor. (p. 809 – 810; p. 815)	see: Tang (1992)	employees of various professions (students, personnel managers, engineers, teachers, workers from banks, churches, university professors, police officers, fire fighters, factory workers) full time, part time and unemployed;	N = 740	1) Success 2) Budget 3) Evil	Likert scales (1–7)	30 items (long scale, see: Tang (1992); the two items with the highest item-total correlation were selected for the short scale 12 items (short scale): 8 items for "Success", 2 items for "Budget", 2 items for "Evil"	Factor analysis 1) Success C-Alpha = 0.76 2) Budget C-Alpha = 0.833) Evil C-Alpha = 0.66 Overall (12-item scale) C-Alpha = 0.70	demographics (sex, age, income, educational level, job tenure); work-related variables (self-esteem, need for achievement); personality variables (internal-external locus of control, Type A behavior pattern, study of values); job satisfaction	
Saving behavior											
Mahdzan and Tabiani (2013)	individual saving; risk-taking behavior; saving regularity; financial literacy/ knowledge;	*Individual saving* refers to the act of setting aside money for future use or emergencies. *Risk-taking behavior* refers to individuals' willingness to take financial risks, which can influence their financial decision-making and saving behavior. (p.43 – 45; p.52)	not specified	Malaysian adults (students, employees, retirees, undergraduate students, housewives, unemployed people);	N = 192; convenience sample;	1) individual saving; 2) risk-taking behavior; 3) saving regularity; FL assessment by using Lusardi (2008) 3 questions: basic FL 9 questions: advanced FL	individual saving: binary (0 = no saving; 1 = positive saving); risk-taking behavior: Likert scale (1–4); saving regularity: Likert scale (1–5);	3 items 1 item for individual saving; 1 item for risk-taking; 1 item of saving regularity;	/	gender; age; marital status; income level; education level; number of children; working experience;	exploratory study;

(continued)

Table A3 (continued)

Author/s (Year)	Name of the construct	Definition of the construct	Cognitive, non-cognitive, or mixed	Target group	Sample size of study	Contents assessed	Item format	Number of items	Measurements features/ psychometric properties/ dimensionality (if applicable)	Additional constructs assessed in the study/relationship to other variables	Comments
Risk attitude / risk tolerance											
Andersen et al. (2008)	risk aversion; risk and time preferences;	The researchers define *risk aversion* as the degree to which individuals are willing to take on risk in exchange for potential rewards. They define *eliciting risk and time preference* as the process of gathering information about individuals' attitudes towards risk and their preferences for receiving rewards at different points in time. (p. 583 – 584)	not explicitly specified (potentially mixed); The authors discuss the meaning of "cognitive burden" for decision-making considering risk and also make "short term temptations" a subject of debate (the latter might be interpreted as an indicator for non-cognitive components in behavioral finance)	representative sample of Danish population between 19 and 75 years of age	N = 253	measuring risk preference by using a multiple price list (MPL); measuring time preferences using a payoff table to assess the individual discount rate	experiment using MPL and payoff tables;	4 risk aversion tasks; 6 discount rate tasks; series of 10 binary choices per task;	/	Binary indicators for gender, age (less than 30; 40 to 50; over 50), living situation, children, home ownership, retirement, student, post-secondary education, higher education, an income level (below 300.000 DKK; 500.000 DKK and more) were included in the estimation (p. 604); + no. of people living in the household;	Experimental design to assess risk and time preference. Procedure and data described in detail in Harrison et al. (2005) Microeconomic paper Was used by Mudzingiri et al. (2018)

| Weber et al. (2002) | risk attitude; risk perception; risk behavior; | The researchers defined the construct of *risk attitude* as the positive or negative weight assigned to the perceived riskiness of an option when determining its overall desirability. Risk attitude refers to an individual's preference for risky options or behaviors based on their evaluation and integration of the risks and returns associated with those options. (p. 264–265) | not explicitly specified (potentially mixed); However, the authors discuss that the interplay of cognitive and affective processes might play a role in risk-taking (p. 283) | undergraduate students at The Ohio State University | Study 1 (Scale development): N = 539 Study 2 (Test-Retest reliability, validity): N = 121 Study 3 (Refinement): N = 343 | 1) Financial investment 2) Financial gambling 3) Health/safety 4) Recreational 5) Ethical 6) Social | Likert scale (1–5) | 40 items (final scale) | Behavior: 6-factor model accounts for 50.3% of the variance; Perception: 6-factor model accounts for 47% of the variance C-Alpha *behavior*: 1) 0.84 2) 0.89 3) 0.77 4) 0.83 5) 0.78 6) 0.70 C-Alpha *perception*: 1) 0.67 2) 0.87 3) 0.76 4) 0.80 5) 0.81 6) 0.70 | demographic variables, personality variables (sensation seeking, tolerance for ambiguity, gender), situational factors (content domain of the decision, outcome framing, aspiration levels), and subjective norms about appropriate levels of risk taking. Various other scales were used to establish convergent and discriminant validity of the newly developed Risk-Behavior-Scale | only parts of the scale are about a financial context => Complete scale is displayed in Appendix C of the paper |

(continued)

Table A3 (continued)

Author/s (Year)	Name of the construct	Definition of the construct	Cognitive, non-cognitive, or mixed	Target group	Sample size of study	Contents assessed	Item format	Number of items	Measurements features/ psychometric properties/ dimensionality (if applicable)	Additional constructs assessed in the study/relationship to other variables	Comments
Interest in financial topics											
Hermansson and Jonsson (2021)	financial interest; risk tolerance; financial literacy;	The researchers use the term *financial interest* to describe a motivational state where the individual is interested in economic issues and financial markets. (p. 2) They differentiate between *situational interest* and *individual interest* and relate financial interest in their study to being situational. *Financial-risk tolerance* is defined as the maximum amount of variability in return that someone is willing to accept when making a financial decision (p. 1). *Financial literacy* is defined in this study as knowledge of financial concepts, i.e., inflation and risk diversification (p. 3).	non-cognitive	Swedish bank customers, age 18+	N = 12,156	financial interest: 1) I am interested in economic matters and financial markets. 2) I follow the media about developments on the financial markets. 3) I follow the media about the developments of new saving products. risk tolerance: subjective measure: 1) I can accept losing part of my savings if the chance of getting a good return is great. 2) I think one has to take risks to gain something. 3) I would like to increase risk because the return is too low. objective measure: the ratio of investments in stock (equity) to total financial wealth	financial interest & risk tolerance: Likert scales (1–7); financial literacy: multiple-choice;	financial interest: 3 items risk tolerance: 3 items financial literacy: 6 items	composite reliabilities: financial interest = 1.00 risk tolerance = 0.99 factor analysis for financial interest scale: factor loadings between 0.76 and 0.93;	age, gender, geographical location, income, financial assets, loan and mortgages, marital and family status, education, employment, housing status, wealth;	"Findings contribute to the literature on risk tolerance, specifically pointing to the relevance of the non-cognitive trait, interest, to individuals risk tolerance". the financial literacy questions by Anderson et al. and Lusardi have been adapted to a Swedish context; the authors used a subjective and an objective measurement of risk tolerance;

Time preferences (= construct includes a time component)

Hastings and Mitchell (2020)	impatience; financial literacy; risk preferences;	no explicit definitions provided; However, the paper mentions that *financial literacy* is measured as the ability to understand basic concepts like inflation, compounding, and investment returns (p. 16). Further, *financial literacy* is perceived as an individual's knowledge and capability of performing calculations needed to make wise financial decisions (p. 3) *Impatience* is measured using a game designed to elicit preferences for current gratification versus future gain and the ability to follow through with it. (p. 16). In this study, impatient people are seen as those who overweight current consumption versus the future (p. 4).	not specified	Chilean adults	N = 8850 game participants; data was taken from a representative bi-annual microeconomic panel study in Chile (EPS);	impatience (1 experiment); financial literacy and risk preference (6 questions): 1) Chance of Disease 2) Lottery Division 3) Numeracy in Investment Context 4) Compound Interest 5) Inflation 6) Risk Diversification	experiment to assess *impatience*: random participants were given a choice to receive a gift card in return for filling out a short questionnaire. The value of the gift card depended on the time span the questionnaire was sent back to the interviewer: 1) Now = 5000 pesos 2) Later = 6000 to 8000 pesos in weekly 500-peso increments (by up to four weeks later); financial literacy and risk preferences: True/false, open answer, single choice;	1 experiment ("game"); 6 items;	/	age; gender; education; wage; employment status; marital status; saving;	the experiment allowed the authors to identify three types of respondents: 1) the *impatient* who took the gift card with the lower value right away; 2) the *efficacious deferrers* who chose the higher value and returned the questionnaire later; 3) the *inefficacious deferrers* who opted for the higher value but failed to send in the questionnaires to activate the gift card in time (p. 4, p. 7)

(continued)

Table A3 (continued)

Author/s (Year)	Name of the construct	Definition of the construct	Cognitive, non-cognitive, or mixed	Target group	Sample size of study	Contents assessed	Item format	Number of items	Measurements features/ psychometric properties/ dimensionality (if applicable)	Additional constructs assessed in the study/relationship to other variables	Comments
Ray and Najman (1986)	deferment of gratification;	no explicit definition provided	not specified	people in the Australian city of Brisbane ("random doorstep sampling")	N = 209	1) Are you good at saving your money rather than spending it straight away? 2) Do you enjoy a thing all the more because you have had to wait for it and plan for it? 3) Did you tend to save your pocket-money as a child? 4) When you are in a supermarket do you tend to buy a lot of things you hadn't planned to buy? 5) Are you constantly "broke"? 6) Do you agree with the philosophy: "Eat, drink and be merry, for tomorrow we may be all dead."? 7) Would you describe yourself as often being too impulsive for your own good? 8) Do you fairly often find that it is worthwhile to wait and think things over before deciding? 9) Do you like to spend your money as soon as you get it? 10) Is it hard for you to keep from blowing your top when someone gets you very angry? 11) Can you tolerate being kept waiting for things fairly easily most of the time? 12) Are you good at planning things way in advance?	yes or no questions; "Pro-deferment" items (No. 1, 2, 3, 8, 11, 12) were scored 3 = yes, 1 = no. The remainder were scored in reverse.	12 items	C-Alpha = 0.72	/	used by Wutke and Aprea (2018) and Siegfried and Wutke (2021); only partly related to financial incidents;

Financial confidence

Morris et al. (2022)	Financial confidence; Financial behavior; Financial knowledge	*Financial confidence* is the self-assurance required to make sound financial decisions (Palameta et al., 2016). It is further described as an individual's belief in their ability to effectively manage day-to-day financial matters and their overall ability to manage their finances. *Financial behavior* refers to the actions and decisions individuals make regarding their personal finances. It includes behaviors such as saving, investing, budgeting, and managing debt. The study aims to understand the factors that influence financial behavior among university students. *Financial knowledge* refers to an individual's understanding of financial concepts and principles. (p. 3 – 5)	not specified (probably mixed)	Canadian university students	N = 1221	financial confidence (Robb & Woodyard, 2011, modified): 1) "I am good at dealing with day-to-day financial matters such as checking accounts, credit and debit cards, and tracking expenses." 2) "I am pretty good at math." 3) "I regularly keep up with economic and financial news." 4) "On a scale, how would you assess your overall financial knowledge?"	Likert scale (1–5)	financial confidence: 4 items financial behavior: 6 items + financial knowledge: 25 items	financial confidence: C-Alpha = 0.747; financial behavior: C-Alpha = 0.793;	gender, age, ethnicity, educational background;	financial confidence questions taken from Robb and Woodyard (2011); financial behavior items adapted from Fernandes et al. (2014); financial knowledge items inspired by various programmes and authors (e.g., Jump$tart; Lusardi & Mitchell; Mandell; Allgood & Walstad);

(continued)

Table A3 (continued)

Author/s (Year)	Name of the construct	Definition of the construct	Cognitive, non-cognitive, or mixed	Target group	Sample size of study	Contents assessed	Item format	Number of items	Measurements features/ psychometric properties/ dimensionality (if applicable)	Additional constructs assessed in the study/relationship to other variables	Comments
Motivation (to deal with financial issues)											
Mandell and Schmid-Klein (2007)	motivation; financial literacy;	The study does not provide a specific definition of the construct "motivation." However, it mentions that motivation is a key driver of individual behavior and refers to theories such as expectancy theory and goal setting theory to explain the motivational influences underlying human behavior. The study also does not provide a specific definition of the construct "financial literacy." However, it mentions that *financial literacy* refers to the knowledge and understanding of financial concepts and skills necessary to make informed financial decisions. It also mentions that financial literacy scores were measured using a financial literacy quiz and were related to financial behavior and practices. (p.106)	not specified	random sample of public high school seniors The samples have been drawn from a list provided by the U.S. Department of Education that includes all public schools in the U.S. Geographic representation is insured through stratification by state.	/	FL assessment by using the Jumpstart Instrument (Mandell, 2008) To measure the impact of motivation questions from the JumpStart questionnaire that are associated with motivation are included in the regression model. Three questions to measure motivation to be financial literate.	three variables: 1) financial difficulties no plan/ credit 2) Not so bad to not pay bills 3) Live well on social security	/	controls for socioeconomic, demographic and aspirational characteristics	c.f. JumpStart	"[…] motivational variables significantly increased our ability to explain differences in financial literacy."

Financial self-efficacy

Lown (2011)	financial self-efficacy "Financial Self-Efficacy Scale" (FSES)	The author defined the construct as "*financial self-efficacy*," which refers to an individual's belief in their ability to effectively manage their financial resources and make financial decisions. Financial self-efficacy means "having the confidence in one's ability to deal with financial situations without being overwhelmed" (Hira, 2010, as cited in Lown, 2011, p. 15). This definition is based on the concept of self-efficacy, which refers to a sense of personal agency and the belief that one can achieve and succeed at a given task.	not specified	university employees	N = 726	1) It is hard to stick to my spending plan when unexpected expenses arise. 2) It is challenging to make progress toward my financial goals. 3) When unexpected expenses occur, I usually have to use credit. 4) When faced with a financial challenge, I have a hard time figuring out a solution. 5) I lack confidence in my ability to manage my finances. 6) I worry about running out of money in retirement.	Likert-scale (1–4)	6 items	Factor analysis C-Alpha = 0.76	gender, marital status, education, age, type of investor, ethnicity, household income, self-perception measures of investment sophistication and financial confidence; + Retirement Personality Type (RPT) inventory: retirement planning type	This study developed a 6-item Financial Self-Efficacy Scale for use by researchers, educators, counselors, and advisors. Scale items were adapted from Schwarzer and Jerusalem's (1995) 10-item General Self-Efficacy Scale (GSES) by incorporating specific references to financial management in six of the original 10 statements. (p. 57).

(continued)

Table A3 (continued)

Author/s (Year)	Name of the construct	Definition of the construct	Cognitive, non-cognitive, or mixed	Target group	Sample size of study	Contents assessed	Item format	Number of items	Measurements features/ psychometric properties/ dimensionality (if applicable)	Additional constructs assessed in the study/relationship to other variables	Comments
Prevett et al. (2020)	self-efficacy; financial literacy;	*Self-efficacy* is defined as the belief in one's own abilities to meet challenges and successfully complete tasks. In the context of financial literacy, self-efficacy refers to the belief in one's ability to apply and use financial knowledge in various contexts and situations of financial practices (p. 232; p. 241). The authors consider financial self-efficacy as situated as it may vary depending on context. *Financial literacy* is defined as comprising two main dimensions: financial knowledge and financial confidence. The researchers use the term *"financial self-efficacy"* instead of confidence and advocate for its wider adoption in conceptualizing financial literacy. They claim that *self-efficacy* is related to *confidence* but it is not the same thing (p. 232)	not specified	recruited from fifteen different educational institutions, including high schools and pre-university colleges; age 16 to 19, sometimes older;	N = 171	1) Managing Money 2) Planning Ahead 3) Choosing Products 4) Staying Informed – self-efficacy in financial knowledge – self-efficacy in financial performance-in-practice – self-efficacy in financial performance-in-practice in various social contexts – self-efficacy in engagement with the financial industry	Likert-scale (1–4) (1 = not confident at all, 2 = not very confident, 3 = fairly confident, 4 = very confident)	29 items: 13 items for Learning Financial Capability 16 items for Personal Financial Practices	validation via Rasch model; DIF analyses;	gender, proxy for socio-economic disadvantage (educational allowance), ethnicity, age, school type; proxy for learning gain;	"financial self-efficacy has been identified in a range of studies as the best predictor of financial behavior" (p. 231)

Financial emotion (= construct contains an emotional component, e.g., stress, anxiety, enjoyment, etc.)							
Archuleta et al. (2013)	financial anxiety; "Financial Anxiety Scale"; financial satisfaction; financial knowledge;	*Financial satisfaction* has been generally defined as perceived satisfaction of one's income, ability to handle financial emergencies, ability to meet basic necessities, debt level, amount of savings, and money for future financial needs and life goals (Hira & Mugenda 1998) (p. 51). The authors refer further to financial mental health and financial disorders (e.g., financial enabling disorder, compulsive buying disorder, compulsive hoarding, pathological gambling, workaholism, financial dependence, financial infidelity, and financial enmeshment). Financial stress and anxiety can be seen as relevant aspects of financial mental health. (p. 50).	college students who sought services at a university peer financial counseling center in a Midwestern state	N = 180	financial satisfaction: 1) "How satisfied are you with your overall current financial situation?" financial anxiety: 1) I feel anxious about my financial situation. 2) I have difficulty sleeping because of my financial situation. 3) I have difficulty concentrating on my school or work because of my financial situation. 4) I am irritable because of my financial situation. 5) I have difficulty controlling worrying about my financial situation. 6) My muscles feel tense because of worries about my financial situation. 7) I feel fatigued because I worry about my financial situation.	financial anxiety: Likert scale (1–7) financial satisfaction: Likert scale (1–10)	financial anxiety: 7 items financial satisfaction: 1 item	financial anxiety: C-Alpha = 0.94 factor loadings range from 0.72 to 0.90;	age, relationship status, gender, primary ancestry ("race"), income, student loans, debt;	financial satisfaction was measured adapting one item from Prawitz et al. (2006);

(continued)

Table A3 (continued)

Author/s (Year)	Name of the construct	Definition of the construct	Cognitive, non-cognitive, or mixed	Target group	Sample size of study	Contents assessed	Item format	Number of items	Measurements features/ psychometric properties/ dimensionality (if applicable)	Additional constructs assessed in the study/relationship to other variables	Comments
Heo et al. (2020)	financial stress "APR Financial Stress Scale"	"Financial stress is a psychophysiological response to the perception of imbalance, uncertainty, and risk in the realm of financial resource management and decision making. As Selye (1956) maintained, a psychophysiological response should be denoted as a measurable response of stress. In addition, financial stress stems from the possible mismanagement of financial resources at the household level." (p. 4)	mixed A = affective (how people feel about the current financial situation P = physiological (how the human body reacts to stressors) R = relational (describes the effect of stress on cognitive and behavioral phenomena)	adults (U.S. citizens), age 19 to 83	Study 1: N = 688 Study 2: N = 1115	1) Affective reaction 2) Relational / Interpersonal Behavior 3) Physiological Responses	Likert scale (1–5)	42 items (initial draft) 24 items (final scale): 8 questions for "Affective Reaction" 8 questions for "Relational / interpersonal behavior" 8 questions for "physiological responses"	exploratory and confirmatory factor analysis; Affective reaction: C-Alpha = 0.95 relational behavior: C-Alpha = 0.91 physiological responses: C-Alpha = 0.94	age, number of children, income, work status, gender, marital status, education; Questionnaires included in confirmatory survey: PANAS, Financial Anxiety, Job Security, Life Satisfaction, Financial well-being;	

| Shapiro and Burchell (2012) | financial anxiety "Financial Anxiety Scale" (FAS) | "*Financial anxiety* has been defined as a psychosocial syndrome whereby individuals have an uneasy and unhealthy attitude towards engaging with, and administering their personal finances in an effective way (Burchell, 2003, as cited in Shapiro & Burchell, 2012, p. 93)." | not specified; probably non-cognitive (emotional) | full-time undergraduate students; | Study 1: N = 38 Study 2: N = 79 | Final scale (after study 2): 1) I prefer not to think about the state of my personal finances. 2) Thinking about my personal finances can make me feel guilty. 3) I am worried about the debt I will have when I complete my university education. 4) Thinking about my personal finances can make me feel anxious. 5) I get myself into situations where do not know where I'm going to get the money to "bail" myself out. 6) Discussing my finances can make my heart race or make me feel stressed. 7) I do not make a big enough effort to understand my finances. 8) I do not think I am doing as well as I could academically because I worry about money. 9) I find opening my bank statements unpleasant. 10) I would rather someone else who I trusted kept my finances organized. | Likert scale (1–4); Note: lower numbers indicate a higher level of financial anxiety; | 10 items | Exploratory factor analysis; Study 1: C-Alpha = 0.83; factor loadings of items between 0.37 and 0.74; Study 2: C-Alpha = 0.85; factor loadings of items between 0.53 and 0.78; | Spielberger's State-Trait Anxiety Inventory (STAI); Center for Epidemiologic Studies Depression Scale (CES-D); | In addition to the development of the FAS, this paper provides insights into the adaption of the Emotional Stroop Test (EST) and the Dot-Probe-Paradigm (DPP) to investigate financial anxiety. |

(continued)

Table A3 (continued)

Author/s (Year)	Name of the construct	Definition of the construct	Cognitive, non-cognitive, or mixed	Target group	Sample size of study	Contents assessed	Item format	Number of items	Measurements features/ psychometric properties/ dimensionality (if applicable)	Additional constructs assessed in the study/relationship to other variables	Comments
Financial well-being											
Consumer Financial Protection Bureau CFPB (2017)	financial well-being; "CFPB Financial Well-Being Scale"	"Financial well-being is a state of being wherein a person can fully meet current and ongoing financial obligations, can feel secure in their financial future, and is able to make choices that allow them to enjoy life" (p. 6).	not specified by the authors; based on the given definition, probably non-cognitive ("feel secure", "enjoy life")	all adults in the United States, age 18 to 61; age 62+;	Round 1: N = 3542 (age 18 to 61) N = 958 (age 62+) Round 2: N = 6350 (age 18 to 61) N = 1549 (age 62+) Round 3: N = 1019 (age 18 to 61) N = 981 (age 62+) Total: N = 14.399	1) I could handle a major unexpected expense. 2) I am securing my financial future. 3) Because of my money situation, I feel like I will never have the things I want in life. 4) I can enjoy life because of the way I'm managing my money. 5) I am just getting by financially. 6) I am concerned that the money I have or will save won't last 7) Giving a gift for a wedding, birthday or other occasion would put a strain on my finances for the month 8) I have money left over at the end of the month 9) I am behind with my finances 10) My finances control my life	2x 5-point categorical response sets: "describes me" (1 = does not describe me at all; 5 = describes me completely) "frequency" (how often; 1 = never; 5 = always)	10 items: 6 items ("describes me"); 4 items ("frequency"); 5 items (short scale): 3 items ("describes me") 2 items ("frequency")	10-item-scale: C-Alpha: 0.89 to 0.90 5-item-scale: C-Alpha: 0.82 to 0.84 (depending on age group and survey method, e.g., online vs. phone); questionnaire was also scaled with an IRT model (p. 33–41)	Validators: Credit ranking, Confidence, having 3 months of expenses in savings, self-rated current financial situation, experience of negative economic events, inability to afford food or medical care;	abbreviated 5-item-scale was also developed for cases where a 10-item scale is not feasible

Other constructs that are in any way related to personal finance

Letkiewicz and Fox (2014)	conscientiousness; asset accumulation;	With reference to the APA Dictionary of Psychology (VandenBos, 2015, p. 236), *conscientiousness* is defined as "the tendency to be organized, responsible, and hardworking". It is comprised of six lower-level facets, including competence (efficiency), order (organization), dutifulness (thorough), achievement striving (ambitious), self-discipline (not lazy), and deliberation (not impulsive) (Costa & McCrae, 1992). Traits related to conscientiousness include perseverance, impulse control, task- and goal-orientation, propensity to plan, and delay of gratification (John & Srivastava, 1999). (p. 275)	not specified	Conscientiousness: 24 to 28-year-olds; Financial literacy: 23 to 27-years-olds;	N = 9000 (approx.) National Longitudinal Survey of Youth (NLSY)	Conscientiousness: 2 questions from the Ten Item Personality Inventory (TIPI), Conscientiousness: Likert scale (1–7) to rate how well two pairs of personality traits apply to the participants;	2 items: 1 item for "dependable – self-disciplined" 1 item for "disorganized – careless"	/	gender, race/ethnicity, education, income, marital status, family socioeconomic status (mother's education), Armed Services Vocational Aptitude Battery (ASVAB) score, inheritance, student loans,	"Findings indicate that both conscientiousness and financial literacy are consistent predictors of asset accumulation among young Americans." "Financial literacy moderates the effect of conscientiousness on net worth."

(continued)

Table A3 (continued)

Author/s (Year)	Name of the construct	Definition of the construct	Cognitive, non-cognitive, or mixed	Target group	Sample size of study	Contents assessed	Item format	Number of items	Measurements features/ psychometric properties/ dimensionality (if applicable)	Additional constructs assessed in the study/relationship to other variables	Comments
Beutler and Gudmunson (2012)	entitlement; conscientiousness;	*Entitlement* is defined as an attitude in which adolescents feel their parents are obligated to provide and pay for the things they want or believe they deserve. Entitlement encompasses adolescents' belief that their parents' financial resources automatically belong to them and their parents should pay for things they desire if they are "extras" (pp. 19–20); Costa and McCrae (1992) defined *conscientiousness* as a personality trait involving caution, thorough-ness, self-discipline, thinking before acting, and acting according to the dictates of one's conscience. (…) In this study, the definition of *conscientiousness* was restricted to adolescents' acknowledgment of responsibility toward their parents for how they spend money allocated to them. It included frugality, paying others back, and cautious spending habits. (p. 21)	not specified	U.S. high school students;	N = 265	Entitlement: 1. I feel it is my parents' job to pay for my everyday needs. 2. My parents should provide me with spending money. 3. I feel my parents should pay for the 'extras.' 4. I feel my parents should pay for my college education. 5. I deserve to get most of the things I want. 6. I feel my parents should help me get the things I want. Conscientiousness: 7. I help my parents save money by being thrifty and frugal. 8. When my parents buy me things, I try to 'pay them back' by helping them out. 9. I am cautious, even when spending my parents' money. 10. I feel personal responsibility when spending my parents' money.	Entitlement: Likert scale (1–4) Conscientiousness: Likert scale (0–4)	10 items: 6 items (entitlement) 4 items (conscientiousness);	Confirmatory factor analysis: chi-square: 48.3 df: 34 CFI: 0.98 TLI: 0.97 RMSEA: 0.04 Factor loadings: entitlement: 0.45 to 0.77 conscientiousness: 0.55 to 0.90	gender, age, race / ethnicity, family arrangements;	The authors consider conscientiousness related to emotional intelligence and impulse control (p. 21);

Xue et al. (2019, 2021);	financial concerns; financial strategies;	no explicit definition is provided;	not specified	retired individuals aged 55 and older	N = 15,000 National Senior Australia survey	financial concerns: C1: You might not have enough money to pay for a long stay in a nursing home or a long period of nursing care at home. C2: You might not have enough money if your spouse or partner requires a nursing home or long-term care at home. C3: Your spouse/partner may not be able to maintain the same standard of living after your death, if you should die first. C4: You might not be able to keep the value of your savings and investments up with inflation. C5: You might not be able to maintain a reasonable standard of living for the rest of your life. C6: You might not be able to afford to stay in your current home for the rest of your life. C7: You might not be able to leave money to your children or other heirs. C8: You might outlive your savings. financial strategies: S1: Cut back on spending	financial concerns: Likert scale with four ordered options: 1) not at all concerned 2) not too concerned 3) somewhat concerned 4) very concerned financial strategies: 4 response possibilities: A) Already done B) Plan to do in future C) No plans D) Do not know/ unsure	financial concerns: 8 items; financial strategies: 16 items;	The eight survey questions about financial concerns are grouped into four broad financial concerns using categorical principal component analysis (CPCA), which reflects four major and popular concerns among elderly people: C1) long-term care; C2) investment performance; C3) current home affordability; C4) bequest;	wealth, age, gender, marital status, health, tenure, income, education, occupation, retirement status, loan, earning, partner's occupation, partners earning,	"We find (1) financial concerns mediate the majority of financial literacy-strategy nexuses; specifically, financially illiterate people are more likely to have financial concerns and are more likely to cut back on spending, seek job opportunities, increase debts and downsize or sell their residence as a result; (2) financially literate people are more likely to seek professional financial advice, purchase a life annuity, contribute more to superannuation and invest more conservatively, regardless of their concerns."

(continued)

Table A3 (continued)

Author/s (Year)	Name of the construct	Definition of the construct	Cognitive, non-cognitive, or mixed	Target group	Sample size of study	Contents assessed	Item format	Number of items	Measurements features/ psychometric properties/ dimensionality (if applicable)	Additional constructs assessed in the study/relationship to other variables	Comments
Xue et al. (2019, 2021);	financial concerns; financial strategies;	no explicit definition is provided;	not specified	retired individuals aged 55 and older	N = 15,000 National Senior Australia survey	S2: Work longer S3: Obtain professional financial advice S4: Buy a life annuity or other product to provide guaranteed income for life S5: Increase contributions to superannuation S6: Increase savings outside superannuation S7: Move assets to more conservative assets S8: Take out or increase reverse mortgage or home refinancing S9: Take out or increase other debt (e.g. credit cards, personal loans) S10: Completely pay off mortgage S11: Pay off all credit cards and personal loans S12: Buy real estate or invest in property (including upsizing or renovations) S13: Move to a smaller home/less expensive area S14: Sell household goods, investment property or other material assets S15: Approach others for financial support/ loan S16: Increase insurance cover (life, disability, trauma, accident or private health)	financial concerns: Likert scale with four ordered options: 1) not at all concerned 2) not too concerned 3) somewhat concerned 4) very concerned financial strategies: 4 response possibilities: A) Already done B) Plan to do in future C) No plans D) Do not know/ unsure	financial concerns: 8 items; financial strategies: 16 items;	The eight survey questions about financial concerns are grouped into four broad financial concerns using categorical principal component analysis (CPCA), which reflects four major and popular concerns among elderly people: C1) long-term care; C2) investment performance; C3) current home affordability; C4) bequest;	wealth, age, gender, marital status, health, tenure, income, education, occupation, retirement status, loan, earning, partner's occupation, partners earning,	"We find (1) financial concerns mediate the majority of financial literacy-strategy nexuses; specifically, financially illiterate people are more likely to have financial concerns and are more likely to cut back on spending, seek job opportunities, increase debts and downsize or sell their residence as a result; (2) financially literate people are more likely to seek professional financial advice, purchase a life annuity, contribute more to superannuation and invest more conservatively, regardless of their concerns."

References

Agarwal, S., Driscoll, J. C., Gabaix, X., & Laibson, D. (2007). *The age of reason: Financial decisions over the lifecycle*. NBER Working Paper 13191. https://doi.org/10.3386/w13191

Allgood, S., & Walstad, W. B. (2016). The effects of perceived and actual financial literacy on financial behaviors. *Economic Inquiry, 54*(1), 675–697. https://doi.org/10.1111/ecin.12255

Andersen, S., Harrison, G. W., Lau, M. I., & Rutström, E. E. (2008). Eliciting risk and time preferences. *Econometrica, 76*(3), 583–618. https://doi.org/10.1111/j.1468-0262.2008.00848.x

Antonides, G., de Groot, I. M., & van Raaij, W. F. (2011). Mental budgeting and the management of household finance. *Journal of Economic Psychology, 32*(4), 546–555. https://doi.org/10.1016/j.joep.2011.04.001

Aprea, C., & Wuttke, E. (2016). Financial literacy of adolescents and young adults: Setting the course for a competence-oriented assessment instrument. In C. Aprea et al. (Eds.), *International handbook of financial literacy* (pp. 397–414). Springer. https://doi.org/10.1007/978-981-10-0360-8_27

Archuleta, K. L., Dale, A., & Spann, S. M. (2013). College students and financial distress: Exploring debt, financial satisfaction, and financial anxiety. *Journal of Financial Counseling and Planning, 24*(2), 50–62.

Atkinson, A., & Messy, F.-A. (2012). Measuring financial literacy. *OECD Working Papers on Finance, Insurance and Private Pensions*, No. 15. https://doi.org/10.1787/5k9csfs90fr4-en.

Aydin, A. E., & Selcuk, E. A. (2019). An investigation of financial literacy, money ethics, and time preferences among college students: A structural equation model. *International Journal of Bank Marketing, 37*(3), 880–900. https://doi.org/10.1108/IJBM-05-2018-0120

Babiarz, P., & Robb, C. A. (2014). Financial literacy and emergency saving. *Journal of Family and Economic Issues, 35*, 40–50. https://doi.org/10.1007/s10834-013-9369-9

Bannier, C. E., & Neubert, M. (2016). Gender differences in financial risk taking: The role of financial literacy and risk tolerance. *Economics Letters, 145*, 130–135. https://doi.org/10.1016/j.econlet.2016.05.033

Barry, D. (2014). *Die Einstellung zu Geld bei jungen Erwachsenen. Eine Grundlegung aus wirtschaftspädagogischer Sicht [Attitudes towards money among young adults. A foundation from a business and economics education perspective]*. Springer.

Bateman, H., Eckert, C., Geweke, J., Louviere, J., Satchell, S., & Thorp, S. (2014). Financial competence, risk presentation, and retirement portfolio preferences. *Journal of Pension Economics & Finance, 13*(1), 27–61. https://doi.org/10.1017/S1474747213000188

Beutler, I. F., & Gudmunson, C. G. (2012). New adolescent money attitude scales: Entitlement and conscientiousness. *Journal of Financial Counseling and Planning, 23*(2), 14.

Bocchialini, E., & Ronchini, B. (2019). A pilot study assessing attitudes toward finance among Italian business students. *International Journal of Business and Management, 14*(10), 44–60. https://doi.org/10.5539/ijbm.v14n10p44

Bocchialini, E., Ronchini, B., & Torti, F. (2022). Predicting students' financial knowledge from attitude towards finance. *International Journal of Business and Management, 17*(6), 13. https://doi.org/10.5539/ijbm.v17n6p13

Bosshardt, W., & Walstad, W. B. (2014). National standards for financial literacy: Rationale and content. *Journal of Economic Education, 45*(1), 63–70. https://doi.org/10.1080/00220485.2014.859963

Braunstein, S., & Welch, C. (2002). Financial literacy: An overview of practice, research, and policy. *Federal Reserve Bulletin, 88*, 446–457. https://www.federalreserve.gov/pubs/bulletin/2002/1102lead.pdf

Calcagno, R., & Monticone, C. (2015). Financial literacy and the demand for financial advice. *Journal of Banking and Finance, 50*, 363–380. https://doi.org/10.1016/j.jbankfin.2014.03.013

CEE. (2013). *National standards for financial literacy*. Council for Economic Education. ISBN: 978-1-56183-734-2. https://www.councilforeconed.org/wp-content/uploads/2013/02/national-standards-for-financial-literacy.pdf

CEE. (2021). *National standards for personal financial education*. Council for Economic Education. ISBN: 978-1-7348096-2-6. https://www.councilforeconed.org/policy-advocacy/k-12-standards/

CFPB. (2015). *Measuring financial well-being: A guide to using the CFPB financial well-being scale*. Consumer Financial Protection Bureau. https://www.consumerfinance.gov/data-research/research-reports/financial-well-being-scale/

CFPB. (2017). *Financial well-being in America*. Consumer Financial Protection Bureau. https://files.consumerfinance.gov/f/documents/201709_cfpb_financial-well-being-in-America.pdf

CFPB. (2019). *A review of youth financial education: Effects and evidence*. Consumer Financial Protection Bureau. https://files.consumerfinance.gov/f/documents/cfpb_youth-financial-education_lit-review.pdf

Charness, G., & Gneezy, U. (2012). Strong evidence for gender differences in risk taking. *Journal of Economic Behavior and Organization, 83*(1), 50–58. https://doi.org/10.1016/j.jebo.2011.06.007

Chen, H., & Volpe, R. (1998). An analysis of personal financial literacy among college students. *Financial Services Review, 7*(2), 107–128. https://doi.org/10.1016/s1057-0810(99)80006-7

Collins, M. J. (2012). Financial advice: A substitute for financial literacy? *Financial Services Review, 21*(4), 307–322. http://www.ssc.wisc.edu/~jmcollin/FSR_12

Cordero, J. M., Gil-Izquierdo, M., & Pedraja-Chaparro, F. (2022). Financial education and student financial literacy: A cross-country analysis using PISA 2012 data. *The Social Science Journal, 59*(1), 15–33. https://doi.org/10.1016/j.soscij.2019.07.011

Costa, P. T., & McCrae, R. R. (1992). *Revised NEO Personality Inventory (NEO-PI-R) and NEO Five-Factor Inventory (NEO-FFI): professional manual*. Psychological Assessment Resources.

Courchane, M., Gailey, A., & Zorn, P. (2008). Consumer credit literacy: What price perception? *Journal of Economics and Business, 60*(1–2), 125–138. https://doi.org/10.1016/j.jeconbus.2007.08.003

Cox, R., Brounen, D., & Neuteboom, P. (2014). Financial literacy, risk aversion, and the choice of mortgage type by households. *Journal of Real Estate Finance and Economics, 50*, 74–112. https://doi.org/10.1007/s11146-013-9453-9

Cude, B. J. (2022). Defining financial literacy. In G. Nicolini & B. J. Cude (Eds.), *The Routledge handbook of financial literacy* (pp. 5–17). Taylor & Francis Group. https://doi.org/10.4324/9781003025221

Dare, S. E., van Dijk, W. W., van Dijk, E., van Dillen, L. F., Galluci, M., & Simonse, O. (2020). The effect of financial education on pupils' financial knowledge and skills: Evidence from a Solomon four-group design. *Journal of Educational Research, 113*(2), 93–107. https://doi.org/10.1080/00220671.2020.1733453

De Winne, R. (2021). Measuring the disposition effect. *Journal of Behavioral and Experimental Finance, 29*(March), 100468. https://doi.org/10.1016/j.jbef.2021.100468

Fernandes, D., Lynch, J. G., & Netemeyer, R. G. (2014). Financial literacy, financial education, and downstream financial behaviors. *Management Science, 60*(8), 1861–1883. https://doi.org/10.1287/mnsc.2013.1849

Förster, M., Happ, R., & Maur, A. (2018). The Relationship among gender, interest in financial topics and understanding of personal finance. *Empirische Pädagogik, 32*(3/4), 292–308.

Förster, M., Happ, R., & Molerov, D. (2017). Using the U.S. test of financial literacy in Germany – Adaptation and validation. *Journal of Economic Education, 48*(2), 123–135. https://doi.org/10.1080/00220485.2017.1285737

Friedline, T., Chen, Z., & Morrow, S. (2021). Families' financial stress & well-being: The importance of the economy and economic environments. *Journal of Family and Economic Issues, 42*(Suppl1), 34–51. https://doi.org/10.1007/s10834-020-09694-9

Furnham, A. F. (1984). Many sides of the coin: The psychology of money usage. *Personality and Individual Differences, 5*(5), 501–509. https://doi.org/10.1016/0191-8869(84)90025-4

Gallery, N., Gallery, G., Brown, K., Furneaux, C., & Palm, C. (2011). Financial literacy and pension investment decisions. *Financial Accountability & Management, 27*(3), 286–307. https://doi.org/10.1111/j.1468-0408.2011.00526.x

Gignac, G. E., & Ooi, E. (2021). Measurement error in research on financial literacy: How much error is there and how does it influence effect size estimates? *Journal of Consumer Affairs, 56*(2), 938–956. https://doi.org/10.1111/joca.12417

Gomes, F., Haliassos, M., & Ramadorai, T. (2021). Household finance. *Journal of Economic Literature, 59*(3), 919–1000. https://doi.org/10.1257/jel.20201461

Grohs-Müller, S., & Greimel-Fuhrmann, B. (2018). Students' money attitudes and financial behaviour: A study on the relationship between two components of financial literacy. *Empirische Pädagogik, 32*(3/4), 369–386.

Gutter, M., & Copur, Z. (2011). Financial behaviors and financial well-being of college students: Evidence from a national survey. *Journal of Family and Economic Issues, 32*, 699–714. https://doi.org/10.1007/s10834-011-9255-2

Harris, M. N., Loundes, J., & Webster, E. (2002). Determinants of household saving in Australia. *Economic Record, 78*(241), 207–223. https://doi.org/10.1111/1475-4932.00024

Harrison, G. W., Lau, M. I., Rutström, E. E., & Sullivan, M. B. (2005). Eliciting risk and time preferences using field experiments: Some methodological issues. In G. W. Harrison, J. Carpenter, & J. A. List (Eds.), *Field experiments in economics (Research in experimental economics, Vol. 10)* (pp. 125–218). Emerald Group Publishing Limited. https://doi.org/10.1016/S0193-2306(04)10005-7

Hastings, J., & Mitchell, O. S. (2020). How financial literacy and impatience shape retirement wealth and investment behaviors. *Journal of Pension Economics & Finance, 19*(1), 1–20. https://doi.org/10.1017/S1474747218000227

Heo, W., Cho, S., & Lee, P. (2020). APR financial stress scale: Development and validation of a multidimensional measurement. *Journal of Financial Therapy, 11*(1), 2. https://doi.org/10.4148/1944-9771.1216

Hermansson, C., & Jonsson, S. (2021). The impact of financial literacy and financial interest on risk tolerance. *Journal of Behavioral and Experimental Finance, 29*, 100450. https://doi.org/10.1016/j.jbef.2020.100450

Hilgert, M. A., Hogarth, J. M., & Beverly, S. G. (2003). Household financial management: The connection between literacy and behavior. *Federal Reserve Bulletin, 89*(7), 309–322. https://www.federalreserve.gov/pubs/bulletin/2003/0703lead.pdf

Hira, T. K., & Mugenda, O. M. (1998). Predictors of financial satisfaction: Differences between retirees and non-retirees. *Financial Counseling and Planning, 9*(2), 75–83.

Houts, C. R., & Knoll, M. A. Z. (2020). The financial knowledge scale: New analyses, findings, and development of a short form. *Journal of Consumer Affairs, 54*(2), 775–800. https://doi.org/10.1111/joca.12288

Huston, S. J. (2010). Measuring financial literacy. *Journal of Consumer Affairs, 44*(2), 296–316. https://doi.org/10.1111/j.1745-6606.2010.01170.x

Jappelli, T., & Padula, M. (2013). Investment in financial literacy and saving decisions. *Journal of Banking and Finance, 37*(8), 2779–2792. https://doi.org/10.1016/j.jbankfin.2013.03.019

Joo, S., & Grable, J. E. (2004). An exploratory framework of the determinants of financial satisfaction. *Journal of Family and Economic Issues, 25*, 25–50. https://doi.org/10.1023/B:JEEI.0000016722.37994.9f

John, O. P., & Srivastava, S. (1999). The Big Five Trait taxonomy: History, measurement, and theoretical perspectives. In L. A. Pervin & O. P. John (Eds.), *Handbook of personality: Theory and research* (2nd ed., pp. 102–138). Guilford Press.

Kaiser, T., Lusardi, A., Menkhoff, L., & Urban, C. (2022). Financial education affects financial knowledge and downstream behaviors. *Journal of Financial Economics, 145*(5), 255–273. https://doi.org/10.1016/j.jfineco.2021.09.022

Kaiser, T., & Menkhoff, L. (2017). Does financial education impact financial literacy and financial behavior, and if so, when. *The Word Bank Economic Review, 31*(3), 611–630. https://doi.org/10.1093/wber/lhx018

Kaiser, T., & Menkhoff, L. (2019). Financial education in schools: A meta-analysis of experimental studies. *Economics of Education Review, 78*, 101930. https://doi.org/10.1016/j.econedurev.2019.101930

Kershaw, M. M., & Webber, L. S. (2008). Assessment of financial competence. *Psychiatry, Psychology and Law, 15*(1), 40–55. https://doi.org/10.1080/13218710701873965

Knoll, M. A., & Houts, C. R. (2012). The financial knowledge scale: An application of item response theory to the assessment of financial literacy. *Journal of Consumer Affairs, 46*, 381–410. https://doi.org/10.1111/j.1745-6606.2012.01241.x

Kraitzek, A., & Förster, M. (2023). Measurement of financial competence – Designing a complex framework model for a complex assessment instrument. *Journal of Risk and Financial Management, 16*(4), 223. https://doi.org/10.3390/jrfm16040223

Kraitzek, A., & Förster, M. (2024). *Adaptation and validation of the U.S. test of financial knowledge for use in Germany*. Poster Presentation at the Annual Conference of the American Educational Research Association (AERA) 2024. https://doi.org/10.3102/IP.24.2104907

Kraitzek, A., Förster, M., & Walstad, W. B. (2022). Comparison of financial education and knowledge in the United States and Germany: Curriculum and assessment. *Research in Comparative and International Education, 17*(2), 153–173. https://doi.org/10.1177/17454999221081333

Kramer, M. M. (2016). Financial literacy, confidence and financial advice seeking. *Journal of Economic Behavior & Organization, 131*(Part A), 198–217. https://doi.org/10.1016/j.jebo.2016.08.016

Letkiewicz, J. C., & Fox, J. J. (2014). Conscientiousness, financial literacy, and asset accumulation of young adults. *Journal of Consumer Affairs, 48*(2), 274–300. https://doi.org/10.1111/joca.12040

Lin, X., Bruhn, A., & William, J. (2019). Extending financial literacy to insurance literacy: A survey approach. *Accounting & Finance, 59*(S1), 685–713. https://doi.org/10.1111/acfi.12353

Lin, J. T., Bumcrot, C., Mottola, G., Valdes, O., Ganem, R., Kieffer, C., Lusardi, A., & Walsh, G. (2022). *Financial capability in the United States: Highlights from the FINRA Foundation National Financial Capability Study* (5th ed.). FINRA Investor Education Foundation. www.FINRAFoundation.org/NFCSReport2021

Lown, J. M. (2011). Development and validation of a financial self-efficacy scale. *Journal of Financial Counseling and Planning, 22*(2), 54. https://ssrn.com/abstract=2006665

Lusardi, A. (2008). *Financial Literacy: An Essential Tool for Informed Consumer Choice?* NBER Working Paper, No. 14084. https://doi.org/10.3386/w14084

Lusardi, A. (2012). Numeracy, financial literacy, and financial decision-making. *Numeracy, 5*(1), 2. https://doi.org/10.5038/1936-4660.5.1.2

Lusardi, A., & Mitchell, O. S. (2007). Baby boomer retirement security: The roles of planning, financial literacy, and housing wealth. *Journal of Monetary Economics, 54*(1), 205–224. https://doi.org/10.1016/j.jmoneco.2006.12.001

Lusardi, A., & Mitchell, O. S. (2009). *How ordinary consumers make complex economic decisions: financial literacy and retirement readiness*. Intertemporal Choice & Growth eJournal. https://www.nber.org/papers/w15350

Lusardi, A., & Mitchell, O. S. (2011). Financial literacy around the world: an overview. *Journal of Pension Economics and Finance, 10*, 497–508. https://doi.org/10.1017/S1474747211000448

Lusardi, A., & Mitchell, O. S. (2014). The economic importance of financial literacy: Theory and evidence. *Journal of Economic Literature, 52*(1), 5–44. https://doi.org/10.1257/jel.52.1.5

Lusardi, A., & Mitchell, O. S. (2017). How ordinary consumers make complex economic decisions: Financial literacy and retirement readiness. *Quarterly Journal of Finance, 7*(3), 1–31. https://doi.org/10.1142/S2010139217500082

Lusardi, A., & Tufano, P. (2015). Debt literacy, financial experiences, and overindebtedness. *Journal of Pension Economics & Finance, 14*(4), 332–368. https://doi.org/10.1017/S1474747215000232

Mahdzan, N., & Tabiani, S. (2013). The impact of financial literacy on individual saving: An exploratory study in the Malaysian context. *Transformations in Business & Economics, 12*(1), 41–55.

Mandell, L. (2008). *The financial literacy of young American adults: Results of the 2008 National Jump $tart Coalition survey of high school seniors and college students.*

Mandell, L., & Schmid-Klein, L. (2007). Motivation and financial literacy. *Financial services review, 16*(2), 105.

Morris, T., Maillet, S., & Koffi, V. (2022). Financial knowledge, financial confidence and learning capacity on financial behavior: A Canadian study. *Cogent Social Sciences, 8*(1), 1996919. https://doi.org/10.1080/23311886.2021.1996919

Muck, P. M. (2013). Entwicklung von Situational Judgment Tests: Konzeptionelle Überlegungen und empirische Befunde [Development of Situational Judgment Tests: Conceptual considerations and empirical findings]. *Zeitschrift für Arbeits- und Organisationspsychologie, 57*(4), 185–205. https://doi.org/10.1026/0932-4089/a000125

Mudzingiri, C., Muteba Mwamba, J. W., & Keyser, J. N. (2018). Financial behavior, confidence, risk preferences and financial literacy of university students. *Cogent Economics & Finance, 6*(1). https://doi.org/10.1080/23322039.2018.1512366

OECD. (2005, July). *Recommendation on principles and good practices for financial education and awareness.* https://legalinstruments.oecd.org/en/instruments/OECD-LEGAL-0338

OECD. (2013). *PISA 2012 assessment and analytical framework: Mathematics, reading, science, problem solving and financial literacy.* PISA, OECD Publishing. https://doi.org/10.1787/9789264190511-en

OECD. (2014). *PISA 2012 results: Students and money: Financial literacy skills for the 21st century* (Vol. VI). PISA, OECD Publishing. https://doi.org/10.1787/9789264208094-en

OECD. (2017). *PISA 2015 results (Volume IV): Students' financial literacy.* PISA, OECD Publishing. https://doi.org/10.1787/9789264270282-en

OECD. (2019). *PISA 2018 assessment and analytical framework.* PISA, OECD Publishing. https://doi.org/10.1787/b25efab8-en

OECD. (2020). *PISA 2018 results (Volume IV): Are student smart about money?* PISA, OECD Publishing. https://doi.org/10.1787/48ebd1ba-en

OECD. (2022). *OECD/INFE Toolkit for measuring financial literacy and financial inclusion 2022.* www.oecd.org/financial/education/2022-INFE-Toolkit-Measuring-Finlit-Financial-Inclusion.pdf

Ouachani, S., Belhassine, O., & Kammoun, A. (2021). Measuring financial literacy: A literature review. *Managerial Finance, 47*(2), 266–281. https://doi.org/10.1108/MF-04-2019-0175

Palameta, B., Nguyen, C., Shek-wai Hui, T., & Gyarmati, D. (2016). *The link between financial confidence and financial outcomes among working-aged Canadians.* Report for the Financial Consumer Agency of Canada. Social Research and Demonstration Corporation SRDC. https://srdc.org/wpcontent/uploads/2022/07/fcac-full-report-on-financial-confidence-en.pdf

Parker, A. M., Bruine de Bruin, W., Yoong, J., & Willis, R. (2012). Inappropriate confidence and retirement planning: Four studies with a national sample. *Journal of Behavioral Decision Making, 25*(4), 382–389. https://doi.org/10.1002/bdm.745

Prawitz, A. D., Garman, E. T., Sorhaindo, B., O'Neill, B., Kim, J., & Drentea, P. (2006). In charge financial distress/financial well-being scale: Development, administration, and score interpretation. *Journal of Financial Counseling and Planning, 17*(1), 34–50.

Prevett, P. S., Pampaka, M., Farnsworth, V. L., Kalambouka, A., & Shi, X. (2020). A situated learning approach to measuring financial literacy self-efficacy of youth. *Journal of Financial Counseling and Planning.* https://doi.org/10.1891/JFCP-18-00038

Ranyard, R., McNair, S., Nicolini, G., & Duxbury, D. (2019). An item response theory approach to constructing and evaluating brief and in-depth financial literacy scales. *Journal of Consumer Affairs, 54*(3), 1121–1156. https://doi.org/10.1111/joca.12322

Ray, J. J., & Najman, J. M. (1986). The generalizability of deferment of gratification. *The Journal of Social Psychology, 126*(1), 117–119. https://doi.org/10.1080/00224545.1986.9713578

Remund, D. L. (2010). Financial literacy explicated: The case for a clearer definition in an increasingly complex economy. *Journal of Consumer Affairs, 44*(2), 276–295. https://doi.org/10.1111/j.1745-6606.2010.01169.x

Robb, C. A., & Woodyard, A. S. (2011). Financial knowledge and best practice behavior. *Journal of Financial Counseling and Planning, 22*(1), 60–70.

Schwarzer, R., & Jerusalem, M. (1995). Generalized Self-Efficacy Scale. In J. Weinman, S. Wright, & M. Johnston (Eds.), *Measures in Health Psychology: A User's Portfolio. Causal and Control Beliefs* (pp. 35–37). NFER-NELSON.

Selye, H. (1956). *The stress of life*. McGraw-Hill.

Shapiro, G. K., & Burchell, B. J. (2012). Measuring financial anxiety. *Journal of Neuroscience, Psychology, and Economics, 5*(2), 92–103. https://doi.org/10.1037/a0027647

Siegfried, C., & Wuttke, E. (2021). What influences the financial literacy of young adults? A combined analysis of socio-demographic characteristics and delay of gratification. *Frontiers in Psychology, 12*, 663254. https://doi.org/10.3389/fpsyg.2021.663254

Stolper, O. A., & Walter, A. (2017). Financial literacy, financial advice, and financial behavior. *Journal of Business Economics, 87*(5), 581–643. https://doi.org/10.1007/s11573-017-0853-9

Tang, T. L.-P. (1992). The meaning of money revisited. *Journal of Organizational Behavior, 13*(2), 197–202. https://doi.org/10.1002/job.4030130209

Tang, T. L.-P. (1995). The development of a short money ethic scale: Attitudes toward money and pay satisfaction revisited. *Personality and Individual Differences, 19*(6), 809–816. https://doi.org/10.1016/s0191-8869(95)00133-6

Tokar Asaad, C. (2015). Financial literacy and financial behavior: Assessing knowledge and confidence. *Financial Services Review, 24*(2), 101–117. https://doi.org/10.61190/fsr.v24i2.3236

VandenBos, G. R. (Ed.). (2015). *APA dictionary of psychology (2nd ed.)*. American Psychological Association. https://doi.org/10.1037/14646-000

van Rooij, M., Lusardi, A., & Alessie, R. (2011a). Financial literacy and stock market participation. *Journal of Financial Economics, 101*(2), 449–472. https://doi.org/10.1016/j.jfineco.2011.03.006

van Rooij, M., Lusardi, A., & Alessie, R. (2011b). Financial literacy and retirement planning in the Netherlands. *Journal of Economic Psychology, 32*(4), 593–608. https://doi.org/10.1016/j.joep.2011.02.004

van Rooij, M., Lusardi, A., & Alessie, R. (2012). Financial Literacy, Retirement Planning and Household Wealth. *The Economic Journal, 122*(560), 449–478. https://doi.org/10.1111/j.1468-0297.2012.02501.x

Walstad, W. B., & Allgood, S. (2022). The likely influence of financial literacy on financial behaviors. In G. Nicolini & B. J. Cude (Eds.), *The Routledge handbook of financial literacy* (pp. 153–170). Routledge.

Walstad, W. B., & Rebeck, K. (2016a). *Basic finance test: Examiner's manual*. Council for Economic Education.

Walstad, W. B., & Rebeck, K. (2016b). *Test of financial knowledge: Examiner's manual*. Council for Economic Education.

Walstad, W. B., & Rebeck, K. (2016c). *Test of financial literacy: Examiner's manual*. Council for Economic Education.

Walstad, W. B., & Rebeck, K. (2017). The test of financial literacy: Development and measurement characteristics. *Journal of Economic Education, 48*(2), 113–122. https://doi.org/10.1080/00220485.2017.1285739

Walstad, W. B., & Rebeck, K. (2018). The measurement properties of the basic finance test for children and the test of financial knowledge for youth. *Empirische Pädagogik, 32*(3/4), 248–248.

Walstad, W. B., Urban, C., Asarta, C. J., Breitbach, E., Bosshardt, W., Heath, J., O'Neill, B., Wagner, J., & Xiao, J. J. (2017). Perspectives on evaluation in financial education: Landscape, issues, and studies. *Journal of Economic Education, 48*(2), 93–112. https://doi.org/10.1080/00220485.2017.1285738

Warmath, D., & Zimmerman, D. (2019). Financial literacy as more than knowledge; the development of a formative scale through the lends of Bloom's domains of knowledge. *Journal of Consumer Affairs, 53*(4), 1602–1629. https://doi.org/10.1111/joca.12286

Weber, E. U., Blais, A.-R., & Betz, N. E. (2002). A domain-specific risk-attitude scale: Measuring risk perceptions and risk behaviors. *Journal of Behavioral Decision Making, 15*(4), 263–290. https://doi.org/10.1002/bdm.414

Wuttke, E., & Aprea, C. (2018). A situational judgement approach for measuring young adults' financial literacy. *Empirische Pädagogik, 32*(3/4), 272–292.

Xiao, J. J., & O'Neill, B. (2016). Consumer financial education and financial capability. *International Journal of Consumer Studies, 40*(6), 712–721. https://doi.org/10.1111/ijcs.12285

Xue, R., Gepp, A., O'Neill, T. J., Stern, S., & Vanstone, B. J. (2021). Financial literacy and financial strategies: The mediating role of financial concerns. *Australian Journal of Management, 46*(3), 437–465. https://doi.org/10.1177/0312896220940762

Xue, R., Gepp, A., O'Neill, T. J., Stern, S., & Vanstone, B. J. (2019). Financial literacy amongst elderly Australians. *Accounting & Finance, 59*, 887–918. https://doi.org/10.1111/acfi.12362

Yamauchi, K. T., & Templer, D. J. (1982). The development of a money attitude scale. *Journal of Personality Assessment, 46*(5), 522–528. https://doi.org/10.1207/s15327752jpa4605_14

Open Access This chapter is licensed under the terms of the Creative Commons Attribution 4.0 International License (http://creativecommons.org/licenses/by/4.0/), which permits use, sharing, adaptation, distribution and reproduction in any medium or format, as long as you give appropriate credit to the original author(s) and the source, provide a link to the Creative Commons license and indicate if changes were made.

The images or other third party material in this chapter are included in the chapter's Creative Commons license, unless indicated otherwise in a credit line to the material. If material is not included in the chapter's Creative Commons license and your intended use is not permitted by statutory regulation or exceeds the permitted use, you will need to obtain permission directly from the copyright holder.

Chapter 6
Development and Validation of a Test for Assessing Financial Competence in a Decision-making Process: Using the Example of Purchasing a Mobile Phone

Manuel Förster ⓘ, Christin Siegfried ⓘ, and Christoph König ⓘ

Abstract This chapter discusses the design and field testing of a computer-based test instrument to assess financial competence. The context for the instrument is decisions to purchase a mobile phone and sign a contract for mobile services within a predetermined budget. The reason for focusing on these decisions is that a significant share of debt has been attributed to telecom services. Since the search for financial information and subsequent purchases or contracts are usually conducted online, our instrument's scenario is also computerized to simulate an actual purchase. This digital scenario tasks participants with selecting mobile phones and contracts based on specified conditions. They must decide whether to purchase the phone and sign the mobile phone contract separately or bundled, eliminating impractical combinations. The remaining choices are realistic and yield the most favorable option. The scenario concludes with signing the purchasing contract. Subsequent queries ask participants to justify their choices and to rate their motivational activation and interest in the scenario. The chapter describes the process of developing the test items based on scientific models. It presents the results from an initial validation study with more than 100 apprentices who took the test in September 2023. It became clear that some items were too difficult for the apprentices, but on the other hand the test is basically a reliable instrument. While correla-

M. Förster (✉)
Business and Economic Education, School of Social Sciences and Technology, Technical University of Munich, Munich, Germany
e-mail: manuel.foerster@tum.de

C. Siegfried
Business Education for the Vocational Teaching Profession, Faculty of Economics and Social Sciences, University of Potsdam, Potsdam, Germany
e-mail: christin.siegfried@uni-potsdam.de

C. König
Educational Psychology, Department of Psychology, Goethe University Frankfurt, Frankfurt, Germany
e-mail: koenig@psych.uni-frankfurt.de

© The Author(s) 2026
M. Förster, M. Hommel (eds.), *Conceptualisation and Measurement of Financial Competence*, SpringerBriefs in Education,
https://doi.org/10.1007/978-3-031-95690-4_6

tions between cognitive and non-cognitive components could be identified, no stronger correlations are found for the analysed dispositions, e.g. mathematics and language ability and personal background such as age.

Keywords Assessment of financial literacy · Financial competence · Process assessment · Decision-making

6.1 Relevance

This chapter discusses the design of a complex and realistic scenario for assessing financial competence in a purchase decision. As noted in the previous chapter, the situation in which the test items are embedded should be sufficiently complex and realistic. One problem with many measurement instruments that are used to measure financial skills and knowledge is that few of them are connected to the reality of the respondents' lives, and if they are, they are not sufficiently complex. This scenario, therefore, attempts to present respondents with a scenario that is as realistic as possible, and contains a high degree of complexity.

Furthermore, usually only the outcomes of decisions are considered in financial competence assessments, while the decision-making process itself is not. Of course, the outcome of a decision plays a significant role in financial situations, as it ultimately determines whether the consumer makes a purchase, what product is chosen and what contract is signed. From an educational and diagnostic perspective, however, this decision-making process also is important, as it reveals when and what kind of errors occur that should be corrected at an early stage. Our task here is also to record such development steps to better differentiate the phases of the decision-making process and assess them.

The choice of a realistic financial situation also is a major consideration in preparing an assessment instrument. It can be argued that there are certain financial situations for youths and young adults that are particularly relevant for financial misconduct such as indebtedness and over-indebtedness. The purchase of mobile phones and the signing of mobile phone contracts are a crucial aspect of financial education for young adults and adolescents in Germany, especially given the central role of mobile phones in the daily lives of this target group. The complexity of mobile phone contracts, which often include device financing and service fees, requires informed decisions to avoid unforeseen financial consequences. According to the Federal Statistical Office of Germany (2020), a significant proportion of debt (65% among under-25 s in 2018) has been attributed to telecommunication contracts. Knowledge about interest rates, installment plans, and financial obligations related to mobile phone contracts is thus of great importance for the financial literacy of young people.

For this reason, the test items presented in this chapter focus on the purchase of mobiles and the associated contracts. Since the search for financial information and subsequent purchases or contracts are usually conducted online, the scenario for our instrument is also computerised to simulate a real purchase situation online. In this digital scenario, participants select mobile phones and contracts based on specified needs. They must decide whether to purchase the phone and sign the mobile phone contract separately or bundled, eliminating impractical combinations. In the following, we first present the underlying understanding of competence before describing the item construction in more detail. We then describe the preliminary results from a pretest to validate the instrument.

6.2 The General Understanding of Financial Competence

In line with the AF in model of financial competence presented in the Chap. 4 of this brief, the framework underlying the instrument and its development process follows Weinert (2001). He defines competence generally as functional, context- and domain-specific cognitive abilities and skills enabling individuals to solve specific problems, as well as associated motivational, volitional, and social dispositions to successfully apply solutions to various contexts. Our model in Chap. 4 assumes that financial competences arise in financially challenging situations and differ depending on the personal, social and systemic context. We also assume that the cognitive and non-cognitive dispositions required for the resolution process are subject to pedagogical influences and interventions (e.g. Artelt et al., 2013). This assumption implies that the facets of financial literacy are not static or fixed individual characteristics, but can be changed through learning and teaching processes (Klieme & Leutner, 2006).

Based on our understanding of competence, we also take into account that the process of solving a financial situation, which results in corresponding financial behaviour, involves an interaction of cognitive and non-cognitive state variables of financial competence. We place special emphasis on the assumption that financial competence is observable only through actual financial performance in situations that provide authentic problems and require cognitive and non-cognitive dispositions such as knowledge and skills, as well as other personal characteristics to solve these problems within a problem solving process.

In our case, the competence assessment is embedded in the situation of buying a mobile phone. Since the processes applied and the dispositions used depend to a large extent on the socio-economic situation of the decision-maker (in the model the personal and social context), we decided to provide a situation in which a decision must be made on behalf of a trainee who does not yet earn much financially and has not saved up a large financial cushion. This scenario most closely represents the group that is most at risk of incurring debt due to mobile phone contracts. The choice of a mobile phone and associated contract should therefore have a high subjective relevance for the trainee, as the contract may consume a large part of the available funds and will do so over the next 2 years.

The high relevance leads us to assume that a decision-making process is initiated, instead of applying heuristics that greatly reduce complexity and shorten the decision-making process. Based on Chap. 4 of this SpringerBrief, the process starts with an intensive *perception* of the available material within the situation, which is followed by the *interpretation* and processing of the relevant information and ends with a *decision* and justification for chosing a particular option of mobile phone. Moreover, the respondent needs cognitive domain-specific and non-specific dispositions in the problem-solving process. In our case, reading and arithmetic skills in particular are required to understand the tasks in order to process the stimuli correctly. The financial-specific prior knowledge required to solve the task was quite low here due to the realistic, real-life situation. It is only assumed that the problem solvers understand that the costs should be covered by the income. Financial competence essentially describes the individual ability to apply financial knowledge and skills to responsible decisions that improve, and should not impair, the financial situation of the individual (European Union & OECD, 2023).

The non-cognitive facets include, among others, attitudes towards money, interest and situational motivation as well as emotional experience during the solving process. Attitudes towards money and its value are considered to be largely fixed and thus more likely to be understood as a trait component, while motivation and emotional experience are interpreted as fluctuating over the problem-solving process and thus as a state variable. It can therefore be assumed that both motivation in the sense of expectation and utility components and emotional experience change in the course of complex problem solving.

6.3 Features of the Instrument

The instrument contains a series of items to assess different aspects of the financial decision-making process: (1) the evaluation of a financial decision by the identification (perception) of relevant financial information, (2) the analysis of this information (interpretation), (3) the decision making based on this information, and (4) the reflection by justifying the decision. These items also require knowledge and skills in core facets of financial competence that are subject to educational influence and interventions. Moreover, during the financial decision-making process, core aspects of motivational and volitional dispositions relevant for financial behaviour are assessed.

The cognitive dispositions of the scenario as described above were measured with several items sharing a common stimulus (a testlet); for the non-cognitive components such as current experience, motivation or interest, an integrated measurement by embedded experience sampling (EES) was used (Rausch et al., 2016). The stimulus asks test takers to make an informed decision on the purchase of a mobile phone given a specific problem situation, namely a broken mobile phone that needs to be replaced. The problem situation discloses key information on technical requirements, such as camera requirements, battery life, data volume usage in recent months and budgetary constraints through available financial resources via bank statements and personal preferences. The participant can choose between reading a text or watching a video to understand the problem situation.

After the introduction to the problem, the participants are asked to extract relevant financial information from the initial situation (perception). Then they must analyse and interpret the given information by (1) calculating the average data volume and (2) determining the available financial budget on the basis of bank statements. Furthermore, in order to measure affective dispositions, the participants were asked about their current experience (Schallberger, 2005) and motivation (FAM, Rheinberg et al., 2001) in relation to the problem using EES.

The participants then receive information about the mobile phones available for selection. This is based on conventional comparison portals by presenting various providers and the associated differences between the mobile phones. A total of four providers (Pear, Samsam, Hurawa and Xiaomai) are used. The information on the mobile phones itself is specified on the basis of price, battery life, storage capacity, and camera data (Fig. 6.1). Participants can then obtain information on various mobile phone contract options. Here too, different options (5GB, 10GB and 20GB) and the associated price conditions are presented based on conventional comparison portals (Fig. 6.2). The price conditions change depending on whether a mobile phone is purchased with or without a mobile phone contract (interpretation).

Finally, the participants are asked to make a decision based on the information given. The decision is structured by various questions. Firstly, the preference for one of the four presented mobile phones and the amount of needed data volume in the mobile phone contract (5 GB, 10 GB and 20 GB) must be stated. Next, a decision must be made as to whether a mobile phone should be purchased with or without a mobile phone contract. Finally, this decision must be justified regarding the following four criteria: (1) available budget, (2) data volume, (3) mobile phone requirements, and (4) total costs. Following the justification, the participants receive further information about the mobile phone purchase—similar to what is known from mobile phone contracts with conventional providers—which includes mobile phone insurance. Participants have to decide whether they want to take this additional insurance or not.

We used single- and multiple-choice items to assess the student's ability to perceive and analyze the situation, while we used constructed responses to evaluate

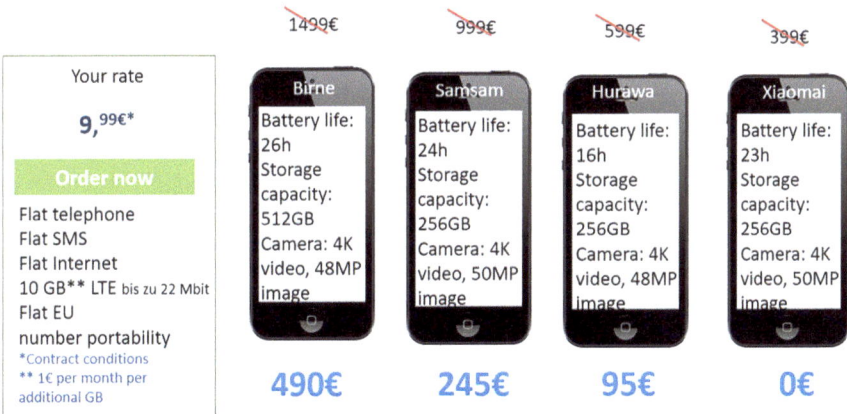

Fig. 6.1 Available mobile phones in the scenario

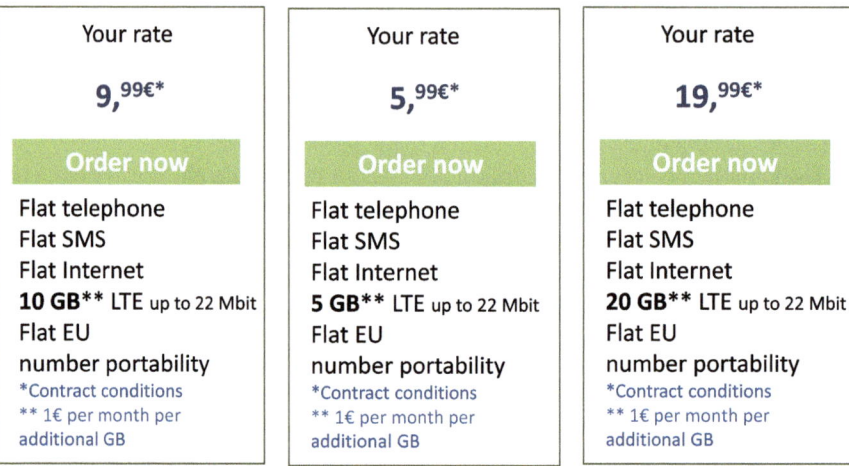

Fig. 6.2 Different rates available in the scenario

their interpretations and decision processes. The format of the constructed-response items varies: whereas some items require only a single word or number as an answer, other items require a more extended solution, especially when test takers are asked to rationalise or justify their decision. The focus on constructed-response items stems from the fact that in relatively ill-structured problems there are several adequate solutions that translate to responsible and informed financial decisions. Moreover, they are better suited to reveal individual decision-making processes than selected-response items. The areas of knowledge necessary to successfully solve the testlet span across knowledge of the contents and structure of bank statements, knowledge and understanding of monthly and overall costs of mobile phone contracts, and knowledge about budgetary constraints. Cognitive processes covered in the testlet include the identification, evaluation, and analysis of financial information contained in bank statements, phone offers, and contract descriptions. The context of the scenario is personal, i.e. a responsible and informed decision improves the financial situation of the individual.

The scenario was technically implemented using the open-source software Moodle, as a large number of vocational schools already use Moodle as a learning management system and learners are therefore familiar with its use. In order to provide orientation for the presentation of information and the associated requirements, participants are informed about the basic sequence of the learning unit. Buttons facilitate navigation in the learning environment.

6.4 Coding Scheme

The first step was to develop a coding scheme for the various items in the instrument. As part of the first question, the test subjects had to identify the relevant requirements for the cell phone from the text or video (perception). If they succeeded in recognizing the two requirements, they received two points; if they named them incorrectly or incompletely, they received partial points or no points. One point was awarded for correctly calculating or estimating the required data volume on the basis of a bar chart (interpretation). In the third question, the available budget had to be calculated (interpretation). A distinction can be made between the existing one-off budget and the monthly amount available. If these are calculated correctly with the help of the materials (bank statements, grandma's gift), two partial points are awarded here. It should be noted that due to the (deliberate) vagueness of the amounts in the bank statements and their change over the months, it was not necessary to specify an exact amount, but a range was defined that was set as correct.

In the subsequent purchase decision, the participant had to choose whether to bundle the mobile phone and contract together in one contract or to buy them separately, which cell phone to buy, and what data volume was required. Full points were awarded if a suitable cell phone was selected that met the previously defined requirements, was within the financial limits, and if the selected data volume met the requirements. It was also taken into account whether the mobile phone was purchased together with the contract or separately, with different conditions for different phone models. In the subsequent reflection, the test subjects' arguments for the decision were evaluated. The aim here was to determine whether the test takers (were able to) correctly justify the purchase they had made. A distinction was made as to whether a sensible reason was given for the selected function, data consumption, and costs. Finally, the respondents were scored on whether they had taken a mobile phone insurance in the final step and how they justified this. Due to large price differences and the rather expensive insurance, the insurance was scored as sensible for expensive phones with adequate justification, but for inexpensive mobile phones, the price-performance ratio was judged to be clearly unfavorable, so buying an insurance was not awarded any points here. Below is an overview of the tasks, the criteria for awarding points and the coding (Table 6.1).

6.5 Sample

The test instrument was administered on 1 day in July 2023 and on 2 days in September 2023 at five total classes in three vocational schools in Germany. A total of 134 test subjects (50 females, 55 males; 19 students with unknow gender) completed the test and were included in the data analysis. On average, the commercial-administrative apprentices were 20 years old ($M = 20.17$, $SD = 4.23$). Of the apprentices, 35% have a migration background. The test participants achieved average grades in German ($M = 2.72$, $SD = 0.91$) and math ($M = 3.07$, $SD = 1.28$), while 1 is the best and 6 the worst grade in the German grading system. The test was carried out either in the school's PC room or in another classroom that provided laptops for the participants. To ensure that the participants had sufficient time to complete the test, two lessons or 90 min were available for each round of the test

Table 6.1 Item coding scheme

Items	Problem solving step/Requirement	Coding
1: What requirements should your new mobile phone meet?	Perception: – Extract (relevant) information from the initial situation	2 mentions relevant [0,2]
2: How many gigabytes (GB) of data do you use on average in a month?	Interpretation (situation analysis): – Average calculation based on an overview of previous data consumption	Correct calculation [0,1]
3: How much money can you budget for the purchase of the mobile phone and the conclusion of the contract?	Interpretation (situation analysis): – Birthday gift (€360) + current account balance (€105) – Current contract costs (20€) + monthly surplus on average (20€)	– Purchase of the cell phone: (360;465] – Monthly for contract: (20;40]
4: Preferred purchase model (single or combined solution), which mobile phone would you like to purchase? Which contract option data volume?	Decision making (product decision): – Features + data consumption + budget + running costs	– Both combined and individual solution for cheapest model permitted [0,2]
5: Explain your decision in detail!	Decision making (justification): – Features + data consumption + budget + running costs	– Arguments for function, data consumption and costs [0,3]
6: Would you like to insure your new mobile phone?	Decision making (extension action plan): – Risk assessment	– Insurance costs for "correct" choice uneconomical, more appropriate for (too) expensive models [0,1]

administration. The test was scheduled to take around 45 min to complete, with a further 45 min planned for preparation and debriefing.

As described in Chap. 4, various variables influence financial behaviour and the underlying competence. Consequently, we controlled for gender and age at the personal level. As personal dispositions, which can be understood as trait variables of competence in our model, we additionally used attitude towards money (Barry, 2014) and the ability to delay gratification (Ray & Najman, 1986). Finally, we collected students' own assessment of their financial competence (Barry, 2014), while the already mentioned FAM can be understood as the assessment of non-cognitive state variables in our study. The initial results of the test are discussed below.

6.6 Preliminary Results

The items were calibrated under the Partial Credit Model (PCM; Masters, 1982). A Wright map is a graphical representation used in Item Response Theory (IRT), including models like the Partial Credit Model, that displays person abilities and item difficulties on the same logit scale. Both person ability and item difficulty are

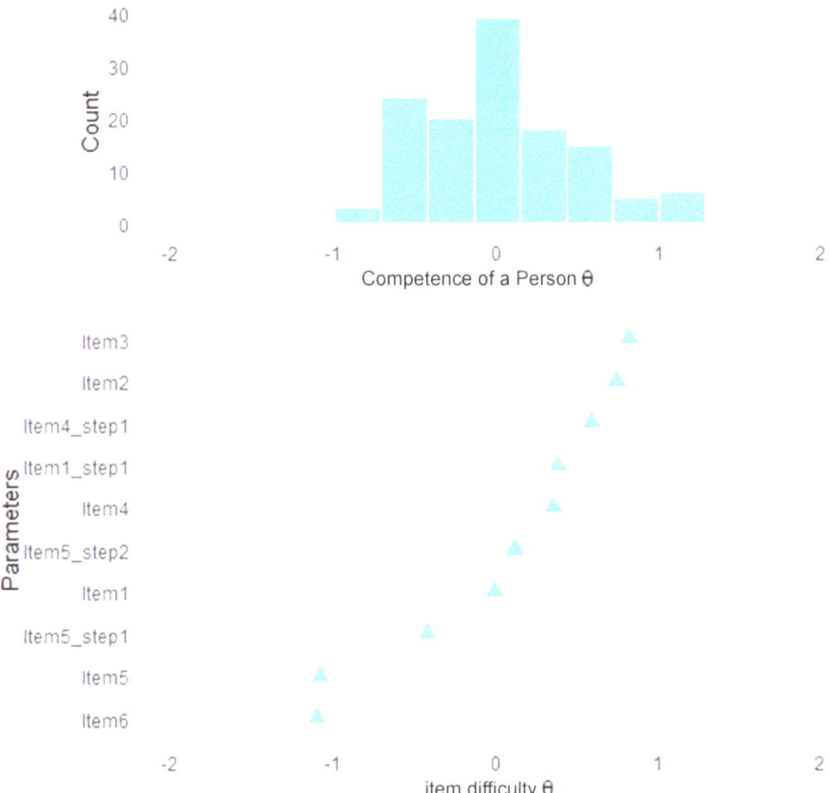

Fig. 6.3 Wright map—Plots of test takers' ability and item difficulty

typically represented by the Greek letter theta (θ), allowing for a direct comparison of how well items target the ability levels of the respondents (Fig. 6.3). As an example, item 1 has a difficulty of -0.014, which means that it measures particularly well and discriminates well among subjects with an ability of 0. The difficulty of the items ranged from -1.100 to 0.814, with a mean difficulty of -0.049. Excluding the items (Item 5 and Item 6) in which the students had to justify their decision, thus focusing directly on the behavioural items, yields a mean difficulty of 0.47, which indicates a relatively difficult test. But in total the item difficulty fits to the ability of the test takers very well (Fig. 6.3). All items exhibited a good model fit, indicated by item-specific mean deviations (*MD*) close to zero and root mean squared deviations (*RMSD*) smaller than 0.06 (Table 6.2).

Similarly, analyses regarding the person-fit of the testlet indicated no problems. Proportions of individuals outside the interval of $[-1.96, 1.96]$ were well below 5% (infit: 3.1%, outfit: 1.5%). Reliability of the testlet was 0.576 (EAP reliability is 0.488). With a strict interpretation of the criteria, Items 1 and 2 would have to be checked for local dependency (Table 6.3). Test information and standard error are, as expected (given the number of items), low and high respectively.

Table 6.2 Summary of item properties

Item	b, (SE)	Infit[a]	Outfit[a]	MD[b]	RMSD[b]
Item1	−0.014 (0.113)	1.002	1.011	−0.002	0.020
Item1 Step1	0.375 (0.211)	0.985	0.965	–	–
Item2	0.738 (0.194)	0.943	0.921	0.002	0.048
Item3	0.814 (0.196)	0.946	0.923	0.003	0.037
Item4	0.346 (0.115)	1.024	1.019	0.001	0.031
Item4 Step1	0.583 (0.232)	0.997	0.994	–	–
Item5	−1.080 (0.134)	1.105	1.152	0.021	0.033
Item5 Step1	−0.426 (0.220)	1.013	1.006	–	–
Item5 Step2	0.109 (0.238)	0.996	0.985	–	–
Item6	−1.100 (0.253)	1.052	1.089	0.005	0.048

Notes. [a]All values $p > 0.05$; [b]good fit indicated by $MD \sim 0.00$ and $RMSD < 0.06$; *SE* Standard Error; *MD* mean deviations; *RMSD* Root-mean-square deviation

Table 6.3 Q3-Matrix—local dependencies among Items

	Item1	Item2	Item3	Item4	Item5	Item6
Item1	—	0.290[a]	0.033	−0.198	−0.109	−0.068
Item2	0.290[a]	—	0.025	0.088	−0.013	−0.180
Item3	0.033	0.025	—	0.177	−0.034	0.150
Item4	−0.198	0.088	0.177	—	−0.176	0.014
Item5	−0.109	−0.013	−0.034	−0.176	—	0.000
Item6	−0.068	−0.180	0.150	0.014	0.000	—

Notes. Adjusted Q3-values (aQ3); Local dependencies in bold. [a]$p_{holm} < .05$

As mentioned above, the tasks embedded in the items also allow to assess the interaction of cognitive and noncognitive aspects of financial competence, since test takers were asked 1) about their emotional and motivational traits prior to starting the test, and 2) about their emotional and motivational states during the test. Trait-variables under investigation were (recent) grades in Mathematics and German, age, language spoken at home, as well as the attitude towards money (Barry, 2014) and delay of gratification (Ray & Najman, 1986). State-variables under investigation were emotional perception (Schallberger, 2005) and (current) motivation in (Rheinberg et al., 2001). Including these variables allowed us to investigate the relationship between the resulting person parameters THETA (the primary indicator of financial competence) and the individual noncognitive aspects. Therefore, we used a correlation analysis to investigate the relationship of cognitive, non-cognitive as well person parameters (Table 6.4).

When looking at the correlation matrix, it is immediately clear that financial ability (THETA) does not correlate significantly with personal characteristics such as linguistic background (native German or not), age, or mathematics and German grades. By contrast, there is a correlation between financial ability and the non-cognitive variables. Higher ability is associated with significantly less positive activation and a lower sense of valence. It should be noted that the negative correlation only exists with positive activation, while the degree of negative activation shows no

6 Development and Validation of a Test for Assessing Financial Competence...

Table 6.4 Correlation of item scores, ability parameter, non-cognitive variables and personal characteristics

	n	M	SD	1	2	3	4	5	6	7	8	9	10	11	12	13	14	15	16	17	18
1. Item1	130	1.01	0.88	–																	
2. Item2	130	0.34	0.48	**0.40**	–																
3. Item3	130	0.32	0.47	**0.20**	0.13	–															
4. Item4	125	0.79	0.88	0.12	**0.25**	**0.30**	–														
5. Item5	98	2.41	0.85	0.09	0.10	0.09	0.03	–													
6. Item6	92	0.76	0.43	-0.01	-0.15	0.15	0.05	0.01	–												
7. THETA	130	-0.02	0.99	**0.66**	**0.55**	**0.53**	**0.62**	**0.49**	**0.26**	–											
8. POS	126	5.35	2.29	**-0.22**	**-0.21**	-0.14	-0.15	**-0.21**	0.05	**-0.27**	–										
9. NEG	126	2.89	1.98	0.00	-0.06	0.04	0.13	0.04	0.00	0.05	-0.03	–									
10. VAL	126	6.49	2.38	**-0.21**	**-0.23**	-0.09	-0.10	-0.10	0.01	**-0.22**	**0.55**	-0.12	–								
11. INT	125	3.34	1.18	-0.07	0.12	0.09	0.02	0.00	0.09	0.06	**0.31**	0.05	**0.27**	–							
12. ERF	123	2.2	0.93	0.03	0.00	-0.04	-0.08	0.09	0.07	0.00	-0.16	**0.29**	**-0.18**	**-0.26**	–						
13. MIS	124	1.85	1.02	0.10	0.06	0.10	-0.01	0.13	0.03	0.12	-0.04	**0.30**	-0.11	0.15	**0.46**	–					
14. HER	125	3.23	1.25	-0.14	-0.01	0.11	-0.08	-0.18	-0.01	-0.09	**0.29**	0.09	**0.25**	**0.61**	0.01	**0.38**	–				
15. LANG	128	3.45	0.8	**0.20**	0.11	0.12	-0.07	-0.08	-0.04	0.08	0.02	0.01	-0.14	0.08	-0.14	-0.12	-0.11	–			
16. AGE	126	20.17	4.23	-0.14	-0.05	0.03	0.05	-0.20	0.13	-0.09	0.17	**0.21**	0.01	0.10	0.02	0.08	0.10	-0.01	–		
17. MATH	121	2.72	0.91	-0.05	-0.01	-0.05	0.05	-0.02	0.01	-0.02	-0.09	-0.10	-0.06	-0.06	0.07	0.01	**-0.19**	-0.12	-0.03	–	
18. GER	123	3.07	1.28	0.03	0.03	0.00	0.01	0.01	0.01	0.02	**-0.25**	0.05	-0.12	-0.06	0.02	0.11	-0.11	-0.05	-0.11	**0.34**	–

Note: Correlations in bold type $p < .05$
Abbreviations: *THETA* Ability to solve the problem; *POS* Positive emotions; *NEG* Negative emotions; *VAL* Values; *INT* Interest; *SUC* Expectations of success; *FAI* Expectations of failure; *HER* challenge; *LANG* spoken language at home; *AGE* age; *MATH* last grade in mathematics (1 best and 5 worst grade); *GER* last grade in German language (1 best and 5 worst grade)

correlation with ability. Furthermore, this negative correlation between the positive activation and the perceived value and the test results can be seen in all tasks except Item 5, while it also becomes significant in Items 1 and 2 (positive activation and value) and Item 5 (only positive activation). Interestingly, the native language only correlates significantly with Item 1, in which information had to be extracted from a text or a video. Students with a different native language performed significantly worse in German. In the other tasks, there are no significant differences with regard to different native languages.

6.7 Discussion and Limitations

The realistic scenario appears to be fundamentally suitable for assessing financial competence, even if it is difficult for the sample used. As the test detects the decision-making process, the results also provide a diagnostic perspective on where students have difficulties in the course of the decision-making process. It is noticeable, for example, that many test subjects already failed at the "information retrieval" stage. The test subjects had problems extracting the important information about the mobile phone requirements from the text or video. This suggests that reading comprehension and the processing of what has been read or heard is already deficient and requires further practice.

Particularly large problems were encountered when calculating the available budget and estimating the data requirements for the mobile phone contract, which could indicate a deficit in the underlying numeracy. The tasks only required simple numerical calculation steps.

The subsequent purchase decision was again difficult for the test subjects, which was made clear by the fact that combinations were often chosen that were not considered sensible. It should be noted that purchasing decisions are always subjective to a certain extent and an expression of individual preferences. This was accounted for in our scoring, with the result that several possible variants were awarded full points. However, some variants could not be financed or the phones did not cover the desired configurations, which are suboptimal decisions. By comparing the purchase decision with the first three items, it was also possible to determine whether the test subjects were able to extract the relevant information from the task and then, in a second step, to translate the information gained into a meaningful and justified action.

With regard to the interaction of cognitive and non-cognitive facets assumed in the model, it becomes clear that we also find these in our test, albeit more strongly for certain items than for others. It is particularly interesting that the positive emotional experience and valence during problem solving are negatively associated. This leads to the assumption that less confidence contributes to a better test solution, possibly because this results in greater effort or more attention during the solution process or different problem solving strategies.

Looking at the correlations between the personality factors and solving the test shows that only the native languages of the test participants are positively associated for the first item (the item in which information must be extracted from the text). Here, students with German as their native language have an advantage over students with a different native language. This is plausible in view of the fact that we are dealing with text comprehension. Other cognitive or non-cognitive dispositions like mathematic skills or interest in the problem do not appear to be related to the test solution.

Nevertheless, limitations should be discussed at this point. Finally, it cannot be ruled out that, due to the low-stakes nature of the test, the test subjects did not have sufficient motivation to complete the test in detail. The individual items in the scenario are not independent of each other; for example, if the test subjects did not manage to calculate the correct budget at the beginning, this also influenced the final decision, as the budget is an important basis for this. Another limitation emerges at this point. The individual items could have initiated relevant considerations for the decision in the first place, i.e. the test subjects might not have focused so strongly on the budget or the features of the mobile phone without the items. This also raises the question of the extent to which the financial competence measured here corresponds to the actual financial competence of the test subjects. Accordingly, when developing similar scenarios, it seems necessary to examine which parameters are actually taken into account in the decision-making process and to what extent these correspond to financially competent behaviour.

6.8 Conclusion

This study developed and validated a computer-based instrument to measure financial competence in the realistic scenario of purchasing a mobile phone under budget constraints—a context significantly contributing to youth indebtedness in Germany. Although the tool demonstrated basic reliability, many of the over 100 apprentices struggled to extract relevant information and perform simple calculations related to budgeting and data usage, indicating deficiencies in reading comprehension and numeracy skills.

An interesting finding was the negative correlation between financial competence and positive emotional activation during problem-solving, suggesting that lower confidence may lead to deeper engagement and better performance. Factors such as age, native language, and prior academic performance had minimal impact on the results.

These findings underscore the need to address both cognitive and non-cognitive aspects in financial education to enhance competence and reduce the risk of indebtedness associated with complex financial products like mobile phone contracts. Future research can look more closely at the connections between cognitive and motivational processes and at the process steps at which problem solvers primarily fail. This would also require the development of more complex scenarios on financial decision-making.

References

Artelt, C., Weinert, S., & Carstensen, C.H. (Eds.) (2013). Assessing competencies across the lifespan within the German National Educational Panel Study (NEPS) [Special Issue]. *Journal for Educational Research Online, 5*(2).

Barry, D. (2014). *Die Einstellung zu Geld bei jungen Erwachsenen: eine Grundlegung aus wirtschaftspädagogischer Sicht [Young adults' attitudes towards money: a foundation from a business and economic education perspective]*. Springer.

European Union & OECD. (2023). *Financial competence framework for children and youth in the European Union*. Publication Office of the European Union.

Federal Statistical Office of Germany [Statistisches Bundesamt] (2020). *Statistik zur Überschuldung privater Personen* 2019. *[Overindebtedness statistics for private individuals]*. Fachserie 15, Reihe 5. Statistisches Bundesamt.

Klieme, E., & Leutner, D. (2006). Kompetenzmodelle zur Erfassung individueller Lernergebnisse und zur Bilanzierung von Bildungsprozessen. Beschreibung eines neu eingerichteten Schwerpunktprogramms der DFG [Competence models for recording individual learning outcomes and assessing educational processes. Description of a newly established priority programme of the German Research Foundation (DFG)]. *Zeitschrift für Pädagogik, 52*(6), 876–903. https://doi.org/10.25656/01:4493

Masters, G. N. (1982). A Rasch model for partial credit scoring. *Psychometrika, 47*, 149–174. https://doi.org/10.1007/BF02296272

Ray, J. J., & Najman, J. M. (1986). The generalizability of deferment of gratification. *The Journal of Social Psychology, 126*(1), 117–119. https://doi.org/10.1080/00224545.1986.9713578

Rausch, A., Seifried, J., Wuttke, E., Kögler, K., & Brandt, S. (2016). Reliability and validity of a computer-based assessment of cognitive and non-cognitive facets of problem-solving competence in the business domain. *Empirical Research in Vocational Education and Training, 8*, 1–23. https://doi.org/10.1186/s40461-016-0035-y

Rheinberg, F., Vollmeyer, R., & Burns, B. D. (2001). FAM: Ein Fragebogen zur Erfassung aktueller Motivation in Lern-und Leistungssituationen (Langversion, 2001) [FAM: A questionnaire for assessing current motivation in learning and performance situations]. *Diagnostica, 2*(2), 57–66. https://doi.org/10.1026/0012-1924.47.2.57

Schallberger, U. (2005). Kurzskalen zur Erfassung der Positiven Aktivierung, Negativen Aktivierung und Valenz in Experience Sampling Studien (PANAVA-KS) [Short scales for measuring positive activation, negative activation and valence in experience sampling studies (PANAVA-KS)]. In *Forschungsberichte aus dem Projekt "Qualität des Erlebens in Arbeit und Freizeit"* (Vol. Nr. 6). Fachrichtung Angewandte Psychologie des Psychologischen Instituts der Universität Zürich.

Weinert, F.E. (2001). Concept of competence: A conceptual clarification. In D. S. Rychen & L. H. Salganik (Eds.), Defining and selecting key competences (pp. 4565). Hogrefe and Huber Publishers.

Open Access This chapter is licensed under the terms of the Creative Commons Attribution 4.0 International License (http://creativecommons.org/licenses/by/4.0/), which permits use, sharing, adaptation, distribution and reproduction in any medium or format, as long as you give appropriate credit to the original author(s) and the source, provide a link to the Creative Commons license and indicate if changes were made.

The images or other third party material in this chapter are included in the chapter's Creative Commons license, unless indicated otherwise in a credit line to the material. If material is not included in the chapter's Creative Commons license and your intended use is not permitted by statutory regulation or exceeds the permitted use, you will need to obtain permission directly from the copyright holder.

Chapter 7
Concluding Remarks on the Work of the Financial Literacy Network AFin

Manuel Förster ⓘ, Mandy Hommel ⓘ, Carmela Aprea ⓘ, Bärbel Fürstenau ⓘ, Roland Happ ⓘ, and Eveline Wuttke ⓘ

Abstract The core achievements and insights gained from the AFin network ("Action-based Financial Literacy – Conceptualization, Assessment and Validation"), a research initiative funded by the German Research Foundation (DFG), are

---

The chapters of this SpringerBrief represent the work and the results of the AFin ("Action-based Financial Literacy – Conceptualization, Assessment and Validation") network funded by the German Research Foundation (DFG, FO 1039/2-1, project number: 460770732). In this concluding chapter, we summarise the results in terms of the network's objectives and provide an outlook on possible further research to advance financial education.

M. Förster (✉)
Business and Economic Education, School of Social Sciences and Technology,
Technical University of Munich, Munich, Germany
e-mail: manuel.foerster@tum.de

M. Hommel
Vocational Education, Faculty of Electrical Engineering, Media and Computer Science,
OTH Amberg-Weiden, Amberg and Weiden, Germany
e-mail: m.hommel@oth-aw.de

C. Aprea
Business and Economic Education – Instructional Systems Design and Evaluation &
Mannheim Institute for Financial Education (MIFE), University of Mannheim,
Mannheim, Germany
e-mail: carmela.aprea@uni-mannheim.de

B. Fürstenau
Business Education and Management Training, Faculty of Business and Economics,
TU Dresden, Dresden, Germany
e-mail: baerbel.fuerstenau@tu-dresden.de

R. Happ
Business Education and Management Training, Leipzig University, Leipzig, Germany
e-mail: happ@wifa.uni-leipzig.de

E. Wuttke
Economics and Business Education, Goethe University Frankfurt, Frankfurt, Germany
e-mail: wuttke@em.uni-frankfurt.de

© The Author(s) 2026
M. Förster, M. Hommel (eds.), *Conceptualisation and Measurement of Financial Competence*, SpringerBriefs in Education,
https://doi.org/10.1007/978-3-031-95690-4_7

summarized in this concluding chapter. The chapter revisits the network's three key objectives: (1) the development of a holistic financial competence model, (2) the systematisation of existing assessment instruments, and (3) the creation of a holistic approach to assessing financial literacy. The AFin network addressed the fragmentation in financial literacy research by analysing and aligning inconsistent terminology, diverse frameworks, and assessment practices. Through systematic literature review and conceptual modelling, the project identified the necessity of integrating cognitive and non-cognitive dimensions, as well as financial behaviour, into competence models.

The chapter outlines how existing frameworks and test instruments often lack theoretical grounding or holistic coverage, and presents a newly developed, generic process model of financial competence. This model allows for flexibility while reflecting the complexity of real-world financial decision-making. A scenario-based prototype assessment tool is also introduced to respond to current measurement limitations. The chapter concludes with a call for further interdisciplinary research, stressing the importance of methodological innovations to enhance ecological validity and ensure the relevance of assessments in real-life contexts. Ultimately, the chapter highlights the significance of research in personal finance in shaping future financial education, policy, and research.

Keywords Financial literacy · Financial competence · Financial education

7.1 First Objective: Development of a Holistic Competence Model

According to the objectives of the AFin network (Chap. 1), Chaps. 2, 3, and 4 provide the foundation for the first objective: the development of a holistic competence model for financial literacy. Therefore, we first analysed, systematised, and thereby untangled the terminology, in particular concepts and definitions that have been used in research on financial literacy and financial competence. Second, we analysed the existing frameworks for financial literacy.

7.1.1 Terminology in the Context of Financial Literacy: Main Results of Chap. 2

The central goal and the basis for further work and a holistic competence model was the clarification and systematisation of terms, definitions, and constructs discussed in the context of financial literacy. Therefore, the chapter took up definitions, terms, and the description of the underlying constructs from studies focusing on financial literacy and/or financial competence. Furthermore, we looked at the content areas included in each case and analysed whether only personal finances or society-related aspects are taken into account. This was intended to systematically detect which constructs are behind which terms and definitions, how broad the respective authors considered content areas as an expression of financial literacy, and which decisions (personal, societal) are included in each case. We also took a first look at whether the constructs include financial behaviour. Ultimately, the aim was to create a framework in which existing and future studies can be located and which forms a basis for comparing different studies and deriving evidence-based support measures.

Despite the striking heterogeneity, two central results can be identified:

- A categorisation system for further classification of contributions to the topic.
- A systematisation of contributions that illustrates the diversity and inconsistency of the terms, constructs, and research approaches that are addressed.

Terminology in the context of financial literacy research is heterogeneous; however, all definitions have one common core, namely financial knowledge (see Chap. 2 of this SpringerBrief). But knowledge is only one important component, which must be activated in the application context in order to lead to effective decision-making. Although studies often include decision-making and/or self-assessments, financial behaviour as performance is seldom taken into account and/or assessed. Few contributions use complex scenarios or situational judgements to measure financial literacy behaviourally (see Chap. 2).

The heterogeneity of terms and constructs behind the terms remains striking. These differences continue in the other categories considered, such as the differences in the consideration of financial behaviour/performance, cognitive, emotional, or volitional components of financial literacy. Subsequently, the differences persist in the content scope, content considered, and the way in which the underlying construct is operationalised in measurements. Not all approaches fulfil the requirements for the development of a holistic competence model. For example, non-cognitive components are not present in many approaches and society-related components and competencies are quite often neglected. Only knowledge can be identified as a common core within competence models.

7.1.2 Financial Literacy Frameworks: Main Results of Chap. 3

Chapter 3 provides a structured overview and description of existing financial literacy frameworks, which serve as key tools for conceptualising financial education and coordinating activities in policy and practice. The frameworks are analysed in terms of their developers, target groups, publication context, conceptual foundations, methodological approaches, and core components. In addition, the strengths and weaknesses of the frameworks are addressed.

The analysis highlights the diversity of financial literacy frameworks, developed by both academic and policy institutions, with no universally-accepted model. Their conceptual foundations vary significantly, with financial competence emerging as a dominant term after 2013, while financial capability remains inconsistently defined. Many frameworks lack a strong theoretical basis, relying on literature reviews rather than empirical validation, limiting their reliability and applicability. Furthermore, framework components, such as content areas and psychological dispositions, are often loosely structured and inconsistently related, making integration into a holistic model difficult.

A key challenge is the lack of a holistic approach that connects systemic and individual perspectives, cognitive and non-cognitive dimensions, and financial behaviour. Most frameworks only cover parts of these aspects. To address these gaps, a holistic competence model for financial literacy ideally should:

- Integrate both systemic and individual perspectives, as well as cognitive and non-cognitive dimensions.
- Be based on a clear and coherent conceptual and theoretical foundation.
- Undergo systematic empirical validation.
- Follow a clear structure with defined components and qualification levels.
- Include relevant topics like digitalisation, sustainability, and social skills.
- Take an interdisciplinary approach incorporating economic, psychological, and sociological perspectives.

These findings support the project's goal of developing a financial literacy competence model that is both theoretically grounded and practically useful.

7.1.3 Towards a Model of Financial Competence: Main Results of Chap. 4

The aim of Chap. 4 was to develop a generic yet holistic process model for the financial competence of individuals, to clarify the basis for the model's development, and to illustrate the model using three examples of financial decision-making. The model is generic to maintain adaptability for specific financial environments and situations. It is holistic, as it includes different state and trait variables of the person, but also the environment, different contexts, and the interaction of all these variables. It is a process model since, firstly, it maintains that the person interacts with the environment, which can be seen as a process in time including interactions between the person and the environment and, secondly, it conceptualises decision-making processes as comprised of several phases (such as perception, interpretation, etc.) taking place within the individual.

The model is strongly based on defining characteristics of financial competence, and it complements existing content and level models. It helps users—be they scientists, education policy makers, or teachers—to be aware of the complexity of factors and their interaction relevant in financial decision-making. Dependent on the purpose of use, the model can be specified and refined. For example, if researchers or educators are interested in just cognition, only the cognitive factors can be regarded. If researchers or educators are interested in the interaction of emotion and cognition, they can specifically assess or foster this interaction. If researchers or educators are interested in measuring or fostering financial competence holistically—just as we are—all components and their respective specifications should be regarded. The model can be used as a basis for fostering financial competence and for aligning learning, instruction, and assessment.

7.2 Second Objective: Systematisation of Existing Test Instruments

By aligning the conceptual insights from Chaps. 1 to 4 with real-world assessment tools, Chap. 5 addresses the second key objective of the AFin network: to systematise and categorise the various instruments used to measure financial literacy and related constructs. The chapter begins by examining a broad range of assessment tools, noting how their underlying theoretical frameworks often diverge from the holistic perspective advocated earlier. It becomes clear that while current instruments tend to focus on factual knowledge, cognitive skills, and non-cognitive dispositions, these constructs are typically measured in isolation. This echoes Chaps. 2 and 3, which highlight the shortcomings of narrowly defined approaches to financial competence.

Chapter 5 offers a structured overview of test instruments, including their methodological foundations and target groups. This mapping reveals both the diversity of existing tools and the need for measurement approaches that simultaneously capture non-cognitive factors alongside cognitive components—factors emphasised in the holistic process model introduced in Chap. 4. By consolidating this information, the chapter provides researchers with a valuable orientation for navigating the array of available cognitive and non-cognitive measures. Moreover, it shows that most instruments are primarily product-oriented, focusing on results or particular states rather than the dynamic process by which individuals build and apply financial competencies over time.

Examining existing instruments' limitations, Chap. 5 paves the way for refining existing or developing new assessments that better reflect the integrative framework of knowledge, behaviour, and socio-emotional aspects. Adopting measurement formats that capture the process-oriented nature of financial decision-making could support the alignment of research, policy, and practice. Ultimately, the systematisation presented here underscores the crucial next step: moving away from isolated measures toward a comprehensive, process-oriented approach that resonates with real-world financial challenges. In this way, stakeholders are better positioned to enhance financial competence effectively and sustainably.

7.3 Third Objective: Development of an Approach for Alternative and Holistic Assessment

Building on the systematisation of existing assessment tools in Chaps. 5, and 6 addresses the third main objective of the AFin network: the development of an initial draft for an alternative and holistic approach to measuring financial competence. Based on the stated limitations of conventional assessments, which often rely on standardised, decontextualised items and focus predominantly on cognitive or product-oriented measures, Chap. 6 emphasises the need to capture not only the knowledge dimension of financial competence, but also behavioural, emotional, and social facets in authentic decision-making contexts.

Central to this new approach is the integration of process-oriented assessment formats that recognise that financial competence develops in the real world through constant interactions with social and environmental factors. This chapter presents a scenario-based task designed to test individuals' ability to apply their knowledge in complex situations. By having learners work in complex contexts, the interplay of motivation, emotions, and cognitive processes should be analysed in specific contexts to gain a more differentiated picture of financial competence.

Moreover, Chap. 6 highlights how a holistic assessment framework can inform targeted interventions. For instance, feedback loops within scenario-based exercises help educators identify specific areas that might be overlooked in conventional measures. In doing so, the chapter offers a roadmap for aligning instructional methods and educational objectives with a broader, more integrative view of financial literacy.

7.4 Prospects for Possible Further Research and Significance of this Volume for Advancing Financial Education and Research

In an era where personal finance intersects with global economic trends, this volume provides a timely, evidence-based perspective on how financial competence can be conceptualised, measured, and fostered. Moving beyond fragmented definitions and narrowly focused assessments, it highlights the importance of integrating cognitive, emotional, behavioural, and societal dimensions to reflect the complexity of real-world financial decisions.

A key contribution lies in the systematic analysis of diverse theoretical frameworks and terminologies. By clarifying and aligning various perspectives, the volume offers a coherent foundation for educators, researchers, and policymakers who have grappled with the heterogeneity of financial literacy concepts. This unified basis serves as a starting point for further empirical studies and more targeted pedagogical interventions.

Another notable aspect is the emphasis on alternative assessment methods. Traditional tests in Financial Education Research often concentrate on isolated knowledge checks, neglecting how contextual factors—such as non-cognitive dispositions or one's personal situation—affect financial behaviour. The volume's scenario-based and interactive approaches encourage deeper engagement and reveal a more accurate picture of an individual's financial competence. These methods also help identify areas where specific support measures may be most effective.

In addition, the volume bridges the gap between theory and practice by combining existing research, models, and survey instruments in a structured way and providing a first approach to a practical assessment tool. This volume is intended to be both scientifically sound and a guide for practical implementation and policy decisions. Overall, the book makes a substantive contribution to advancing financial education by championing an integrative, holistic model. By balancing conceptual rigour with practical strategies, it offers valuable insights for those seeking to develop inclusive and effective financial education in an ever-evolving financial landscape. In the future, research must aim to operationalise complex competence models by developing and validating new holistic competence test procedures. These must be able to capture the various components of the competence models as simultaneously as possible and take into account the complexity of financial decisions in reality as much as possible. These demanding requirements make validation in the form of a systematic process of collecting empirical evidence for the interpretation and use of the test results more difficult. A large number of complex procedures are required here, which enable not only an assessment of the quality of the test results but also the quality of the problem-solving process. This requires procedures such as multidimensional Rasch models to assess the product of the test, but also longitudinal methods such as think-aloud studies or eye-tracking to better assess the progress of financial problem solving. Finally, it is also important that the instruments developed allow conclusions to be drawn about real-life behaviour to a high degree, which can be improved by involving experts from the field in the development process and designing scenarios to be as realistic and sufficiently complex as possible. At the same time, it is also necessary to deal with the challenge that complex decision-making situations, which are presented with a large number of texts or other stimuli, take longer to process. This usually means that fewer tasks within a content area are solved in the same period of time compared to a pure knowledge test, so that we have to weigh up (ecological) validity and high reliability. Considering the above, it is a challenge to measure financial competence in this holistic way and thus to contribute to targeted and situation-appropriate financial education. Therefore, it requires joint research efforts to implement such an intention, but those research efforts can be richly rewarded with deeper understanding of interactions between the diverse factors that influence real-life financial decision-making and behaviour.

Open Access This chapter is licensed under the terms of the Creative Commons Attribution 4.0 International License (http://creativecommons.org/licenses/by/4.0/), which permits use, sharing, adaptation, distribution and reproduction in any medium or format, as long as you give appropriate credit to the original author(s) and the source, provide a link to the Creative Commons license and indicate if changes were made.

The images or other third party material in this chapter are included in the chapter's Creative Commons license, unless indicated otherwise in a credit line to the material. If material is not included in the chapter's Creative Commons license and your intended use is not permitted by statutory regulation or exceeds the permitted use, you will need to obtain permission directly from the copyright holder.

References

Andersen, S., Harrison, G. W., Lau, M. I., & Rutström, E. E. (2008). Eliciting risk and time preferences. *Econometrica, 76*(3), 583–618. https://doi.org/10.1111/j.1468-0262.2008.00848.x

Aprea, C., & Wuttke, E. (2016). Financial literacy of adolescents and young adults: Setting the course for a competence-oriented assessment instrument. In C. Aprea et al. (Eds.), *International handbook of financial literacy* (pp. 397–414). Springer. https://doi.org/10.1007/978-981-10-0360-8_27

Archuleta, K. L., Dale, A., & Spann, S. M. (2013). College students and financial distress: Exploring debt, financial satisfaction, and financial anxiety. *Journal of Financial Counseling and Planning, 24*(2), 50–62.

Barry, D. (2014). *Die Einstellung zu Geld bei jungen Erwachsenen: eine Grundlegung aus wirtschaftspädagogischer Sicht [Young adults' attitudes towards money: a foundation from a business and economic education perspective]*. Springer.

Beutler, I. F., & Gudmunson, C. G. (2012). New adolescent money attitude scales: Entitlement and conscientiousness. *Journal of Financial Counseling and Planning, 23*(2), 14.

Bocchialini, E., & Ronchini, B. (2019). A pilot study assessing attitudes toward finance among Italian business students. *International Journal of Business and Management, 14*(10), 44–60. https://doi.org/10.5539/ijbm.v14n10p44

Bocchialini, E., Ronchini, B., & Torti, F. (2022). Predicting Students' Financial Knowledge from Attitude towards Finance. *International Journal of Business and Management, 17*(6), 13–33. https://doi.org/10.5539/ijbm.v17n6p13

Chen, H., & Volpe, R. (1998). An analysis of personal financial literacy among college students. *Financial Services Review, 7*(2), 107–128. https://doi.org/10.1016/s1057-0810(99)80006-7

Consumer Financial Protection Bureau. (2017). *CFPB financial well-being scale: scale development technical report*. https://files.consumerfinance.gov/f/documents/201705_cfpb_financial-well-being-scale-technical-report.pdf

Costa, P. T., & McCrae, R. R. (1992). *Revised NEO Personality Inventory (NEO-PI-R) and NEO Five-Factor Inventory (NEO-FFI): professional manual*. Psychological Assessment Resources.

CEE. (2013). *National standards for financial literacy*. Council for Economic Education. ISBN: 978-1-56183-734-2. https://www.councilforeconed.org/wp-content/uploads/2013/02/national-standards-for-financial-literacy.pdf

Federal Statistical Office of Germany [Statistisches Bundesamt] (2020). *Statistik zur Überschuldung privater Personen* 2019. *[Overindebtedness statistics for private individuals]*. Fachserie 15, Reihe 5. Statistisches Bundesamt.

Fernandes, D., Lynch, J. G., & Netemeyer, R. G. (2014). Financial literacy, financial education, and downstream financial behaviors. *Management Science, 60*(8), 1861–1883. https://doi.org/10.1287/mnsc.2013.1849

Förster, M., Happ, R., & Maur, A. (2018). The Relationship among gender, interest in financial topics and understanding of personal finance. *Empirische Pädagogik, 32*(3/4), 292–308.

Förster, M., Happ, R., & Molerov, D. (2017). Using the U.S. test of financial literacy in Germany—adaptation and validation. *The Journal of Economic Education, 48*(2), 123–135. https://doi.org/10.1080/00220485.2017.1285737

Furnham, A. F. (1984). Many sides of the coin: The psychology of money usage. *Personality and Individual Differences, 5*(5), 501–509. https://doi.org/10.1016/0191-8869(84)90025-4

Grohs-Müller, S., & Greimel-Fuhrmann, B. (2018). Students' money attitudes and financial behaviour: A study on the relationship between two components of financial literacy. *Empirische Pädagogik, 32*(3–4), 369–386.

Harrison, G. W., Lau, M. I., Rutström, E. E., & Sullivan, M. B. (2005). Eliciting risk and time preferences using field experiments: Some methodological issues. In G. W. Harrison, J. Carpenter, & J. A. List (Eds.), *Field experiments in economics (Research in experimental economics, Vol. 10)* (pp. 125–218). Emerald Group Publishing Limited. https://doi.org/10.1016/S0193-2306(04)10005-7

Hastings, J., & Mitchell, O. S. (2020). How financial literacy and impatience shape retirement wealth and investment behaviors. *Journal of Pension Economics & Finance, 19*(1), 1–20. https://doi.org/10.1017/S1474747218000227

Heo, W., Cho, S., & Lee, P. (2020). APR financial stress scale: Development and validation of a multidimensional measurement. *Journal of Financial Therapy, 11*(1), 2. https://doi.org/10.4148/1944-9771.1216

Hermansson, C., & Jonsson, S. (2021). The impact of financial literacy and financial interest on risk tolerance. *Journal of Behavioral and Experimental Finance, 29*, 100450. https://doi.org/10.1016/j.jbef.2020.100450

Hira, T. K., & Mugenda, O. M. (1998). Predictors of financial satisfaction: Differences between retirees and non-retirees. *Financial Counseling and Planning, 9*(2), 75–83.

John, O. P., & Srivastava, S. (1999). The Big Five Trait taxonomy: History, measurement, and theoretical perspectives. In L. A. Pervin & O. P. John (Eds.), *Handbook of personality: Theory and research* (2nd ed., pp. 102–138). Guilford Press.

Klieme, E., & Leutner, D. (2006). Kompetenzmodelle zur Erfassung individueller Lernergebnisse und zur Bilanzierung von Bildungsprozessen. Beschreibung eines neu eingerichteten Schwerpunktprogramms der DFG [Competence models for recording individual learning outcomes and assessing educational processes. Description of a newly established priority programme of the German Research Foundation (DFG)]. *Zeitschrift für Pädagogik, 52*(6), 876–903. https://doi.org/10.25656/01:4493

Knoll, M. A., & Houts, C. R. (2012). The financial knowledge scale: An application of item response theory to the assessment of financial literacy. *Journal of Consumer Affairs, 46*, 381–410. https://doi.org/10.1111/j.1745-6606.2012.01241.x

Kraitzek, A., & Förster, M. (2024). *Adaptation and validation of the U.S. test of financial knowledge for use in Germany*. Poster Presentation at the Annual Conference of the American Educational Research Association (AERA) 2024. https://doi.org/10.3102/IP.24.2104907

Kraitzek, A., Förster, M., & Walstad, W. B. (2022). Comparison of financial education and knowledge in the United States and Germany: Curriculum and assessment. *Research in Comparative and International Education, 17*(2), 153–173. https://doi.org/10.1177/17454999221081333

Letkiewicz, J. C., & Fox, J. J. (2014). Conscientiousness, financial literacy, and asset accumulation of young adults. *Journal of Consumer Affairs, 48*(2), 274–300. https://doi.org/10.1111/joca.12040

Lown, J. M. (2011). Development and validation of a financial self-efficacy scale. *Journal of Financial Counseling and Planning, 22*(2), 54. https://ssrn.com/abstract=2006665

Lusardi, A. (2008). *Financial Literacy: An Essential Tool for Informed Consumer Choice?* NBER Working Paper, No. 14084. https://doi.org/10.3386/w14084

Lusardi, A., & Mitchell, O. S. (2009). *How ordinary consumers make complex economic decisions: financial literacy and retirement readiness*. Intertemporal Choice & Growth eJournal. https://www.nber.org/papers/w15350

Lusardi, A., & Mitchell, O. S. (2011). Financial literacy around the world: an overview. *Journal of Pension Economics and Finance, 10*, 497–508. https://doi.org/10.1017/S1474747211000448

Mahdzan, N. S., & Tabiani, S. (2013). The impact of financial literacy on individual saving: An exploratory study in the Malaysian context. *Transformations in Business & Economics, 12*(1), 41–55.

Mandell, L. (2008). *The financial literacy of young American adults: Results of the 2008 National Jump $tart Coalition survey of high school seniors and college students*.

Mandell, L., & Schmid-Klein, L. (2007). Motivation and financial literacy. *Financial services review, 16*(2), 105.

Morris, T., Maillet, S., & Koffi, V. (2022). Financial knowledge, financial confidence and learning capacity on financial behavior: a Canadian study. *Cogent Social Sciences, 8*(1), 1996919. https://doi.org/10.1080/23311886.2021.1996919

Muck, P. M. (2013). Entwicklung von Situational Judgment Tests: Konzeptionelle Überlegungen und empirische Befunde [Development of Situational Judgment Tests: Conceptual considerations and empirical findings]. *Zeitschrift für Arbeits- und Organisationspsychologie, 57*(4), 185–205. https://doi.org/10.1026/0932-4089/a000125

Mudzingiri, C., Muteba Mwamba, J. W., & Keyser, J. N. (2018). Financial behavior, confidence, risk preferences and financial literacy of university students. *Cogent Economics & Finance, 6*(1). https://doi.org/10.1080/23322039.2018.1512366

OECD. (2013). *PISA 2012 assessment and analytical framework: Mathematics, reading, science, problem solving and financial literacy*. PISA,OECD Publishing. https://doi.org/10.1787/9789264190511-en

OECD. (2014). *PISA 2012 results: students and money (Volume VI): Financial literacy skills for the 21st Century*. PISA, OECD Publishing. https://doi.org/10.1787/9789264208094-en

OECD/INFE (2023). *International survey of adult financial literacy*. Organisation for Economic Co-operation and Development (OECD).

Palameta, B., Nguyen, C., Shek-wai Hui, T., & Gyarmati, D. (2016). *The link between financial confidence and financial outcomes among working-aged Canadians*. Report for the Financial Consumer Agency of Canada. Social Research and Demonstration Corporation SRDC. https://srdc.org/wpcontent/uploads/2022/07/fcac-full-report-on-financial-confidence-en.pdf

Prawitz, A. D., Garman, E. T., Sorhaindo, B., O'Neill, B., Kim, J., & Drentea, P. (2006). In charge financial distress/financial well-being scale: Development, administration, and score interpretation. *Journal of Financial Counseling and Planning, 17*(1), 34–50.

Prevett, P. S., Pampaka, M., Farnsworth, V. L., Kalambouka, A., & Shi, X. (2020). A situated learning approach to measuring financial literacy self-efficacy of youth. *Journal of Financial Counseling and Planning*. https://doi.org/10.1891/JFCP-18-00038

Ray, J. J., & Najman, J. M. (1986). The generalizability of deferment of gratification. *The Journal of Social Psychology, 126*(1), 117–119. https://doi.org/10.1080/00224545.1986.9713578

Rheinberg, F., Vollmeyer, R., & Burns, B. D. (2001). FAM: Ein Fragebogen zur Erfassung aktueller Motivation in Lern-und Leistungssituationen (Langversion, 2001) [FAM: A questionnaire for assessing current motivation in learning and performance situations]. *Diagnostica, 2*(2), 57–66. https://doi.org/10.1026/0012-1924.47.2.57

Robb, C. A., & Woodyard, A. S. (2011). Financial knowledge and best practice behavior. *Journal of Financial Counseling and Planning, 22*(1), 60–70.

Schallberger, U. (2005). Kurzskalen zur Erfassung der Positiven Aktivierung, Negativen Aktivierung und Valenz in Experience Sampling Studien (PANAVA-KS) [Short scales for measuring positive activation, negative activation and valence in experience sampling studies (PANAVA-KS)]. In *Forschungsberichte aus dem Projekt "Qualität des Erlebens in Arbeit und Freizeit"* (Vol. Nr. 6). Fachrichtung Angewandte Psychologie des Psychologischen Instituts der Universität Zürich.

Schwarzer, R., & Jerusalem, M. (1995). Generalized Self-Efficacy Scale. In J. Weinman, S. Wright, & M. Johnston (Eds.), *Measures in Health Psychology: A User's Portfolio. Causal and Control Beliefs* (pp. 35–37). NFER-NELSON.

Selye, H. (1956). *The stress of life*. McGraw-Hill.

Shapiro, G. K., & Burchell, B. J. (2012). Measuring financial anxiety. *Journal of Neuroscience, Psychology, and Economics, 5*(2), 92–103. https://doi.org/10.1037/a0027647

Siegfried, C., & Wuttke, E. (2021). What influences the financial literacy of young adults? A combined analysis of socio-demographic characteristics and delay of gratification. *Frontiers in Psychology, 12*, 663254. https://doi.org/10.3389/fpsyg.2021.663254

Stolper, O., & Walter, A. (2017). Financial literacy, financial advice, and financial behavior. *Journal of Business Economics, 87*, 581–643. https://doi.org/10.1007/s11573-017-0853-9

Tang, T. L.-P. (1992). The meaning of money revisited. *Journal of Organizational Behavior, 13*(2), 197–202. https://doi.org/10.1002/job.4030130209

Tang, T. L.-P. (1995). The development of a short money ethic scale: Attitudes toward money and pay satisfaction revisited. *Personality and Individual Differences, 19*(6), 809–816. https://doi.org/10.1016/s0191-8869(95)00133-6

VandenBos, G. R. (Ed.). (2015). *APA dictionary of psychology (2nd ed.)*. American Psychological Association. https://doi.org/10.1037/14646-000

van Rooij, M., Lusardi, A., & Alessie, R. (2012). Financial Literacy, Retirement Planning and Household Wealth. *The Economic Journal, 122*(560), 449–478. https://doi.org/10.1111/j.1468-0297.2012.02501.x

Walstad, W. B., & Rebeck, K. (2016a). *Basic finance test: Examiner's manual*. Council for Economic Education.

Walstad, W. B., & Rebeck, K. (2016b). *Test of financial knowledge: Examiner's manual*. Council for Economic Education.

Walstad, W. B., & Rebeck, K. (2016c). *Test of financial literacy: Examiner's manual*. Council for Economic Education.

Walstad, W. B., & Rebeck, K. (2017). The test of financial literacy: Development and measurement characteristics. *The Journal of Economic Education, 48*, 113–122. https://doi.org/10.1080/00220485.2017.1285739

Walstad, W. B., & Rebeck, K. (2018). The measurement properties of the basic finance test for children and the test of financial knowledge for youth. *Empirische Pädagogik, 32*(3/4), 248–248.

Weber, E. U., Blais, A. R., & Betz, N. E. (2002). A domain-specific risk-attitude scale: Measuring risk perceptions and risk behaviors. *Journal of Behavioral Decision Making, 15*(4), 263–290. https://doi.org/10.1002/bdm.414

Wuttke, E., & Aprea, C. (2018). A situational judgement approach for measuring young adults 'financial literacy. *Empirische Pädagogik, 32*(3/4), 272–292.

Xue, R., Gepp, A., O'Neill, T. J., Stern, S., & Vanstone, B. J. (2019). Financial literacy amongst elderly Australians. *Accounting & Finance, 59*, 887–918. https://doi.org/10.1111/acfi.12362

Xue, R., Gepp, A., O'Neill, T. J., Stern, S., & Vanstone, B. J. (2021). Financial literacy and financial strategies: The mediating role of financial concerns. *Australian Journal of Management, 46*(3), 437–465. https://doi.org/10.1177/0312896220940762

Yamauchi, K. T., & Templer, D. J. (1982). The development of a money attitude scale. *Journal of Personality Assessment, 46*(5), 522–528. https://doi.org/10.1207/s15327752jpa4605_14

MIX
Papier aus verantwortungsvollen Quellen
Paper from responsible sources
FSC® C105338

If you have any concerns about our products,
you can contact us on
ProductSafety@springernature.com

In case Publisher is established outside the EU,
the EU authorized representative is:
**Springer Nature Customer Service Center GmbH
Europaplatz 3, 69115 Heidelberg, Germany**

Printed by Libri Plureos GmbH
in Hamburg, Germany